Pearson
Revise

Pearson Edexcel GC

German

Revision Guide

Author: Heather Murphy

This book includes Pearson Revise Online access with a revision planner, retrospective tracker, plus make your own flashcards!

Quizzes, videos and flashcards to boost your progress – on every page!

Scan the **Digital resources QR codes** for more ways to revise.

Digital resources

- **Quick quizzes**: Quick-fire practice to check your knowledge.
- **Vocabulary quizzes**: Improve your understanding and retention of all the required vocabulary with just a few minutes' practice each day.
- **Videos**: Help with tricky grammar and tips for the exams.
- **Vocab flashcards**: Test your understanding of all the required vocabulary with ready-made flashcards

Audio for Speaking and Listening at your fingertips

Scan the **green audio QR codes** to immediately launch high-quality recordings of native speakers.

Listen to the recording

- **Exam-style tracks** for realistic assessment practice
- **Targeted pronunciation practice** of German sounds helps build your confidence.
- **Answer-section audio** brings Speaking activities to life.

Transcripts for all audio files can be accessed on the Pearson Revise Online platform.

Higher and Foundation tiers

You can use this book no matter which tier you are doing.

Higher tier vocabulary and grammar are highlighted with the purple background or H symbol.

Everything else is relevant for both Foundation and Higher tier.

Beziehungen

Beziehung (f)	relationship
Einstellung (f)	attitude
Streit (m)	argument
Typ...	

Um ... zu (H ONLY)

Ich treibe Sport, **um** gesund **zu** bleiben.
I do sport to stay healthy.
Er spielt Tennis, **um** starke Muskeln **zu** haben.

Difficulty scale

The icon next to each exam-style question tells you how difficult it is.

Target grade 4

Some questions cover a range of difficulties.

Target grade 7-8

Also available:

The Revision Workbook provides additional practice with hundreds more exam-style questions along with hints on writing the most effective responses PLUS a full set of practice papers – one for each of Foundation and Higher tier – at the back of the book.

How can this book help me revise?

On the page...

1 **Topics** make vocabulary easier to revise.

✓ Revise the words, then see and use them again in many topics!

2 Key **vocabulary**, taken from the approved vocabulary list.

✓ Check which words you already know and learn some new words.

✓ Refer to vocabulary pages at the back of the book for a complete list.

Words/grammar which will only appear on the Higher tier papers look like this: erreichen . The rest may appear on either paper.

Health | Had a look ☐ | Nearly there ☐ | Nailed it! ☐

Digital resources

Sport

Sport macht Spaß!

Bewegung (f)	exercise
Knochen (m)	bone
Muskel (m)	muscle
Wettbewerb (m)	competition
schwierig / leicht	hard / easy
stark	strong
gewinnen	to win
sich bewegen	to exercise
sich interessieren für	to be interested in
sich konzentrieren auf	to concentrate on
sich treffen (mit)	to meet up (with)
spazieren gehen	to go for a walk
Sport treiben	to do / play sport
teilnehmen an	to take part in
verlieren	to lose
wandern	to hike

Reflexive verbs Grammar page 107

Reflexive verbs need a reflexive pronoun.

Ich interessiere **mich** nicht für Sport.
I'm not interested in sport.
Wir treffen **uns** im Park.
We meet up in the park.
Man soll **sich** jeden Tag bewegen.
You should exercise every day.

Um ... zu H ONLY

Ich treibe Sport, **um** gesund **zu** bleiben.
I do sport to stay healthy.
Er spielt Tennis, **um** starke Muskeln **zu** haben.
He plays tennis to have strong muscles.

Remember to include the comma before um.

Worked example READING Target grade 2-3

Read these comments about sport.
Answer the following questions **in English**. You do not need to write in full sentences.

Mia: Ich spiele jeden Tag Tennis, weil ich so gesund bleibe.
Leon: Wir gehen immer samstags an der Küste wandern, denn wir brauchen die frische Luft.
Arda: Nach der Schule spiele ich mit Freunden Fußball. Das macht Spaß.
Yasmin: Es ist wichtig, sich zu bewegen, sonst wird man gestresst.
Sofie: Wenn ich Sport mache, treffe ich mich mit Freunden. Toll!

(a) Why does Mia play tennis?
It keeps her healthy.
(b) Why does Leon go for a walk?
He needs the fresh air.
(c) When does Arda play football?
After school.
(d) Why does Yasmin think exercise is important?
To avoid getting stressed.
(e) What does Sofie do when she plays sport?
Meets up with friends.

(5 marks)

Flexible phrases

Frische Luft ist für jeden wichtig.
Fresh air is important for everyone.

Sport zu treiben ist gut für die Gesundheit.
Playing sport is good for your health.

Now try this WRITING Target grade 5

Write to a Swiss friend about sport and exercise.
You **must** include the following points:
- why sport is important to you, or why not
- the pros and cons of doing sport
- what exercise you have done recently
- your plans for next weekend's activities.

Write your answer **in German**. You should aim to write between 80 and 90 words.

(18 marks)

18

3 Short reminders on **grammar** points help you revise how to form the language correctly and add 'complexity' to aim for higher grades. Grammar points which are only needed on the Higher papers are marked H ONLY. **Videos** cover key or tricky areas.

✓ If you need more detail, you can look in the longer grammar section on pages 94–117, watch one of the accompanying videos, or ask your teacher.

4 **Flexible phrases** can be used in many contexts.

✓ Learn these to use in your writing and speaking exams to help boost your confidence.

5 Now, look at the **Worked examples** to see how a student might use this language in an exam-style question. Hints tell you how to approach similar questions, things to look out for and how to improve your answer.

✓ Use some of the language you've learned to answer this question.

6 Then put it all into practice. The **Now try this** is an exam-style question to help you bring everything together and have a go yourself.

✓ Check your answer with the model answer in the answer section – this may include an audio file to help with pronunciation.

You'll see a range of question types – **Speaking, Listening, Reading** and **Writing** – including the new read aloud and dictation tasks, plus audio files for Listening and Speaking questions.

On Pearson Revise Online...

7 Give your knowledge a quick check with the **quick quiz!**

✓ Scan the QR code to access a set of multi-choice questions relating to what you've just revised.

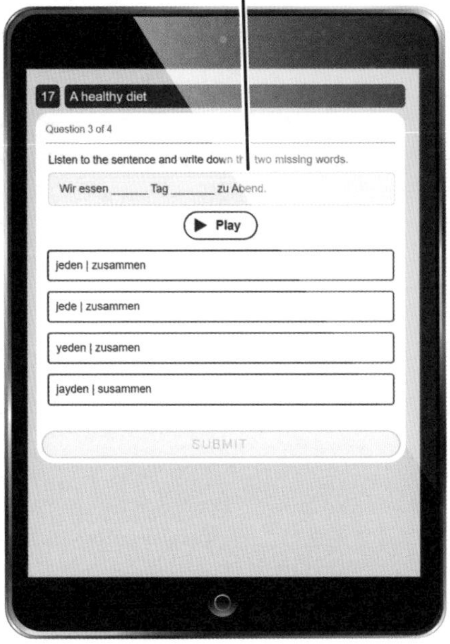

8 Power up your vocabulary with the **vocab test!** Scan the QR code for quick-fire questions to boost your knowledge.

✓ Do this every day to really build your vocabulary – and see your progress grow!

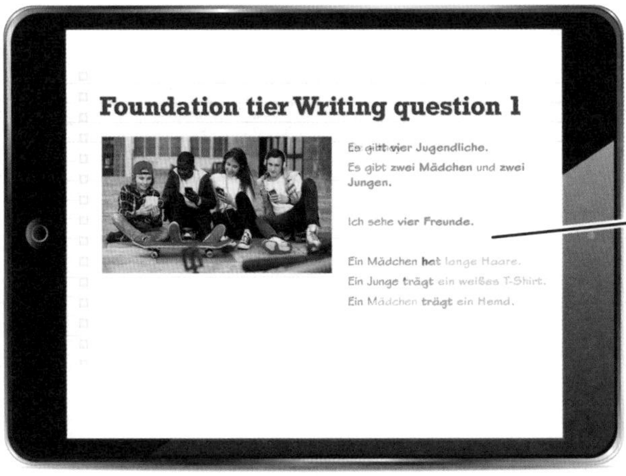

9 **Videos** help you focus in on mastering your grammar, plus provide overall tips from experienced teachers and examiners.

10 Ready made flashcards covering all the required vocabulary help you test your understanding at the touch of a button.

Pearson Revise

Your Pearson Revise Online access also includes a revision planner, progress tracker, plus make your own flashcards!

Contents

…ge match with the German Revision Workbook ISBN 9781292471747

A small bit of small print:
Pearson Edexcel publishes Sample Assessment Material and the Specification on its website. This is the official content and this book should be used in conjunction with it. The questions in Now try this have been written to help you practise every topic in the book. Remember: the real exam questions may not look like this.

Physical descriptions

Digital resources

Wie sieht er / sie aus?

dünn / dick	thin / fat
groß / klein	tall / small
jung / alt	young / old
lang / kurz	long / short
schmal	slender / narrow
aussehen	to look / appear
Ich bin sechzehn Jahre alt.	I am sixteen.
Ich bin ziemlich / sehr groß.	I am quite / very tall.
Ich habe blaue / grüne / braune Augen.	I have blue / green / brown eyes.
Ich habe schwarze / blonde / braune / rote / graue / hellbraune Haare.	I have black / blond / brown / red / grey / light brown hair.
Ich trage eine Brille.	I wear glasses.
Ich trage modische Kleidung.	I wear fashionable clothing.
Sie hat ein rundes / schmales Gesicht.	She has a round / narrow face.
Wie alt ist er / sie?	How old is he / she?

Sein and haben

Grammar page 111

Make sure you know how to use sein (to be) and haben (to have) in the present tense.

	sein	haben
ich	bin	habe
du	bist	hast
er / sie / es	ist	hat
wir	sind	haben
ihr	seid	habt
Sie	sind	haben
sie	sind	haben

Worked example

READING — Target grade 1-3

Read the message from Lea.

Meine Schwester Sofie ist zwölf Jahre alt, also vier Jahre jünger als ich. Sie sieht sportlich aus. Sofie ist groß, dünn und hat – wie ich – grüne Augen und lange braune Haare. Ich finde, sie trägt schöne modische Kleidung.

Put a cross ✗ in each one of the **three** correct boxes.

☐	**A** Lea is younger than Sofie.
☐	**B** Sofie is quite small.
☒	**C** Sofie looks sporty.
☒	**D** Lea and Sofie both have green eyes.
☐	**E** Sofie has long blond hair.
☒	**F** Lea likes Sofie's fashion style.

(3 marks)

There are lots of descriptive adjectives in the text, many of which can be used for comparison. Read them all carefully to answer the questions.

Making comparisons

Grammar page 101

For most adjectives, just add **-er**.

Er ist klein**er** als ich.
He is smaller than me.

For some adjectives, add an umlaut to the vowel and then **-er**.

jung → **jünger**
alt → **älter**
groß → **größer**
lang → **länger**

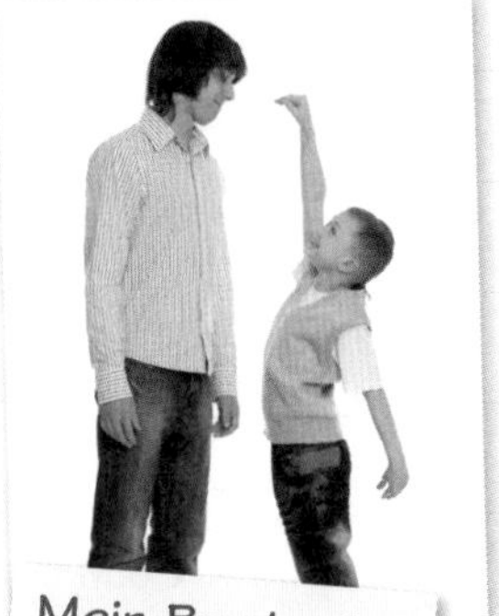

Mein Bruder ist größer als ich.
My brother is taller than me.

Now try this

WRITING — Target grade 3-4

Write a description of a friend or family member.
You **must** include the following points:

- their name and age
- what they look like
- any other feature or detail about the person.

Write your answer **in German**. You should aim to write between 40 and 50 words. **(14 marks)**

Remember that for Foundation Question 2, one of the bullet points will need a future time reference. You can practise this later in the Guide.

Digital resources

Character and personality

Was für eine Person ist er / sie?

beliebt	popular	lustig	funny / amusing
böse	angry / cross	offen	open
ehrlich	honest	ruhig	calm / quiet
ernst	serious	sauer	sour
fleißig	hard-working	streng	strict
freundlich	friendly	unabhängig	independent
glücklich	happy	verantwortlich	responsible
lieb	kind	zufrieden	contented

Meine ältere Schwester ist ziemlich unabhängig.
My older sister is quite independent.

Vocabulary in action

Mein Bruder ist oft böse auf mich.
My brother is often cross with me.
Meine Mama ist sehr lieb und immer ruhig.
My mum is very kind and always calm.
Meine Freundin Yasmin ist fleißig.
My friend Yasmin is hard-working.
Ich würde sagen, ich bin freundlich und lustig.
I would say I'm friendly and funny.
Der Mathelehrer ist beliebt, obwohl er streng ist.
The maths teacher is popular, although he's strict.

Worked example

LISTENING TRACK 1 — Target grade 5-6

Lukas is talking about family. What does he say?

Meine Eltern sind lieb aber manchmal etwas zu ernst. Mama ist ruhig und nie böse, und Papa ist sehr lustig. Meine beiden Brüder sind immer fleißig.

Listen to the recording

Complete the gap in each sentence using a word from the box below. There are more words than gaps.

boring open friendly serious cross
happy funny kind hard-working

(a) Lukas's parents are sometimes too serious.
(b) His mum is never cross.
(c) His dad is very funny.
(d) Lukas says his brothers are hard-working.

(4 marks)

Worked example

READING — Target grade 7-8

Read this comment on a student forum.

Viele Schüler finden unseren Direktor streng und gar nicht freundlich. Ich würde sagen, er ist nur so, weil er fleißig und für uns verantwortlich ist und will, dass wir unser Bestes tun. **Max G.**

Complete the gaps in each sentence using words from the box below. There are more words than gaps.

strict disliked unfriendly kind
hard-working serious responsible

(a) Many school pupils think the head is strict and unfriendly.
(b) Max says the head is like this because he's hard-working and responsible for them.

(4 marks)

Flexible phrases

Expressing opinions

Meiner Meinung nach ... In my opinion ...
Ich finde ihn / sie ... I think he / she is ...
Ich würde sagen, ich bin ... I'd say that I am ...
Ich denke, dass ... I think that ...

Now try this

WRITING — Target grade 3-5

Write about yourself as part of a job application. You **must** include the following points:

- positive aspects of your character
- one negative aspect of your character
- what your family / friends say about you.

Write your answer **in German**. You should aim to write between 40 and 50 words. **(14 marks)**

My family

Digital resources

Meine Familie

Bruder (m)	brother
Erwachsene (m/f)	adult
Geschwister (pl)	siblings
Groß	grand
Kind (nt)	child
Mutter (f)	mother
Opa (m) / Oma (f)	grandma / grandad
Onkel (m)	uncle
Partner (m) / Partnerin (f)	partner
Person (f)	person
Schwester (f)	sister
Stief-	step-
Tante (f)	aunt
Vater (m)	father
Zwilling (m)	twin
traditionell	traditional
typisch	typical
heiraten	to marry
trennen	to separate

Nominative and accusative

Grammar page 96

Use the **nominative case** when a noun is the subject of a verb.

Use the **accusative case** when a noun is the direct object of a verb.

Meine Schwester hat **einen** Freund.
My sister has a boyfriend.

Masculine accusative articles end in ***-en***.

Mein Onkel hat **einen** Hund.
My uncle has a dog.

Worked example

READING — Target grade 1-3

Read the messages about families.

Malik: Meine Familie ist traditionell – zwei Eltern und zwei Kinder – mein jüngerer Bruder und ich.

Sofie: Es gibt drei Personen bei mir zu Hause – meinen Vater und meine Großmutter und mich. Meine Mama ist tot.

Complete the following table **in English**. You do not need to write in full sentences.

(a) One detail about Malik's family.	traditional
(b) Two people in Sofie's family.	her dad and her grandmother

(2 marks)

Worked example

LISTENING — TRACK 2 — Target grade 6-7

Anna is describing her family. What does she say?

Mein Vater wohnt nicht mehr bei uns. Er hat eine neue Frau und wohnt seit zwei Jahren in der Schweiz. Meine Mama ist auch wieder verheiratet, und mein Stiefvater heißt Martin. Er hat einen Sohn, Leon, der mein Stiefbruder ist.

Listen to the recording

Listen to the recording and complete the sentences by putting a cross ✗ in the correct box for each question.

(a) Anna's father has …

✗	**A** remarried.
☐	**B** left Switzerland.
☐	**C** a two-year-old son.

(b) Martin is Anna's …

☐	**A** brother.
☐	**B** stepbrother.
✗	**C** stepfather.

(2 marks)

Now try this

WRITING — Target grade 5-7

das macht Spaß means 'that is fun'

Translate the paragraph **into German**.

> My family is not a typical family with two parents and two children. I live with my dad and his partner, Helmut, and with my stepbrother, who is called Noah. We get on well and often play sport together. I see my mum every weekend and that is always fun.

(10 marks)

Digital resources

Friends

Die Freunde

Beziehung (f)	relationship
Frau (f)	woman
Freund (m) / Freundin (f)	friend
Junge (m)	boy
Mädchen (nt)	girl
Mann (m)	man
Unterstützung (f)	support
Verhältnis (nt)	relationship
eng	close
gemeinsam	in common
nötig	necessary
verschieden	different / diverse
wichtig	important
brauchen	to need
helfen	to help
sich verstehen mit	to get on with
verbringen	to spend (time)

Explaining opinions

Grammar page 104

Giving reasons counts as complex language in the exam.

You can use denn or weil.

Max ist mein Freund, **weil** wir viel gemeinsam **haben**.

Max is my friend because we have lots in common.

Remember the word order with **weil** puts the verb at the end.

Ich mag meine Freundin, **denn** sie hilft mir mit Problemen.

I like my friend because she helps me with problems.

Worked example

READING — Target grade 5

Read these comments about friendships. Complete the gap in each sentence using a word from the box below. There are more words than gaps.

(a) Ich finde meine Freundin Mika toll, denn sie ist immer sehr lustig.

(b) Ich liebe meine Freunde, weil sie alle so verschieden sind.

(c) Meine Freundin Lara ist mir wichtig, weil sie so lieb ist.

(d) Jonas ist ein fantastischer Freund, denn er ist immer für mich da.

important sporty funny helpful different necessary kind close fantastic

(a) Mika is great because she is very ....funny.... .

(b) I love my friends because they are all so ....different.... .

(c) Lara is important to me because she's ....kind.... .

(d) Jonas is always there for me. He is ....fantastic.... .

(4 marks)

Note how **denn** and **weil** are used in these sentences, with commas, and how **weil** sends the verb to the end of the sentence.

Now try this

LISTENING TRACK 3 — Target grade 6-7

Listen to the recording

Dictation

You are going to hear someone talking about friends.

Sentences 1–2: write down the missing words in the gaps provided. In each gap, you will write one word **in German**.

Sentence 3: write down the full sentence that you hear in the space provided, **in German**.

1 Ich habe ______ Freunde und ______, die mir ______ sind.

2 Ich bin ______ elf Jahren mit Lea ______ – wir waren zusammen in der ____________ .

3 ____ . **(6)**

Relationships

Digital resources

Beziehungen

Beziehung (f)	relationship
Einstellung (f)	attitude
Streit (m)	argument
Typ (m)	guy
Unterschied (m)	difference
Verhältnis (nt)	relationship
Verständnis (f)	understanding
kompliziert	complicated
schwierig	difficult
stolz auf	proud of
zuständig	responsible
gefallen	to please
sich fühlen	to feel
sich verstehen mit	to get on with
unterstützen	to support

Using gefallen

Grammar page 102

This is an impersonal verb, meaning it can only be used with es, another third person pronoun or a noun. The person the verb refers to is in the dative case (mir / dir / uns / euch).

This literally means 'Sport pleases to me very much'.

Sport gefällt mir sehr.
I like sport very much.
Diese Jungen gefallen mir nicht.
I don't like these boys.

Diese Jungen is plural, so the verb gefallen is in the plural.

Die Party hat mir gut gefallen!
I liked the party!

Worked example

LISTENING TRACK 4 — Target grade 6-7

Max is talking about his father. What does he say? Listen to the recording and put a cross ✗ in each one of the **three** correct boxes.

Listen to the recording

Ich verstehe mich nicht gut mit meinem Vater, weil er zu streng ist und mir nicht genug Freiheit gibt. Das gefällt mir nicht, und unser Verhältnis ist deshalb schwierig. Seine Einstellung ist altmodisch, und ich fühle mich oft wie ein kleines Kind. Ich bin so gestresst!

Max …

☐	**A** doesn't understand his father.
☒	**B** doesn't get on with his father.
☐	**C** has a lot of freedom.
☐	**D** finds his dad fashionable.
☒	**E** feels he is treated like a child.
☒	**F** is suffering from stress.

(3 marks)

Using reflexive verbs

Grammar page 107

Reflexive verbs have an extra part: the reflexive pronoun (mich / dich / sich …).
Ich fühle **mich** sehr glücklich. I feel very happy.
Sie versteht **sich** gut mit ihm. She gets on well with him.

Worked example

LISTENING TRACK 5 — Target grade 5

Yasmin is talking about relationships. What does she say? Listen to the recording and complete the following statements **in English**.

Listen to the recording

Aktivitäten mit Freunden gefallen mir sehr, weil das immer Spaß macht, aber meine jüngere Schwester gefällt mir gar nicht, denn sie ist laut.

Yasmin ...

(a) likes ...activities with friends...
because ...it's fun... **(2 marks)**

(b) dislikes ...her younger sister...
because ...she's noisy... **(2 marks)**

Now try this

WRITING — Target grade 4-5

Write a response to a questionnaire about relationships. You **must** include the following points:

- who you get on well with and why
- who you don't get on with and why
- where you will make new friends in the future.

Write your answer **in German**. You should aim to write between 40 and 50 words. **(14 marks)**

Digital resources

Dealing with problems

Probleme

Druck (m)	pressure
Gespräch (nt)	conversation
Hoffnung (f)	hope
Leistung (f)	achievement
Lösung (f)	solution
Ruhe (f)	silence / peace
Stimmung (f)	mood / atmosphere
Wirklichkeit (f)	reality
geistig	mental / psychological
schwer / schwierig	hard / difficult
Angst haben	to be scared
sich entschuldigen	to apologise

Worked example

READING — Target grade 5-6

Read these problems and answers from an online help page.

Paul: Ich habe Angst, dass meine Noten nicht gut genug sind.
Am besten sprichst du mit deinen Lehrern, die dir helfen können.

Sofie: Ich bin immer müde, aber ich kann nicht schlafen.
Du brauchst Ruhe, bevor du ins Bett gehst. Du kannst lesen oder Musik hören.

Noah: Ich bin traurig, weil meine Eltern getrennt sind.
Das Einzige, was du tun kannst, ist mit beiden Eltern sprechen und sie regelmäßig sehen.

Remember how to use modal verbs like **müssen**, **können** and **sollen**. See page 112.

Who says what? Choose the correct answers.

Put a cross ✗ in the correct column for each question.

	Who …	Paul	Sofie	Noah
(a)	… should speak to their parents?			✗
(b)	… is always tired?		✗	
(c)	… could speak to their teachers?	✗		

(3 marks)

Worked example

WRITING — Target grade 7-8

Write to an Austrian friend about problems and pressures.

You **must** include the following points:

- a problem at school
- what you can do to solve the problem
- a problem you have had recently at school
- how you will avoid this problem in future.

Write your answer **in German**. You should aim to write between 80 and 90 words.

Ein guter Freund ist heute böse auf mich: ich bin mit einem Mädchen, das er liebt, ins Kino gegangen.

Ich kann mit ihm darüber sprechen und ich muss mich entschuldigen. Wenn wir darüber sprechen, können wir eine Lösung finden.

In der Schule habe ich Probleme mit dem Mathelehrer gehabt. Er war sehr ziemlich negativ, weil ich nichts verstanden habe.

Ich denke, ich werde mit dem Lehrer sprechen und ihn um Hilfe bitten. Er wird vielleicht alles erklären.

(18 marks)

In this question, the first two bullet points are in the present tense, the third is in the past and the fourth is in the future. The student has used has answered using the correct time frames.

Now try this

SPEAKING — Target grade 1-9

(a) Was machst du, wenn dein Freund ein Problem hat?
(b) Was machst du gern mit Freunden?

(4 marks)

Exam alert

After describing the picture in the Speaking exam, your teacher will ask you two related questions like these. You should reply in short full sentences.

Daily routine

Digital resources

Mein Alltag

Alltag (m)	daily routine / everyday life
Frühstück (nt)	breakfast
jeden Tag / Morgen	every day / morning
gegen	at around (time)
um	at (time)
zu Fuß	on foot
ankommen	to arrive
aufstehen	to get up
sammeln	to collect / gather
sich anziehen	to get dressed
verlassen	to leave
vorbereiten	to prepare

Um wie viel Uhr?

um halb sieben

um sieben Uhr

um Viertel vor neun

um Viertel nach eins

Ich stehe um sechs Uhr auf. I get up at 6 am.
Um halb acht verlasse ich das Haus.
I leave the house at half past seven.

Worked example

WRITING — Target grade 5-7

Translate the paragraph **into German**.

> I get up early every day when I have to go to school. I get dressed and eat breakfast. Yesterday I ate fruit. After breakfast I collect my books and leave the house at about half past seven. I always go to school on foot. It's not very far.

Ich stehe jeden Tag früh auf, wenn ich zur Schule gehen muss. Ich ziehe mich an und esse das Frühstück. Gestern habe ich Obst gegessen. Nach dem Frühstück sammele ich meine Bücher und verlasse gegen halb acht das Haus. Ich gehe immer zu Fuß zur Schule. Es ist nicht sehr weit.

(10 marks)

Worked example

LISTENING TRACK 6 — Target grade 3-4

Listen to the recording

Emily and Mika are talking about their daily routine. What do they say?

Listen to the recording and complete the sentences by putting a cross ✗ in the correct box for each question.

Emily: Ich stehe immer zu spät auf und habe dann keine Zeit, das Frühstück zu essen.

Mika: Ich muss das Haus um halb sieben verlassen, um mit dem Zug zur Schule zu fahren.

(a) Emily always …

☐	**A** eats breakfast.
☐	**B** gets up on time.
☒	**C** gets up late.

(b) Mika leaves the house at …

☒	**A** 6:30 am
☐	**B** 7:00 am
☐	**C** 7:30 am

(2 marks)

Separable verbs

Grammar page 107

Separable verbs like aufstehen have two parts, the main verb and the prefix, which moves to the end of the clause / sentence.

Ich stehe früh **auf**. I get up early.
Ich bin früh **auf**gestanden.
I got up early.
Ich werde früh **auf**stehen.
I'll get up early.

Now try this

LISTENING TRACK 7 — Target grade 5

Listen to the recording

Paul is talking about his daily routine. What does he say?

Listen to the recording and answer the following questions **in English**. You do not need to write in full sentences.

(a) How does Paul find getting up early?

(b) Why?

(c) What time does he set off for school?

(3 marks)

Clothing and fashion

Digital resources

Kleidung und Mode

Hemd (nt)	shirt
Hose (f)	trousers
Hut (m)	hat
Jacke (f)	jacket
Kleid (nt)	dress
Kleidung (f)	clothing
Krawatte (f)	tie
Marke (f)	brand / label
Mode (f)	fashion
Pullover (m)	jumper
Schuhe (m, pl)	shoes
Socken (f, pl)	socks
T-Shirt (nt)	T-shirt
bequem	comfortable
passen	to fit / suit
tragen	to wear
wählen	to choose
Modetrends folgen	to follow fashion

The verb **passen** also works with a dative pronoun. **Das Hemd passt mir gut.** The shirt fits me well.

Expressing likes and preferences

Grammar page 101

Ich mag die aktuelle Mode.
I like current fashion.
Ich trage **gern** bunte Kleidung.
I **like** wearing colourful clothing.
Ich trage **lieber** lockere Kleidung.
I **prefer** wearing loose clothing.
Ich trage **am liebsten** eine Jeans.
I like wearing jeans **best**.

Using gefallen

Grammar page 102

As gefallen literally means 'to please' rather than 'to like', the thing(s) you like become the subject(s) and the dative pronoun mir is used to say 'to me'.
Diese Marke gefällt **mir** sehr.
I really like this brand.
Der Pullover gefällt **mir** nicht.
I don't like the jumper.

Worked example

LISTENING TRACK 8 — Target grade 5 — Listen to the recording

Lea is talking about her favourite clothes.
What does she like and why?

Meine Lieblingskleidungsstücke sind ein graues Kleid, das sehr modisch ist, und meine bequemen schwarzen Schuhe. Meine alte grüne Jacke gefällt mir auch, weil sie praktisch ist.

Listen to the recording and complete the following table **in English**.

You do not need to write in full sentences. **(6 marks)**

Lea …

(a) likes … grey dress	
because … it's fashionable	
(b) likes … black shoes	
because … comfortable	
(c) likes … green jacket	
because … it's practical	

Now try this

SPEAKING TRACK 9 — Target grade 5-9 — Listen to the recording

Describe this picture. Your description must cover:

- people
- location
- activity.

When you have finished your description, listen to the recording to hear two questions and give your answers. You should say a few words or a short phrase / sentence in response to each question. One-word answers will not be sufficient to gain the full marks. **(8 marks)**

Identity

Digital resources

Wer bin ich?

Charakter

Ich bin … / Er / Sie ist …
I am … / He / She is …

beliebt	popular	modisch	fashionable
ehrlich	honest	nett / lieb	nice
freundlich	friendly	religiös	religious
gestresst	stressed	sportlich	sporty
gesund	healthy	süß	sweet
glücklich	happy	verantwortlich	responsible

Interessen

Ich interessiere mich für … I am interested in …

Mode (f)	fashion	Gaming (nt)	gaming
Natur (f)	nature	Lesen (nt)	reading
Sport (m)	sport	Musik (f)	music
Tiere (nt, pl)	animals	Tanzen (nt)	dancing

Leistungen und Wünsche

Leistung (f)	achievement / performance
Beziehung (f)	relationship
Wunsch (m)	wish
gewinnen	to win
stolz auf … sein	to be proud of

Woher kommst du?

Afrika	Africa
Amerika	America
Asien	Asia
Deutschland	Germany
Europa	Europe
Großbritannien	Great Britain
Österreich	Austria
die Schweiz	Switzerland
die Türkei	Turkey

Wichtige Ideen

Die Familie (f)	Family
Die Freiheit (f)	Freedom
Der Frieden (m)	Peace
Die Religion (f)	Religion
Die Umwelt (f)	The environment
… ist mir wichtig	… is important to me

Sexualität

lesbisch	lesbian
schwul	gay
hetero(sexuell)	heterosexual
nicht binär	non-binary

Worked example

LISTENING TRACK 10 — Target grade 4-5

Listen to the recording

Lea and Noah are describing themselves. What do they mention? Listen to the recording and put a cross ✗ in each one of the **three** correct boxes.

Lea: Ich bin die Lea, ich bin achtzehn. Ich habe eine nette Partnerin und ich mag Käse.

Noah: Hier ist Noah … mmm … Ich bin türkisch und ich habe einen Zwillingsbruder. Meine Religion ist mir wichtig.

☐	**A** Lea is seventeen.
☒	**B** Lea likes cheese.
☐	**C** Lea has a nice boyfriend.
☐	**D** Noah is an only child.
☒	**E** Noah is not German.
☒	**F** Religion is important to Noah.

(3 marks)

Ich bin freundlich, mein Rollstuhl ist gelb und Mode ist mir wichtig.
I'm friendly, my wheelchair is yellow and fashion is important to me.

Now try this

WRITING — Target grade 5-7

Translate the paragraph **into German**.

> I have many friends, who are all different. They are all important to me. My best friend Mika is sporty and also very hard-working. Yesterday we went shopping with Mika's sister. Layla is always happy and uses a wheelchair. We all bought new clothes and then had lunch in a café.

(10 marks)

Digital resources

Celebrations

Wir feiern!

Chance (f)	chance
Erfolg (m)	success
Fest (nt)	festival / party
Freude (f)	joy
Geburtstag (m)	birthday
Geschenk (nt)	present
Licht (nt)	light
Prüfung (f)	exam
Tradition (f)	tradition
bestehen	to pass (an exam)
feiern	to celebrate

Um … zu + infinitive = in order to …
Remember **zu** + infinitive go to the end of the clause / sentence.

H ONLY

Using question words

Wann hat er Geburtstag? **When** is his birthday?
Wer hat heute Geburtstag? **Who** has a birthday today?
Wie alt ist sie heute? **How** old is she today?
Mit wem wirst du feiern? **Who** will you celebrate with?
Was trägst du für das Fest?
What are you wearing for the party?
Wo ist die Party? **Where** is the party?
Welche Geschenke hast du bekommen?
Which presents did you get?

Was machen wir, **um** deinen Geburtstag **zu** feiern?
What shall we do to celebrate your birthday?
Wir werden eine Party haben, **um** das Ende der Prüfungen **zu** feiern.
We'll have a party to celebrate the end of the exams.

Worked example

READING — Target grade 3-4

Read these comments about birthday celebrations.

Jan: Ich feiere meinen Geburtstag am liebsten mit meinen Eltern und meinen Schwestern.

Malik: Bei mir zu Hause gibt es immer eine große Party – dann kann ich alle meine Freunde einladen! Weil es im Garten dunkel ist, gibt es immer Lichter zwischen den Bäumen. Das sieht schön aus.

Leonie: Ich gehe lieber aus, um meinen Geburtstag zu feiern. Dieses Jahr war ich auf einem Konzert. Das war toll!

Who says what? Choose the correct answers. Put a cross ✗ in the correct column for each question.

	Who …	Jan	Malik	Leonie
(a)	… doesn't celebrate at home?			✗
(b)	… likes to celebrate with family?	✗		
(c)	… decorates for the party?		✗	
(d)	… always has a big party?		✗	

(4 marks)

Now try this

LISTENING TRACK 11 — Target grade 4-5

Listen to the recording

Alina is talking about her last birthday. What does she say?
Listen to the recording and put a cross ✗ in each one of the **three** correct boxes.
Alina …

☐	**A** loved her party last year.	☐	**D** had about thirty guests.
☐	**B** celebrated by the sea.	☐	**E** provided the sausages for her party.
☐	**C** had her party in July.	☐	**F** came home at midnight.

(3 marks)

When I was younger

Digital resources

Als ich jünger war

Er hatte oft Angst in der Schule.
He was often scared in school.
Mit acht Jahren konnte ich (schwimmen).
I could (swim) at eight years old.
Sie wollte (Lehrer) werden.
She wanted to become (a teacher).
Wir durften nicht alleine zur Schule gehen.
We were not allowed to go to school by ourselves.

Note that **es gibt** (there is / there are) becomes **es gab** (there was / were) in the imperfect tense.

The imperfect tense

Grammar page 115

Use this tense to talk about how things used to be.

ich spielte	I played / used to play
ich wohnte	I lived / used to live
ich hatte	I had
ich war	I was
ich konnte	I was able to
ich musste	I had to
ich wollte	I wanted to
es gab	there was

In the imperfect tense, the **er / sie / es** form is the same as the **ich** form.

Worked example

LISTENING TRACK 12

Target grade 6

Alina is talking about when she was younger.
What does she say?
Listen to the recording and put a cross ✗ in each one of the **three** correct boxes.

Listen to the recording

> Als ich jünger war, hatte ich keine Probleme. Ich war in einer kleinen Schule, wo ich Schreiben und Lesen lernte und keine Hausaufgaben hatte. Damals hatte ich eine Katze, mochte Kindersendungen im Fernsehen und war immer glücklich. Das Leben war nicht so schwierig wie heute.

When she was younger, Alina ...

✗	**A** had a pet.
	B was not happy at school.
✗	**C** learned to read.
✗	**D** found life easier.
	E had homework twice a week.
	F didn't like watching television.

(3 marks)

'When' in the past tense

Grammar page 115

Use als to say 'when' if the verb is in the past.
Als ich jünger **war**, **wohnte** ich in London.
When I was younger, I lived in London.
Use wenn to say 'whenever'.
Wenn es warm **war**, **spielten** wir immer Tennis.
Whenever it was warm we played tennis.

Both **als** and **wenn** send the verb to the end of the clause; then the verb of the next clause comes straight after the comma.

Mein Leben war nicht so kompliziert, als ich jünger war.
My life was not so complicated when I was younger.

Now try this

READING

Target grade 5

Translate the following sentences **into English**.

(a) Als ich ein Kind war, hatte ich ein Kaninchen.
(b) Ich spielte oft im Garten.
(c) Ich sah gerne Kindersendungen.
(d) Ich malte oft Bilder.
(e) Ich hatte auch einen kleinen schwarzen Hund, den ich liebte.

(10 marks)

Digital resources

My life in the future

Die Zukunft

Traum (m)	dream
beitragen zu	to contribute to
besitzen	to own
erfahren	to experience
gelingen	to succeed
heiraten	to marry
hoffen	to hope
schaffen	to manage
sich freuen auf	to look forward to
wählen	to choose
werden	to become

Useful phrases

Ich freue mich auf meine Zukunft.
I'm looking forward to my future.
Ich würde nie heiraten.
I would never get married.
Mein Traum ist es, im Ausland zu leben.
My dream is to live abroad.
Ich hoffe, ich werde es schaffen.
I hope I'll manage it.
Ich hoffe, es gelingt mir.
I hope I'll succeed.

Ich möchte das Leben in Amerika erfahren.
I'd like to experience life in America.

Future and conditional

Grammar pages 116 and 117

Note how the infinitive goes at the end.

Ich werde ins Ausland **fahren**.
I **will** travel abroad.

Ich würde ins Ausland **fahren**.
I **would** travel abroad.

Ich möchte ins Ausland **fahren**.
I **would like** to travel abroad.

Zu + infinitive clauses

H ONLY

Grammar page 105

Use this clause to express 'to do something'. Remember to include a comma after the first clause and put zu + infinitive at the end of the sentence.

Es ist mein Traum, reich **zu werden**.
It's my dream **to become** rich.

Ich hoffe, in Deutschland **zu leben**.
I hope **to live** in Germany.

Modals need an infinitive at the end but **no zu**!
Sie muss fleißig arbeiten. She has to work hard.

Worked example

READING — Target grade 5

Read Yusuf's plans for the future.

Ich interessiere mich für Fremdsprachen und möchte in der Zukunft im Ausland leben. Es ist mein Traum, andere Kulturen zu erfahren, und ich hoffe, ich werde es schaffen. Ich will nicht heiraten, weil meine Freiheit mir wichtiger ist als eine Partnerin und Kinder.

Answer the following questions **in English**. You do not need to write in full sentences.

(a) How will Yusuf benefit in the future from his love of languages?
living overseas / abroad

(b) What is his dream?
experience other cultures

(c) Why doesn't he plan to marry and have children?
his freedom is more important to him

(3 marks)

Now try this

LISTENING TRACK 13 — Target grade 5

Listen to the recording

Mia is talking about her future plans. What does she mention? Listen to the recording and put a cross ✗ in each one of the **three** correct boxes.

Mia …

☐	**A** looks forward to the future.	☐	**D** wants to get married.
☐	**B** wants to be wealthy.	☐	**E** has a boyfriend called Malik.
☐	**C** dreams of owning a fast car.	☐	**F** plans to have more than one child.

(3 marks)

Food and drink

Digital resources

Was gibt es zu essen und zu trinken?

Brot (nt)	bread
Butterbrot (nt)	sandwich
Ei (nt)	egg
Eis (nt)	ice cream
Essen (nt)	food, meal
Fisch (m)	fish
Fleisch (nt)	meat
Gemüse (nt)	vegetables
Getränk (nt)	drink
Kaffee (m)	coffee
Kuchen (m)	cake
Mahlzeit (f)	meal
Obst (nt)	fruit
Pommes (pl)	chips
Schokolade (f)	chocolate
Tee (m)	tea
Wasser (nt)	water

Mahlzeiten

Frühstück (nt)	breakfast
Mittagessen (nt)	lunch
Abendessen (nt)	evening meal
zum Frühstück	for breakfast
zum Abend- / Mittagessen	for dinner / lunch
Guten Appetit!	Enjoy your meal!

- Remember to write in **full sentences**.
- Keep in mind who? where? what?
- Say **who** is in the picture, **where** they are and **what** they are doing.

Worked example

LISTENING TRACK 14 — Target grade 2-3

Frida is planning tomorrow's meals. Which foods does she mention? Listen to the recording and put a cross in each one of the **three** correct boxes.

Listen to the recording

Also … Zum Frühstück gibt es heiße Schokolade, Brot mit Käse … und dann zum Mittagessen Butterbrote, frisches Obst und ein Glas Wasser und zum Abendessen essen wir Fisch mit Gemüse … kein Problem …

X	**A** fruit	X	**D** vegetables
	B cake		**E** ice cream
X	**C** cheese		**F** eggs

(3 marks)

Worked example

WRITING — Target grade 1-3

Describe the photo. Write four short sentences **in German**. **(8 marks)**

1 Es gibt eine Familie mit vier Personen.
2 Sie essen das Frühstück zu Hause.
3 Die Eltern trinken Kaffee.
4 Die Kinder essen vielleicht Obst mit ihrem Frühstück.

Now try this

LISTENING TRACK 15 — Target grade 6

Listen to the recording

Dictation

You are going to hear someone talking about food.

Sentences 1–2: write down the missing words in the gaps provided. In each gap, you will write one word **in German**.

Sentences 3–6: write down the full sentences that you hear in the spaces provided, **in German**.

1 Am ________ esse ich ________ und ________ .
2 Zum ________ mag ich ________ mit ________ .
3 ________________________________ .
4 ________________________________ .
5 ________________________________ .
6 ________________________________ .

(10 marks)

Digital resources

Meals at home

Flexible phrases

Ich habe keine Zeit, ... zu ...
I don't have time to ...

Das ist einfach meine Meinung.
That is simply my opinion.

Die Menschen sind völlig unterschiedlich / verschieden.
People are completely different.
H ONLY

Mein Bruder ist Vegetarier, aber meine Schwester mag kein Gemüse. Sie sind völlig unterschiedlich!
My brother is vegetarian, but my sister doesn't like vegetables. They are completely different!

Relative clauses

Grammar page 105

Relative clauses give further information about a noun.

Mein Vater, **der Schweizer ist**, kann gut kochen.
My Dad, **who is Swiss**, can cook well.

Additional information is given about the father here.

The **relative pronoun** translates as 'who', 'that' or 'which'. It agrees with the noun it is referring to and sends the verb to the end of the clause.

Der Käse, **den** ich gekauft **habe**, ist lecker.
The cheese **which I bought** is delicious.

The commas are very important in German – don't leave them out.

Worked example

READING — Target grade 4-5

Read these opinions from a magazine.

Layla: Ich habe keine Zeit, das Frühstück zu essen, aber ich trinke jeden Morgen Kaffee.
Milan: Wir essen immer zusammen zu Abend. Das mag ich, denn wir können über den Tag sprechen.
Bente: Mein Vater kocht fantastisches Essen, weil er Italiener* ist. Bei uns isst man sehr gut.
Joel: Wir essen nie zusammen, weil meine Eltern lange Stunden arbeiten. Ich koche einfaches Essen.

* *Italiener* = Italian

Who says what? Choose the correct answers.
Put a cross ✗ in the correct column for each question.

Who says ...		Layla	Milan	Bente	Joel
(a)	... we eat well at home?			✗	
(b)	... we don't have family meals?				✗
(c)	... I don't have time to eat in the morning?	✗			
(d)	... I enjoy the conversations at dinner?		✗		

(4 marks)

Now try this

WRITING — Target grade 5

Write to a friend about meals at home. You **must** include the following points:

- what you eat and drink for breakfast
- what your favourite meal is
- what you ate recently for dinner at home
- what you will eat later today.

Write your answer **in German**. You should aim to write between 80 and 90 words. **(18 marks)**

Shopping for food

Digital resources

Role plays in the Speaking exam are transactional, so the scenarios will be set in locations like hotels, tourist offices, doctor's surgeries, cinemas and shops.

Einkaufen

Dose (f)	tin / can
Flasche (f)	bottle
Kilo (nt)	kilo
Kleingeld (nt)	change (money)
Tüte (f)	bag
Würste (pl)	sausages
brauchen	to need

Transactional language

Ich möchte …	I would like …
Ich hätte gern …	I would like …
Haben Sie …?	Do you have …?
bitte	please
danke	thank you

Was kostet das? / Was macht das? What does that come to?

Worked example

LISTENING TRACK 16 — Target grade 2-3

Listen to the recording

Samira is shopping for groceries. Which items does she mention?

Listen to the recording and put a cross ✗ in each one of the **three** correct boxes.

Samira: Hallo. Ich möchte Brot, bitte.
Man: Bitte schön.
Samira: Haben Sie auch Würste?
Man: Ja, wie viele?
Samira: Fünf, bitte … und dazu eine Tüte Kaffee und sechs Eier.

☐	**A** cake	☐	**D** chocolate
☒	**B** bread	☐	**E** tea
☒	**C** sausages	☒	**F** eggs

(3 marks)

Worked example

LISTENING TRACK 17 — Target grade 5-6

Listen to the recording

Some people are paying for items at the checkout. What do they pay?

Listen to the recording and put a cross ✗ in the correct box for each question.

(a) So … Fleisch, Würste, Eier … macht zusammen 28.55 Euro.
(b) Danke … das kostet 37.90 Euro.

(a)

☐	**A** 25.80 Euro
☒	**B** 28.55 Euro
☐	**C** 82.55 Euro

(b)

☒	**A** 37.90 Euro
☐	**B** 73.19 Euro
☐	**C** 39.70 Euro

(2 marks)

Revise your numbers on page 118. You'll need them for both prices and times!

Now try this

SPEAKING — Target grade 1-5

Read aluod

Your German friend Leonie has sent you information about going shopping. Read out the text below.

Ich kaufe heute im Supermarkt ein.
Ich brauche Kaffee, Eier, Brot, Milch und Käse.
Auf dem Markt kaufe ich jeden Samstag Obst und Gemüse.
Ich möchte auch Schokolade kaufen.
Später werde ich das Abendessen kochen.

(8 marks)

Digital resources

Eating out

Im Restaurant

Wir möchten bitte einen Tisch für … Personen.
We would like a table for … people, please.
Wo wollen Sie sitzen?
Where do you want to sit?
Ich hätte gern einen Tisch am Fenster.
I would like a table by the window.
Können Sie uns die Karte bringen?
Can you bring us the menu?
Wir möchten bestellen. We would like to order.
Haben Sie heute Fisch?
Have you got fish today?
Können Sie mir bitte ein Messer / eine Gabel / einen Löffel bringen?
Please could you bring me a knife / fork / spoon?
Die Rechnung, bitte. The bill please.

Note that **ich möchte** is a pleasant and polite way of saying what you would like, and is often better than **ich will** (I want).

Remember to use the more polite **Sie** form in shops/restaurants, not the **du** form. You'll need to understand the **Sie** form for the Speaking test role play.

Modal verbs + infinitive

Grammar page 112

Modal verbs like können, dürfen and wollen all need an infinitive at the end.
Können Sie mir **helfen**? Can you help me?
Darf ich die Karte **sehen**?
May I see the menu?
Wollen Sie für heute Abend eine Reservierung **machen**?
Do you want to make a reservation for this evening?

Was möchten Sie essen?
What would you like to eat?

Worked example

LISTENING TRACK 18 | Target grade 4-5 | Listen to the recording

These people are in a restaurant.
What does each person say?
Listen to the recording and complete the sentences by putting a cross ✗ in the correct box for each question.

(a) Wo ist der Kellner? Ich habe kein Glas!
(b) Ich möchte die Karte sehen.
(c) Meine Pommes sind kalt!
(d) Haben sie keinen Fisch?

(a) I don't have a …

☐	**A**	plate.
☐	**B**	menu.
☒	**C**	glass.

(b) I want to see the …

☐	**A**	table.
☒	**B**	menu.
☐	**C**	waiter.

(c) My … are cold.

☒	**A**	chips
☐	**B**	vegetables
☐	**C**	feet

(d) Don't you have …

☐	**A**	meat?
☒	**B**	fish?
☐	**C**	sausages?

(4 marks)

Now try this

LISTENING TRACK 19 | Target grade 6-7 | Listen to the recording

In the exam, there will be more sentences.

Dictation
You are going to hear someone talking about eating out.
Write down the three full sentences that you hear in the spaces provided, **in German**.
1 ____ .
2 ____ .
3 ____ . **(6 marks)**

A healthy diet

Digital resources

Gesund essen!

Fastfood (nt)	fast food
Gesundheit (f)	health
Veganer (m) / Veganerin (f)	vegan
Vegetarier (m) / Vegetarierin (f)	vegetarian
gesund / ungesund	healthy / unhealthy
mindestens	at least
essen	to eat
… schmeckt / schmecken mir	… tastes / taste (good) / I like the taste of …
trinken	to drink
vermeiden	to avoid
versuchen	to try
Ich esse leider zu viel Schokolade und zu wenig Gemüse.	Unfortunately, I eat too much chocolate and too few vegetables.

Choosing tenses

Grammar pages 106, 113–114 and 116

PRESENT – What you eat and drink now.
Ich esse Obst und Gemüse und trinke Wasser.
PERFECT – What you ate and drank earlier.
Zum Frühstück habe ich Brot gegessen und Kaffee getrunken.
FUTURE – What you'll eat and drink later.
Heute Abend werde ich Fisch und Pommes essen und heiße Schokolade trinken.

Ich esse mindestens drei Stück Obst pro Tag. Obst schmeckt mir!
I eat at least three pieces of fruit per day. I like the taste of fruit!

How often?

täglich / jeden Tag every day / daily	normalerweise usually	manchmal sometimes	nicht (sehr) oft not (very) often

Immer Always ← Wie oft? How often? → Nie Never

(sehr) oft (very) often	häufig frequently	regelmäßig regularly	selten rarely

Worked example

LISTENING TRACK 20 — Target grade 6-7 — Listen to the recording

Yusuf is talking about his diet. What does he say?

Ich versuche, gesund zu essen und bin seit vier Jahren Vegetarier. Deshalb vermeide ich Fleisch und esse meistens Gemüse und manchmal Fisch. Gestern zum Frühstück habe ich ein Ei gegessen. Heute Abend werde ich Brot mit Käse essen.

Listen to the recording and put a cross ✗ in each one of the **three** correct boxes. Yusuf …

✗	**A** aims to eat a healthy diet.	☐	**D** enjoys eating chips.
☐	**B** has been a vegetarian for six years.	✗	**E** ate an egg for breakfast yesterday.
☐	**C** never eats fish.	✗	**F** will eat cheese later.

(3 marks)

Now try this

WRITING — Target grade 6-9

Write an article about healthy eating. You must include the following points:

- details about your usual diet
- why it's important to eat well
- a great meal you have eaten recently
- how you will eat more healthily in the future.

Write your answer **in German**. You should aim to write between 130 and 150 words. **(22 marks)**

Digital resources

Sport

Sport macht Spaß!

Bewegung (f)	exercise
Knochen (m)	bone
Muskel (m)	muscle
Wettbewerb (m)	competition
schwierig / leicht	hard / easy
stark	strong
gewinnen	to win
sich bewegen	to exercise
sich interessieren für	to be interested in
sich konzentrieren auf	to concentrate on
sich treffen (mit)	to meet up (with)
spazieren gehen	to go for a walk
Sport treiben	to do / play sport
teilnehmen an	to take part in
verlieren	to lose
wandern	to hike

Reflexive verbs

Grammar page 107

Reflexive verbs need a reflexive pronoun.

Ich interessiere **mich** nicht für Sport.
I'm not interested in sport.

Wir treffen **uns** im Park.
We meet up in the park.

Man soll **sich** jeden Tag bewegen.
You should exercise every day.

Um ... zu

H ONLY

Ich treibe Sport, **um** gesund **zu** bleiben.
I do sport to stay healthy.

Er spielt Tennis, **um** starke Muskeln **zu** haben.
He plays tennis to have strong muscles.

Remember to include the comma before **um**.

Worked example

READING — Target grade 2-3

Read these comments about sport.
Answer the following questions **in English**. You do not need to write in full sentences.

Mia: Ich spiele jeden Tag Tennis, weil ich so gesund bleibe.

Leon: Wir gehen immer samstags an der Küste wandern, denn wir brauchen die frische Luft.

Arda: Nach der Schule spiele ich mit Freunden Fußball. Das macht Spaß.

Yasmin: Es ist wichtig, sich zu bewegen, sonst wird man gestresst.

Sofie: Wenn ich Sport mache, treffe ich mich mit Freunden. Toll!

(a) Why does Mia play tennis?
It keeps her healthy.

(b) Why does Leon go for a walk?
He needs the fresh air.

(c) When does Arda play football?
After school.

(d) Why does Yasmin think exercise is important?
To avoid getting stressed.

(e) What does Sofie do when she plays sport?
Meets up with friends.

(5 marks)

Flexible phrases

Frische Luft ist für jeden wichtig.
Fresh air is important for everyone.

Sport zu treiben ist gut für die Gesundheit.
Playing sport is good for your health.

Now try this

WRITING — Target grade 5

Write to a Swiss friend about sport and exercise.

You **must** include the following points:

- why sport is important to you, or why not
- the pros and cons of doing sport
- what exercise you have done recently
- your plans for next weekend's activities.

Write your answer **in German**. You should aim to write between 80 and 90 words. **(18 marks)**

Advantages of sport

Digital resources

Sport und mein Leben

Gefühl (nt)	feeling	helfen	to help
Körper (m)	body	relaxen	to relax
Risiken (pl)	risk	reduzieren	to reduce
Risiko (nt)	risks	schützen	to protect
Wirkung (f)	effect	verändern	to change
empfehlen	to recommend	verbessern	to improve
führen zu	to lead to		

Was sagen die Experten?

Sport verbessert die Schlafqualität.
Sport improves your quality of sleep.
Sport reduziert das Krankheitsrisiko.
Sport reduces the risk of illness.
Bewegung schützt das Herz.
Exercise protects your heart.
Man hat durch Sport ein längeres Leben.
Sport can give you a longer life.

Verbs + dative

Grammar page 97

Some verbs are followed by the dative case. These include:

verb		+ dative	
antworten	to answer	mir	me
danken	to thank	dir	you
erlauben	to allow	ihm	him
geben	to give	ihr	her
gefallen	to please	ihm	it
gehören	to belong to	uns	us
glauben	to believe	euch	you (plural)
helfen	to help	Ihnen	you (formal)
		ihnen	them

Bewegung hilft **ihr**, in Form zu bleiben.
Exercise helps her to stay fit.

Schwimmen gibt **mir** ein wunderbares Gefühl.
Swimming gives me a wonderful feeling.

Tennis gefällt **uns** nicht so sehr.
We don't like tennis very much.

Der Ball gehört **mir**!
The ball belongs to me!

Worked example

LISTENING TRACK 21 — Target grade 5

Samira is talking about the importance of sport. Which points does she mention?

Listen to the recording and put a cross ✗ in each one of the **three** correct boxes.

> Sport ist gut für das Herz und hilft mir, nicht krank zu werden. Wenn man Sport macht, hat man positivere Gefühle und schläft auch besser.

hilft mir is an example of a verb used with the dative case.

☐	**A**	teamwork
☒	**B**	heart health
☐	**C**	weight loss
☐	**D**	improved appetite
☒	**E**	feeling good
☒	**F**	quality of sleep

Listen to the recording

(3 marks)

Now try this

WRITING — Target grade 5

Write to a friend about the importance of sport. You **must** include the following points:

- how often you play sport / do exercise
- the positive effects of sport
- what sporting activity you did last week
- how sport will improve your life in the future.

Write your answer **in German**. You should aim to write between 80 and 90 words. **(18 marks)**

Digital resources

Physical wellbeing

Körperliche Gesundheit

Bewegung (f)	exercise
Körper (m)	body
Sorge (f)	worry
ernst	serious
genug	enough
gesund	healthy, healthily
körperlich	physical / physically
müde	tired
schlafen	to sleep

Using sondern (H ONLY)

Grammar page 104

Sondern means 'but' and is only used when there is kein or nicht in the sentence.

Ich spiele **nicht** Tennis, **sondern** Handball.
I don't play tennis but handball.

Ich trinke **keinen** Kaffee, **sondern** Tee.
I don't drink coffee but tea.

Ich spiele **nicht nur** regelmäßig Fußball, **sondern auch** Tennis.
I don't only play football regularly, but also tennis.

Worked example (READING, Target grade 2-3)

Read Johanna's answers to a fitness survey.

Frage	Antwort
1. Wie oft machst du Sport in der Woche?	dreimal
2. Was isst du gewöhnlich?	Fleisch und Gemüse
3. Wirst du schnell müde, wenn du läufst?	nicht oft
4. Gehst du jeden Tag an die frische Luft?	ja
5. Hast du gute Muskeln?	nein
6. Fühlst du dich oft müde?	manchmal
7. Möchtest du gesünder sein?	ja

Complete the gap in each sentence using a word from the box below. There are more words than gaps.

month	week	day
fish	vegetables	fruit
park	fresh air	gym
balance	concentration	muscles

(a) Johanna does sport three times a ...week... .

(b) She eats mostly meat and ...vegetables... .

(c) She spends time daily in the ...fresh air... .

(d) She doesn't have good ...muscles... .

(4 marks)

Worked example (READING, Target grade 7)

Read this blog entry from Paul.

Jugendliche brauchen nicht nur Bewegung, sondern auch genug Schlaf und gutes Essen. Man muss vermeiden, sich zu viele Sorgen zu machen. Kurz gesagt – man soll seinen Lebensstil ernst nehmen. **Paul**

Complete the sentences below. Put a cross ✗ in the correct box for each question.

(a) Paul thinks young people need exercise and …

☒	**A** enough sleep.
☐	**B** lots of fun.
☐	**C** good friends.

(b) They should avoid too much …

☐	**A** smoking.
☒	**B** worrying.
☐	**C** dieting.

(2 marks)

Now try this (SPEAKING, Target grade 2-5)

Read aloud

Lara, your friend, has written about her health and wellbeing. Read out the text below.

Ich bin ziemlich gesund. Wir essen Gemüse zu Hause. Ich mag Sport und laufe oft. Im Sommer spiele ich mit meiner Schwester Handball. Ich möchte gern in ein Fitnesszentrum gehen.

(8 marks)

Mental wellbeing

Digital resources

Wie fühlst du dich?

Schmerz (m)	pain
Stimmung (f)	mood / atmosphere
akzeptieren	to accept
erfahren	to experience
ernst nehmen	to take seriously
leiden	to suffer
leisten	to achieve / perform
lösen	to solve
reden	to talk
sich fühlen	to feel
verbessern	to improve
vergessen	to forget
zuhören	to listen to

Compound nouns made up of more than one word are a German speciality. The noun takes the gender of the last word.

Useful cognates / near cognates

Stress (m)	stress
emotional	emotional
psychologisch	psychological

A cognate / near cognate is a word which looks the same / almost the same in German as in English.

Useful compound nouns

Kopfschmerzen (pl)	headache
Kopfmassage (f)	head massage
Leistungsdruck (m)	pressure to achieve
Meinungsverschiedenheit (f)	difference of opinion
Problemlösung (f)	problem-solving
Schulstress (m)	stress at school
Wohlsein (nt)	wellbeing

H ONLY

Worked example

READING

Target grade 5-6

Read the advice on a problem page.

- Schlafprobleme wegen Stress? Hör Musik vor dem Schlafengehen.
- Zu viel Druck? Mach eine Pause an der frischen Luft!
- Du fühlst dich allein? Ruf einen Freund an!

These phrases use the imperative form to give instructions.

What does the problem page say you should do? Complete the table **in English**. You do not need to write in full sentences.

(a) If you're feeling lonely …	phone a friend.
(b) If you're under pressure …	take a break in the fresh air.
(c) If you can't sleep …	listen to music before bed.

(3 marks)

Now try this

WRITING

Target grade 7-8

Write to a friend about looking after your mental health.

You **must** include the following points:

- what you do to be happy
- what causes you stress
- a problem you have had recently
- what you will do in future to deal with problems.

Write your answer **in German**. You should aim to write between 80 and 90 words. **(18 marks)**

Digital resources

Feeling unwell

Ich bin krank

Arzt (m) / Ärztin (f)	doctor
Bauch (m)	stomach
Bein (nt)	leg
Fieber (nt)	temperature
Knie (nt)	knee
Rücken (m)	back
Schmerzen (m, pl)	pains
gebrochen	broken
Durst (m) haben	to be thirsty
(sich) verletzen	to injure (oneself)

Useful phrases

Ich habe Kopfschmerzen.	I have a headache.
Ich bin immer müde.	I'm always tired.
Mir ist zu warm.	I feel hot.
Ich fühle mich krank.	I feel ill.
Ich fühle mich nicht wohl.	I feel unwell.
Was ist los?	What's wrong?
Wie ist das passiert?	How did that happen?
Wie ist das geschehen?	How did that happen?
Das tut weh.	That hurts.
Es geht mir nicht gut.	I don't feel well.

Ich habe **dich** verletzt. Entschuldigung!
I've hurt you. Sorry!

Worked example

LISTENING TRACK 22 — Target grade 3-4

Elif is feeling unwell. What does she say?

Listen to the recording and complete the sentences by putting a cross ✗ in the correct box for each question.

– Ach, Mutti. Ich bin krank. Ich habe Bauchschmerzen und mir ist zu warm.
– Bleib im Bett. Den Arzt brauchen wir noch nicht. Ich hole dir ein Glas Wasser.

Listen to the recording

(a) Elif has a …

☐	**A** headache.
☐	**B** sore throat.
✗	**C** stomach ache.

(b) Her mum will …

☐	**A** call the doctor.
✗	**B** bring Elif a drink.
☐	**C** drive Elif to the surgery.

(2 marks)

Worked example

LISTENING TRACK 23 — Target grade 6

What has happened to Malik? What does he say?

Listen to the recording and put a cross ✗ in each one of the **three** correct boxes.

Listen to the recording

– Ich habe mich verletzt! Die Schmerzen sind schlimm! Mein linkes Bein tut weh.
– Wie ist das geschehen?
– Beim Handballspielen. Ich wollte nur den Ball von einem anderen Spieler bekommen und bin gefallen, weil der Platz nass war.

Malik …

☐	**A** has injured his hand.
✗	**B** has hurt his leg.
✗	**C** was playing handball.
☐	**D** was tackled by another player.
☐	**E** fell over another player.
✗	**F** fell on the wet surface.

(3 marks)

Now try this

WRITING — Target grade 3-5

Translate the following sentences **into German**.

(a) I am not often ill.
(b) Today I have a headache.
(c) My sister can't sleep and is always tired.
(d) At the weekend my father had backache.
(e) He wants to see the doctor.

(10 marks)

Avoiding health risks

Digital resources

Die Gesundheit

Droge (f)	drug
Gefahr (f)	danger
Gefühl (nt)	feeling
Risiken (nt, pl)	risks
gefährlich	dangerous
nehmen	to take
probieren	to try
rauchen	to smoke
schlecht	bad
schlimm	bad
vermeiden	to avoid

Note that the imperative **du** form may sometimes have an **-e** on the end – so either **Trink** or **Trinke** are possible.

Nimm keine Drogen!
Don't take drugs!

The imperative

H ONLY

Grammar page 106

This is used to give an instruction or command.

- Using **du**
  Use the present tense **du** form of the verb minus the **-st** ending. You don't need the pronoun.
  Trink Wasser! Drink water!

Some verbs are irregular in the **du** form.

haben (to have)	**Hab!** Have!
sein (to be)	**Sei!** Be!
essen (to eat)	**Iss!** Eat!
fahren (to drive)	**Fahr!** Drive!
geben (to give)	**Gib!** Give!
lassen (to leave)	**Lass!** Leave!
nehmen (to take)	**Nimm!** Take!

- Using **ihr**
  Use the present tense **ihr** form of the verb. You don't need the pronoun.
  Raucht nicht! Don't smoke!
- Using **Sie**
  Swap the present tense round, so the verb comes before the pronoun.
  Treiben Sie viel Sport! Do a lot of sport!

Another way to give an instruction is to use **müssen** or **sollen** – 'you must' or 'you should'.

Du **musst** Pausen machen.
You must take breaks.

Man **soll** nicht vor Kindern rauchen.
You should not smoke in front of children.

Worked example

LISTENING TRACK 24 — Target grade 4-5

Jan is giving health advice to his friend Tim. What advice does he give?

Listen to the recording and put a cross ✗ in each one of the **three** correct boxes.

Tim, ich denke, du bist gestresst, und das ist schlecht. So, was du machen sollst: rauch nicht mehr und verbringe nicht so viele Stunden im Büro! Du sollst auch versuchen, früher ins Bett zu gehen und mehr Schlaf zu bekommen.

Tim should …

☐	**A** stop eating cakes.
☒	**B** stop smoking.
☒	**C** sleep longer.
☐	**D** avoid drugs.
☐	**E** stop drinking.
☒	**F** work fewer hours.

Listen to the recording

(3 marks)

Now try this

READING — Target grade 5

Translate the following sentences **into English**.

(a) Trink mehr Wasser! Der Körper braucht acht Gläser pro Tag.
(b) Ich soll versuchen, früher ins Bett zu gehen.
(c) Ich kenne Jugendliche, die Drogen nehmen, aber ich finde das gefährlich und würde es nie probieren.
(d) Ich habe nie geraucht und ich werde in der Zukunft nicht rauchen.
(e) Wir versuchen, weniger Schokolade zu essen.

(10 marks)

Digital resources

Sports stars

Sportstars

Rollstuhl (m)	wheelchair
Unfall (m)	accident
Vorbild (nt)	role model
Wettbewerb (m)	competition
behindert	disabled
bekannt	famous
erreichen	to reach
gewinnen	to win
leisten	to achieve
teilnehmen an	to take part in

Prepositions

Grammar pages 97 and 98

Prepositions in German are used with particular cases. Here are some examples:

- with the accusative: für (for), durch (through), ohne (without)
- with the accusative or dative: an (on / at), in (in / into), auf (on)
- with the dative: aus (out of), zu (to), von (of), mit (with)

in with the **accusative** means 'into' and shows **movement** = in **das** Zimmer (**into** the room); whereas in with the **dative** refers to a **fixed position** = in **dem** Zimmer (**in** the room).

Worked example

READING Target grade 6

Read the article about the Austrian snowboarder Rene Eckhart.

Rene Eckhart ist ein österreichischer Para-Snowboarder, der 1987 geboren wurde. Als Kleinkind hatte er eine Amputation eines Teils von seinem linken Bein. Er hat an vielen paralympischen Winterspielen teilgenommen und war 2022 in Beijing in zwölfter Position. Er glaubt, es gibt für ihn keine Grenzen!

Complete the gap in each sentence using a word from the box below. There are more words than gaps.

Austria	Switzerland	Germany
second	twelfth	twentieth
belief	hope	dream

(a) Rene Eckhart comes from ....Austria.........

(b) At the Beijing games, he came in ....twelfth..... place.

(c) His .....belief...... is that there are no limits to what he can achieve.

(3 marks)

You may come across cognates or near-cognates (words which look the same in German and English).

Amputation (f)	amputation
blind	blind
paralympisch	paralympic
Ski fahren / Ski laufen	to ski
Snowboard (nt)	snowboard

Worked example

READING Target grade 6

Read about the tennis player Britta Wend.

Britta Wend ist als Rollstuhltennisspielerin sehr bekannt. Sie kommt aus Bielefeld* und wurde 1996 geboren. Sie hat in 2023 an der Europameisterschaft** teilgenommen, wo Deutschland auf dem dritten Platz im Damendoppel war.

* Bielefeld is a town in Germany.

** *Europameisterschaft* – European Championships

Answer the following questions **in English**. You do not need to write in full sentences.

(a) What is Britta Wend famous for?

Playing wheelchair tennis.

(b) What happened in the women's doubles at the European championships in 2023?

Germany took third place.

(2 marks)

Now try this

READING Target grade 3-5

Translate the following sentences **into English**.

(a) Ich mag viele Sportstars.

(b) Manchmal gehe ich mit Freunden zum Fußballspiel.

(c) Im Sommer gehe ich dreimal pro Woche laufen.

(d) Gestern habe ich Rollstuhltennis im Fernsehen gesehen.

(e) Das war wirklich schnell und sehr spannend.

(10 marks)

Hobbies and interests

Digital resources

In meiner Freizeit

Interesse (nt)	interest
Kultur (f)	culture
Kunst (f)	art
Leichtathletik (f)	athletics
Mitglied (nt)	member
Mode (f)	fashion
Museum (nt)	museum
Pferd (nt)	horse
Verein (m)	club / association
entdecken	to discover
wandern	to hike

In English you can change the order, e.g. I go to the castle by bus on Sunday. In German, you must follow the time-manner-place rule.

Time – Manner – Place

Grammar page 103

This is an important word order rule.

	1. Time (when)	2. Manner (how)	3. Place (where)
Ich gehe	jeden Samstag	mit meinem Freund	in das Kunstmuseum.

I go every Saturday with my boyfriend to the art gallery.

Or the sentence can start with the 'when' information.

1. Time		2. Manner	3. Place
Sonntags	fahre ich	mit dem Bus	zum Schloss.

On Sundays I go to the castle by bus.

Worked example

READING — Target grade 3-4

Read what Ben, Mia and Tim say about hobbies.

Ben: Mein Onkel wohnt an der Küste, und ich mag es sehr, einmal in der Woche mit ihm eine Bootsfahrt zu machen. Ich lerne, wie man ein Boot fährt.

Mia: Ich bin Tierfan und habe ein Pferd, das ich sehr liebe. Ich gehe sonntags mit ihm auf das Land.

Tim: Ich interessiere mich für Geschichte und gehe zweimal im Monat in das Schloss nicht weit von meiner Stadt.

Who says what? Choose the correct answers. Put a cross ✗ in the correct column for each question.

	Who …	Ben	Mia	Tim
(a)	… likes old buildings?			✗
(b)	… has a water-based hobby?	✗		
(c)	… loves animals?		✗	

(3 marks)

Now try this

LISTENING TRACK 25 — Target grade 5-7

Listen to the recording

Dictation

You are going to hear someone talking about hobbies.

Sentences 1–2: write down the missing words in the gaps provided. In each gap, you will write one word **in German**.

Sentences 3–6: write down the full sentences that you hear in the spaces provided, **in German**.

1 In meiner __________ gehe ich mit __________ wandern.

2 Ich __________ gern und mache __________ einen __________ .

3 ______________________________ .

4 ______________________________ .

5 ______________________________ .

6 ______________________________ .

(10 marks)

Nächsten Sonntag fahren wir mit dem Zug zu meinen Großeltern.

Next Sunday we're taking the train to my grandparents'.

Digital resources

Music and dance

Was für Musik hörst du gern?

Art (f)	type
Band (f)	band
klassische Musik (f)	classical music
Lied (nt)	song
Popmusik (f)	pop
Rockmusik (f)	rock music

Ich höre gern Metal, House, Hip Hop usw.
I like listening to metal, house, hip hop, etc.

The German equivalent of 'etc.' (etcetera) is **usw** – an abbreviation of **und so weiter**.

Using cognates

You might see words that are not on the vocabulary list but are very similar to the same word in English. These are called cognates. It is fine for you to use them in your work as well. Types of music are often cognates.

music cognates: Rapmusik, Metal, Dubstep / House / Trap, Andere Musikarten, Hip Hop, Metalcore, Rockmusik, Tanzmusik

Worked example

WRITING — Target grade 1-5

Describe the photo. Write four short sentences **in German**. **(8 marks)**

1 Es gibt ein Konzert.
2 Die Band spielt Rockmusik.
3 Viele Leute tanzen und singen.
4 Die Musik ist laut.

Now try this

LISTENING — TRACK 26 — Target grade 3-5

Dictation

You are going to hear someone talking about music.

Write down the missing words in the gaps provided. In each gap, you will write one word **in German**.

Listen to the recording

1 Ich ____________ sehr ____________ Musik.
2 Mein ______________ spielt ____________ .
3 Ich _______ in der Zukunft _______ spielen.

(6 marks)

Worked example

READING — Target grade 6-7

Read the music magazine article.

Chart-Informationen!

Diese Woche gibt es Toni & Tim mit ihrem neuen Lied *Wo ist sie?* Das ist ein Liebeslied mit einem tollen Video.

Dann noch *Irgendwas* von der jungen Rapper-Band Maximilian X. Das ist nochmal ein stilvolles Video, das früh am Morgen gefilmt wurde.

Aber auf Platz eins für die dritte Woche ist Yasmin mit ihrem traurigen Lied *Verständnis*. Leider ist diesmal das Video nichts Besonderes.

What do you find out?

Put a cross ✗ next to each of the **three** correct statements.

[X]	**A** *Where is she?* is the title of Toni & Tim's hit song.
[ ]	**B** *Irgendwas* is a pop song.
[ ]	**C** The rap video was filmed at night.
[X]	**D** Maximilian X are rappers.
[ ]	**E** There is a new number one song this week.
[X]	**F** Yasmin's video is not brilliant.

(3 marks)

Arranging to go out

Digital resources

Gehen wir ins Kino?

Morgen (m)	morning
Nachmittag (m)	afternoon
Abend (m)	evening
heute	today
morgen	tomorrow
heute Morgen / Nachmittag / Abend / Nacht	this morning / afternoon / evening / tonight
morgen früh	tomorrow morning
morgen Nachmittag / Abend	tomorrow afternoon / evening
am Dienstag	on Tuesday
nächsten Freitag	next Friday
nächstes Wochenende	next weekend
besuchen	to visit
plaudern	to chat

Wann treffen wir uns?

um halb acht	at half past seven / 7:30
gegen Mittag	at about / around midday
um 20 Uhr	at 8 pm
nach der Schule	after school

Wo treffen wir uns?

vor dem Kino	in front of / outside the cinema
in dem Café	in the café
am Strand	on the beach
am Bahnhof	at the station
auf dem Marktplatz	in the market square

Sie treffen sich in einem Café und plaudern.
They meet in a café and chat.

Worked example

LISTENING TRACK 27 — Target grade 3-4

Listen to the recording

Finn and Toni are making plans.
What do they say?
Listen to the recording and complete the sentences by putting a cross ✗ in the correct box for each question.

Finn: Hast du Lust, morgen einen Kaffee zu trinken?
Toni: Ja, gerne! Um wie viel Uhr?
Finn: Halb elf? Wenn dir das passt?
Toni: Ja. Treffen wir uns vor dem Café! Bis dann.
Finn: Toll, bis morgen.

(a) Finn invites Toni …

✗	**A** for coffee.
☐	**B** for tea.
☐	**C** for lunch.

(b) They arrange to meet …

☐	**A** at 10:00.
✗	**B** at 10:30.
☐	**C** at 11:30.

(2 marks)

12-hour clock

zwei Uhr

fünf nach zwei

Viertel nach zwei

halb drei

Viertel vor drei

zehn vor drei

Be careful! **Halb drei** is half past two (literally, half **to** three).

Now try this

LISTENING TRACK 28 — Target grade 6

Listen to the recording

Emily and Joel are arranging to go out. Listen to the recording and answer the following questions **in English**. You do not need to write in full sentences.

(a) When does Joel ask Emily to go out?
(b) What will they do?
(c) Where and when will they meet? (**two** details)

(4 marks)

Digital resources

Reading

Lesen

Abenteuer (nt)	adventure
Geschichte (f)	story / history
Hauptperson (f)	main character
Krimi (m)	detective story
Person (f)	person / character
Roman (m)	novel
Schriftsteller (m) / Schriftstellerin (f)	author / writer
Thema (nt)	theme / subject
historisch	historical
beschreiben	to describe
entdecken	to discover
entwickeln	to develop
erzählen	to tell / relate
passieren	to happen

Talking about reading

Ich lese oft Krimis.
I often read detective stories.

Mein Lieblingsroman ist eine historische Geschichte.
My favourite novel is a historical story.

Das Hauptthema ist Familienverhältnisse.
The main theme is family relationships.

Das Buch ist voller Abenteuer.
The book is full of adventure.

Die Schriftstellerin beschreibt die schöne Landschaft.
The author describes the beautiful landscape.

Die Hauptperson ist ein deutscher Polizist.
The main character is a German policeman.

Remember: you can join nouns together to make compound words.

Qualifiers

These make another word's meaning stronger or less strong.

gar nicht	not at all	meistens	mostly
ein bisschen	a little	ab und zu	from time to time
ein wenig	a little	eigentlich nicht	not really
ganz / ziemlich	quite	vielleicht	perhaps

Ich lese ganz oft Bücher, aber Zeitungen lese ich gar nicht.
I read books quite often, but I don't read newspapers at all.

Worked example

LISTENING TRACK 29 | Target grade 4-5 | Listen to the recording

Max is talking about reading. What does he say?

Ich mag lesen und nehme mein Buch immer mit. Meine Lieblingsbücher sind Abenteuergeschichten, die voller Spannung sind und wo alles schnell passiert. Manchmal lese ich einen historischen Roman, denn Geschichte interessiert mich. Liebesgeschichten sind nichts für mich.

Complete the gap in each sentence using a word from the box below.

never	always	probably	sometimes
crime	horror	adventure	love

(a) Max ...always... has a book with him.
(b) He ...sometimes... reads a historical novel.
(c) His favourite books are ...adventure... stories.
(d) He doesn't enjoy ...love... stories. **(4 marks)**

Flexible phrases

Es ist mir egal. I don't mind.
Es kommt darauf an. It depends.
Daran gibt es keinen Zweifel.
There's no doubt about it.
Das stimmt. That's true.
Das ist auf jeden Fall meine Meinung.
That's my opinion, in any case.

Now try this

LISTENING TRACK 30 | Target grade 6-9 | Listen to the recording

You are going to hear someone talking about reading. Write down the full sentences that you hear, **in German**.

1 ______________________________.
2 ______________________________.
3 ______________________________.

(6 marks)

Television

Digital resources

Was siehst du gern im Fernsehen?

Dokumentarfilm (m)	documentary
Inhalt (m)	content
Komödie (f)	comedy
Krimi (m)	detective story
Nachrichten (f, pl)	news
Sendung (f)	programme
Serie (f)	series
Zuschauer (m, pl)	viewers
im Fernsehen	on TV
über	about
ansehen	to watch
anschauen	to watch
fernsehen	to watch TV

Ansehen, **anschauen** and **fernsehen** are separable verbs. Revise how you use them on page 107 of this Guide.

Was gibt es im Fernsehen?

Heute Abend gibt es eine Sendung über die Arbeit in einem Krankenhaus.
There's a programme on tonight about work in a hospital.

Um 19 Uhr schaue ich die Nachrichten an.
I'm watching the news at 7 pm.

Gibt es keine Komödien heute?
Aren't there any comedies today?

Hast du den Dokumentarfilm über kranke Tiere gesehen?
Did you see the documentary about sick animals?

The 24-hour clock

This way of stating 24-hour clock times is used a lot in German. You just need to say:

	the hour	Uhr	the minutes
15:20	fünfzehn	Uhr	zwanzig
19:55	neunzehn	Uhr	fünfundfünfzig

09:30	neun Uhr dreißig
12:45	zwölf Uhr fünfundvierzig
16:15	sechzehn Uhr fünfzehn
20:40	zwanzig Uhr vierzig
23:00	dreiundzwanzig Uhr

Remember: in order to convert the hours after midday to the 12-hour clock, subtract 12 from the first number.
20:30 – **zwanzig Uhr dreißig**
8:30 pm – **acht Uhr dreißig / halb neun**

Worked example

LISTENING TRACK 31 — Target grade 3-4

Listen to the recording

You hear this information about tonight's television programmes.

What do you learn?

Listen to the recording and complete the sentences by putting a cross ✗ in the correct box for each question.

Heute Abend um 19:30 Uhr gibt es die Serie *Nachbarn* und danach um 20 Uhr eine neue Dokumentarsendung über schmutzige Meere. Um 21:30 Uhr sind die Nachrichten … Später um 22 Uhr ist die Deutsche Verkehrspoliziei nochmal unterwegs …

(a) At 7:30 pm you can watch …

☐	**A**	the news.
☐	**B**	a film.
☒	**C**	a series.

(b) The traffic police programme is at …

☐	**A**	9:30 pm.
☒	**B**	10 pm.
☐	**C**	10:30 pm.

(2 marks)

Now try this

WRITING — Target grade 5

Write to someone you know about TV. You **must** include the following points:

- what you watch on television
- what you think of television programmes
- what you have watched recently
- what you would like to see on television.

Write your answer **in German**. You should aim to write between 80 and 90 words. **(18 marks)**

Digital resources

Film and cinema

Kino

fantastisch	fantastic
komisch	funny (strange)
spannend	exciting
toll	great
traurig	sad

Ich habe … im Kino gesehen.
I saw … at the cinema.

Es war ein Abenteuerfilm / Horrorfilm / Liebesfilm.
It was an adventure / horror / romantic film.

Das Hauptthema war Liebe / Familie.
The main theme was love / family.

Die Geschichte war kompliziert / romantisch.
The story was complicated / romantic.

Der Film spielte in Köln. The film was set in Cologne.

Flexible phrases

These phrases can be used for a variety of topics to give a balanced view. **H ONLY**

vor allem above all
im Großen und Ganzen in general
einerseits on the one hand
andererseits on the other hand
Hier sind die Vorteile / Nachteile: …
Here are the advantages / disadvantages: …

Im Großen und Ganzen macht es Spaß, ins Kino zu gehen, vor allem wenn ein Horrorfilm läuft.
In general, it's fun to go to the cinema, above all when a horror film is on.

Worked example

READING — Target grade 5

Read these film reviews.
Complete the sentences. Put a cross ✗ in the correct box for each question.

TOP FILME für JUGENDLICHE
Der Virus – Spannender Actionfilm. Kann unser Superheld* die Welt retten?
Getrennt – Kompliziertes deutsches Drama. Eine Familie kämpft darum, zusammenzubleiben.
Polizei drei – Abenteuerfilm. Drei junge Detektive auf der Suche nach Antworten.
Durch die Bäume – Schwarze Komödie mit traurigen Momenten.
Wien und die Wahrheit – Animationsfilm. Kampf gegen Kriminelle in Österreich.

* *Superheld* – superhero

(a) *Durch die Bäume* is …

☐	**A** an action film.
☐	**B** an adventure film.
✗	**C** a black comedy.

(b) A family is in trouble in …

☐	**A** *Polizei drei.*
✗	**B** *Getrennt.*
☐	**C** *Der Virus.*

(c) A struggle against lawbreakers features in …

✗	**A** *Wien und die Wahrheit.*
☐	**B** *Polizei drei.*
☐	**C** *Der Virus.*

(d) Young investigators feature in …

✗	**A** *Polizei drei.*
☐	**B** *Der Virus.*
☐	**C** *Durch die Bäume.*

(4 marks)

Now try this

LISTENING TRACK 32 — Target grade 6-7

Listen to the recording

Charlotte is talking about the cinema.
What does she like and dislike?

Listen to the recording and complete the following table **in English**. You do not need to write in full sentences.

(a) Like (2 details)	
(b) Dislike (2 details)	

(4 marks)

Mobile technology

Digital resources

Die Technologie

App (f)	app
Daten (pl)	data
Gefahr (f)	danger
Handy (nt)	mobile phone
Kommunikation (f)	communication
Kosten (pl)	costs
Webseite (f)	website
negativ / positiv	negative / positive
notwendig	necessary essential
nützlich	useful
unmöglich	impossible
unterwegs	on the way
vorsichtig sein	to take care / be careful
herunterladen	to download

Flexible phrases

Es gibt sowohl Nachteile als auch Vorteile.
There are disadvantages as well as advantages.

Es gibt Risiken, aber wenn man vorsichtig ist, ist das kein Problem.
There are risks, but if you take care, it's not a problem.

... ist toll und nicht nur zum ...
... is great and not just for ...

... ist heute total notwendig.
... is absolutely essential nowadays.

Ohne ... kann ich nichts tun!
Without ... I can't do anything!

Worked example

LISTENING TRACK 33

Target grade 4-5

Listen to the recording

Yannie and Sascha are talking about their phones. What do they like and dislike about them?

Listen to the recording and complete the following tables **in English**.

You do not need to write in full sentences.

(a) Yannie

Likes	the (many) useful apps
Dislikes	the camera/the bad photos

(b) Sascha

Likes	the colour
Dislikes	not being able to listen to music

(4 marks)

– Yannie, wie findest du dein Handy?

– Ich mag es sehr, weil ich viele nützliche Apps habe, die ich oft benutze, aber die Fotos, die ich damit mache, sind nicht immer so gut, und das gefällt mir nicht. Und du, Sascha?

– Ich habe ein altes Handy, das nicht sehr schnell ist, aber das ist mir egal. Ich mag die Farbe. Ich denke aber, es ist kaputt, denn ich kann meine Musik nicht mehr hören.

Sascha says **das ist mir egal** ('I don't mind') that the phone is slow.

Now try this

WRITING

Target grade 5

Write to a friend about mobile phone use. You **must** include the following points:

- what you like about your mobile
- what you think is the biggest advantage of a mobile
- how you have used your mobile phone recently
- what sort of phone you would like next.

Write your answer **in German**. You should aim to write between 80 and 90 words. **(18 marks)**

Digital resources

Social media

Soziale Netzwerke

Cybermobbing (nt)	cyberbullying
Daten (pl)	data
Fremde (m, pl)	strangers
Gefahr (f)	danger
Inhalt (m)	content
Netzwerk (nt)	network
Risiken (nt, pl)	risks
soziale Medien (pl)	social media
persönlich	personal
sicher	safe / secure
vorsichtig	careful
chatten	to chat online
schicken	to send
schützen	to protect
sich äußern	to express oneself

Modal verbs

Grammar page 112

Modal verbs are useful to talk about what you can / can't, must / mustn't, should / shouldn't do.

Man soll keine persönlichen Daten mit Fremden teilen.
You should not share personal details with strangers.

Du musst dein Passwort regelmäßig ändern, um dich zu schützen.
You must change your password regularly, in order to protect yourself.

Man kann rund um die Uhr in Kontakt bleiben.
You can keep in touch around the clock.

Man kann mit Menschen aus der ganzen Welt chatten.
You can chat with people from around the world.

Man kann sich äußern.
You can express yourself.

Worked example

READING — Target grade 5-6

Read these online messages.

Lara: Ich finde soziale Medien lustig. Mit Instagram kann ich alles sehen, was meine Freundinnen machen.

Jan: Meine Lieblingsplattform ist YouTube, denn ich kann Musik hören und Tanzvideos sehen.

Robin: Ich benutze WhatsApp, wo ich Modefotos hochladen* kann. Ich bin vorsichtig und teile keine Informationen mit Fremden.

Yasmin: Soziale-Medien-Plattformen kann ich nicht leiden, weil ich meine Aktivitäten lieber privat halte.

* *hochladen* – to upload

Answer the following questions **in English**. You do not need to write in full sentences.

(a) Why does Lara use Instagram?
to see what friends are doing

(b) Why does Jan like YouTube?
music / dance videos

(c) What does Robin use social media for?
uploading fashion photos

(d) Why does Yasmin not use social media?
keeps activities private

(4 marks)

Now try this

WRITING — Target grade 5-9

Translate the following paragraph **into German**.

> Social media can be a positive experience for young people but there are also risks, and you should be careful online. It's not a good idea to share personal data with people you don't know. But it's fun to see what your friends are doing. Yesterday I uploaded some holiday photos.

(10 marks)

Internet

Digital resources

Online-Leben

Cyberkriminalität (f)	cybercrime
Daten (pl)	data
Gefahr (f)	danger
Kommunikation (f)	communication
Laptop (m, nt)	laptop
Möglichkeit (f)	possibility
Nachrichten (f, pl)	news
Streaming (nt)	streaming
Tablet (nt)	tablet
Webseite (f)	website
falsch	untrue
chatten	to chat online
erkennen	to recognise
verbringen	to spend time

Making comparisons

Grammar page 101

H ONLY

adjective	comparative	superlative
praktisch	praktisch**er**	**am** praktisch**sten**
schnell	schnell**er**	**am** schnell**sten**

Das Internet ist praktisch.
The internet is practical.
WhatsApp ist praktisch**er** als E-Mail.
WhatsApp is more practical than email.
Snapchat ist **am** praktisch**sten**.
Snapchat is the most practical.
Junge Menschen müssen lernen.
Young people must learn.

Use the word **als** for 'than' in 'more practical than'.

Using man

Remember to use man to make general statements about what people should / can do. It's better than using du!

Man soll nicht mit Fremden chatten.
One / you shouldn't chat with strangers.

Man soll Daten schützen.
You should protect data.

Modal verbs like **müssen**, **sollen** and **können** are used with an infinitive. Remember: **zu** is not needed before the infinitive with modals.

Worked example

READING — Target grade 7-8

Read this article extract.

> Viele Jugendliche sind sich nicht bewusst, dass das Internet neben all seinen Möglichkeiten auch Gefahren mit sich bringt. Um sich zu schützen, müssen junge Menschen lernen, wie soziale Medien funktionieren, wie man seine Daten und Privatsphäre* schützen kann und wie man falsche Nachrichten erkennt.

* *Privatsphäre* – privacy

Answer the following questions **in English**. You do not need to write in full sentences.

(a) What are many young people unaware of?
The internet can be dangerous.

(b) What do young people need to learn? (**2** details)
How social media function and how to protect their data / privacy.

(c) What do they also need to recognise?
Fake news / messages / announcements.

(4 marks)

Now try this

SPEAKING — TRACK 34 — Target grade 5-9

Read aloud

Max, your friend, has sent you some comments about technology. Read out the text below.

(8 marks)

Listen to the recording

> Die digitale Technologie hat sowohl Risiken als auch viele Vorteile.
> Mein Handy ist mir nützlich, da ich mit Freunden in Kontakt bleiben kann.
> Ich finde das Internet notwendig, weil ich dort alle Informationen finde, die ich für mein Studium brauche.
> Das hilft mir besonders, denn ich interessiere mich für den Klimawandel.

Now listen to the follow-on questions and speak your answers in the pauses.

(4 marks)

Digital resources

Computer games

Computerspiele

Abenteuer (nt)	adventure
Gaming (nt)	gaming
Gewalt (f)	violence
Kampf (m)	struggle / battle
Konflikt (m)	conflict
Lernspiel (nt)	educational game
Spieler (m) / Spielerin (f)	player
Spielkonsole (f)	games console
erfolgreich	successful
weltweit	worldwide

Compound nouns

You can join words together in German to make compound nouns. Remember that the gender is determined by the last word.

Das Abenteuer + **das** Spiel → **das** Abenteuerspiel (adventure game)

Die Rolle + **das** Spiel → **das** Rollenspiel (role playing game)

Die Action + **das** Spiel → **das** Actionspiel (action game)

H ONLY

Das Überleben + **das** Spiel → **das** Überlebensspiel (survival game)

Der Kampf + **das** Spiel → **das** Kampfspiel (battle game)

Worked example

READING — Target grade 5-6

Read this games review.

Minecraft ist heute das erfolgreichste Videospiel aller Zeiten, mit über 140 Millionen Spielern weltweit. In diesem Spiel ist man in einer anderen Welt und muss alles neu bauen.

Mario Kart ist ein Rennspiel*, das fast jährlich in einer neuen Version erscheint. In jeder neuen Version gibt es neue Charaktere und Dinge zu finden.

FIFA ist ein beliebtes Fußballspiel mit realistischem Gameplay, das schnell und spannend ist.

Fortnite ist ein Kampfspiel, in dem man entweder allein oder mit anderen Spielern spielt.

* *Rennspiel* – racing game

What do we learn?

Put a cross ✗ next to each one of the **three** correct statements.

✗	**A** *Minecraft* is the most popular game.
✗	**B** *Mario Kart* is regularly updated.
✗	**C** *Mario Kart* features a search for people and objects.
☐	**D** *FIFA* is no longer as popular as it was.
☐	**E** *Fortnite* must be played solo.
☐	**F** *Fortnite* features sporting heroes.

(3 marks)

Worked example

READING — Target grade 5

Read the extract about computer games.

Diese ersten Spiele sind für Gamer ab einem Alter von 12 Jahren, weil sie keine realistischen Gewaltszenen enthalten.

Terminator Genisys: Future War ist voller Spielspaß. Das Game testet das strategische Denken der Spieler, deshalb könnte es für sehr junge Teenager etwas zu komplex sein.

What does it tell you?

Answer the questions **in English**. You do not need to write in full sentences.

(a) Who are the first games for?

Gamers from 12 years old

(b) Why do this age group play them?

Don't show realistic violence scenes

(c) What does the *Terminator Genisys* game test?

Strategic thinking

(d) What might be a problem for young teenagers?

Too complex **(4 marks)**

Now try this

WRITING — Target grade 1-3

Describe the photo. Write four short sentences **in German**.

(8 marks)

Pros and cons of technology

Digital resources

Auf der einen Seite ... ☺
On the one hand ...

... ist das Internet voller Informationen.
... the internet is full of information.
... kann man schnell kommunizieren.
... you can communicate quickly.
... kann man gut informiert sein.
... you can be well informed.
... ist Online-Einkaufen praktisch.
... online shopping is practical.
... kann man von zu Hause aus arbeiten.
... you can work from home.
... kann man Essen bestellen.
... you can order food.
... kann man viel lernen.
... you can learn a lot.

Auf der anderen Seite ... ☹
On the other hand ...

... verbringt man zu viel Zeit online.
... people spend too much time online.
... sieht man zu viel Gewalt.
... you see too much violence.
... gibt es Risiken.
... there are risks.
... muss man immer vorsichtig sein.
... you always have to be careful.
... sind persönliche Daten nicht immer sicher.
... personal data are not always secure.
... gibt es Cyberkriminalität.
... there is cybercrime.
... kann es falsche Informationen geben.
... there can be false information.

Auf der einen Seite kann man tolle Filme herunterladen.
On the one hand, you can download great films.

Auf der anderen Seite gibt es Cybermobbing.
On the other hand, there is online bullying.

Worked example

LISTENING TRACK 35 — Target grade 5

Listen to the recording

Leonie is talking about technology. Listen to the recording and complete the sentence by putting a cross ✗ in the correct box.

> Das Internet ist heute nützlich, weil alle Leute jetzt Internet haben. Für mich ist der Vorteil, dass es mit meinem Studium hilft. Auf der anderen Seite habe ich Angst, dass man manchmal Nachrichten sieht, die nicht wahr sind.

Leonie thinks that a disadvantage of the internet is ...

☒	**A**	fake news.
☐	**B**	cybercrime.
☐	**C**	cheating at school.

(1 mark)

This is the second part of the Foundation dictation task, where you are asked to write down whole sentences.

Now try this

LISTENING TRACK 36 — Target grade 3-5

Listen to the recording

Dictation

You are going to hear someone talking about technology. Write down the full sentences that you hear in the spaces provided, **in German**.

1 ______________________________ .
2 ______________________________ .
3 ______________________________ .

(6 marks)

Digital resources

Films on the internet

Filme im Internet

Streaming (nt)	streaming
streamen	to stream

Some additional useful cognates:

Streaming-Plattform (f)	streaming platform
Streaming-Service (m)	streaming service
legal / illegal	legal / illegal

Gern, lieber, am liebsten

Grammar page 101

A simple way of showing a preference is to use gern (like), lieber (prefer) and am liebsten (like most of all).

gern ♥ lieber ♥♥ am liebsten ♥♥♥

Worked example

READING — Target grade 4-5

Read about different streaming services.
What do you find out?

Der beste Streaming-Service in Deutschland ist Netflix. Andere wie Amazon Prime, Sky, Apple TV und WOW haben auch viele Zuschauer*. Es kostet natürlich etwas, wenn man einen Streaming-Service benutzen will. Es gibt jetzt ein gutes Angebot – Netflix kostet nur €7,99 pro Monat, was sehr ***günstig*** ist!

Für Musikfans ist YouTube die beliebteste Plattform.

Für Sportfans ist WOW vielleicht die beste, aber auch die teuerste.

Noch etwas: seien Sie vorsichtig – nutzen Sie keinen Streaming-Service, der nicht legal ist!

* *Zuschauer* – viewer / audience member

Put a cross ✗ in each one of the **three** correct boxes.

☐	**A** Amazon is the number 1 provider.
☐	**B** You don't have to pay for legal streaming.
☒	**C** Netflix is cheaper now than usual.
☐	**D** WOW is great for music.
☒	**E** WOW is not a cheap option.
☒	**F** Using illegal streaming services is not recommended.

(3 marks)

Which of these is the best translation for the word ***günstig***? Put a cross ✗ in the correct box.

☐	**A** surprising
☒	**B** good value
☐	**C** popular

(1 mark)

Ich schaue **gern** Filme. Ich schaue **lieber** Actionfilme als Liebesgeschichten, aber **am liebsten** schaue ich mir traurige Filme an.
I like watching films. I prefer action films to love stories, but most of all I like watching sad films.

Talking about prices

€ means Euro (pronounce it 'oyro').
To state a price, say the number of euros, then the word Euro, then the number of cents.
So, €10,25 = zehn Euro fünfundzwanzig.
€90,70 = neunzig Euro siebzig.

Note that the euros and cents are separated by a comma, not a full stop / decimal point.

Now try this

SPEAKING — Target grade 1-5

Describe the picture. Your description must cover people, location and activity. **(8 marks)**

Now listen to the recording for a sample response in the Answer section.

My home

Digital resources

Zu Hause

Bett (nt)	bed
Dach (nt)	roof
Dorf (nt)	village
Ecke (f)	corner
Garten (m)	garden
Haus (nt)	house
Küche (f)	kitchen
Lage (f)	position
Rand (m)	edge
Schlafzimmer (nt)	bedroom
Stock (m)	floor / storey
Treppe (f)	stairs
Wand (f)	interior wall
Wohnung (f)	flat

Ich bin **zu** Hause.
I am at home.

Ich gehe **nach** Hause.
I am going home.

Ich gehe nach oben / unten.
I'm going up- / downstairs.

Some useful compound nouns

Like Schlafzimmer – made up of Schlaf (sleep) and Zimmer (room) – you can also use these neuter compound nouns for rooms:

Badezimmer	bathroom
Esszimmer	dining room
Wohnzimmer	living / sitting room

Im ersten Stock gibt es drei Schlafzimmer und ein Badezimmer.

On the first floor there are three bedrooms and a bathroom.

Using the dative case

Grammar page 98

To describe the position of things, you need the dative case.

vor dem Haus
in front of the house

in der Wohnung
in the flat

am Tisch
at the table

neben der Tür
next to the door

an dem can be shortened to **am** and **in dem** can be shortened to **im**.

Worked example

READING — Target grade 3

Read this property advertisement.

Schönes Haus mit kleinem Garten und Garage. Moderne Küche, großes Wohnzimmer. Im 1. Stock: drei Schlafzimmer und zwei Badezimmer.

Complete the tables **in English**. You do not need to write in full sentences.

(a)

Two things about the outside space	
Has a small garden	Has a garage

(2 marks)

(b)

Four details about the rooms	
Modern kitchen	3 bedrooms
Big living room	2 bathrooms

(4 marks)

Now try this

WRITING — Target grade 5

Write to someone you know about your house or flat.

You **must** include the following points:

- what your home is like
- what you think of your house / flat
- what you did at home yesterday
- what sort of home you would like in the future.

Write your answer **in German**. You should aim to write between 80 and 90 words.

(18 marks)

My town

Digital resources

Meine Stadt

Ausstellung (f)	exhibition
Bibliothek (f)	library
Brücke (f)	bridge
Campingplatz (m)	campsite
Einwohner (m)	inhabitant
Fluss (m)	river
Gegend (f) / Region (f)	area
Hochschule (f) / Universität (f)	university
Krankenhaus (nt)	hospital
Laden (m) / Geschäft (nt)	shop
Strand (m)	beach
Verkehr (m)	traffic

Using weil

Grammar page 104

Weil (because) always sends the **verb to the end.**

Ich wohne gern in meinem Dorf, **weil** es dort ruhig **ist**.

I like living in my village because it is quiet.

If the sentence with weil is in the perfect tense, haben and sein go after the past participle.

Die Gegend ist nicht interessant, **weil** viele Geschäfte **geschlossen haben**.

The area is not very interesting because lots of shops have closed.

If the sentence with weil has a modal verb, the modal verb goes after the infinitive.

Ich wohne gerne in meiner Stadt, **weil** ich dort meine Freunde **treffen kann**.

I like living in my town because I can meet my friends there.

Worked example

READING — Target grade 5

Read these opinions about the places people live from a social media discussion.

Finn: Ich wohne in einer Kleinstadt an der Küste. Die Luft ist sauber, aber das Leben ist zu ruhig.

Laura: Ich wohne in einem Dorf auf dem Land. Es gibt viele Bäume und Felder, aber nichts zu tun.

Ben: Ich wohne in einer Großstadt. Es gibt viele große Gebäude und zu viel Verkehr. Das Leben in der Stadt ist aber spannend.

Complete the tables **in English**.

You do not need to write in full sentences.

(a) Finn

One thing he likes Clean air.

One thing he dislikes Life is too quiet.

(b) Laura

One thing she likes Trees / fields.

One thing she dislikes Nothing to do.

(c) Ben

One thing he likes Exciting.

One thing he dislikes Too much traffic.

(6 marks)

Living in and going to

Grammar page 98

Prepositions like an and in are followed by the **accusative** when there is movement towards something, and by the **dative** when there is not.

Ich gehe **an die** Küste.

I go to the coast.

Ich wohne **an der** Küste.

I live on the coast.

Ich gehe **in ein** Dorf.

I go to a village.

Ich wohne **in einem** Dorf.

I live in a village.

Now try this

SPEAKING — Target grade 1-9

Describe the picture. Your description must cover:

- people
- location
- activity.

(8 marks)

Facilities in town

Digital resources

Was kann man in der Stadt machen?

Was gibt es zu tun? What is there to do?

Für Touristen gibt es das Schloss, die Altstadt und das Museum.

For tourists there's the castle, the old town and the museum.

Für Jugendliche gibt es Clubs, das Kino, Cafés, Konzerte und tolle Geschäfte.

For young people there are clubs, the cinema, cafés, concerts and great shops.

Für die Einwohner gibt es die Bäckerei, die Apotheke, den Supermarkt, das Theater, die Post und ein Fitnesszentrum.

For residents there is the bakery, the pharmacy, the supermarket, the theatre, the post office and a gym.

Ich **wäre** glücklich, wenn die Stadt einen Bahnhof **hätte**.

I would be happy if the town had a station.

Verb in second place

Grammar page 103

①	②	③	④
Es	**gibt**	Geschäfte.	
Für Touristen	**gibt**	es	das Schloss.
Die Jugendliche	**sind**	ins Kino	**gegangen**.

In the perfect tense, the part of **haben** or **sein** goes in second place and the past participle goes to the end.

Using dass

Dass is a conjunction that joins two ideas. It is used with a comma and sends the verb to the end.

Ich bin froh. Es gibt ein Schwimmbad in unserer Stadt. → Ich bin froh, **dass** es in unserer Stadt ein Schwimmbad **gibt**.

Es gibt so viel Verkehr. Es ist für Kinder gefährlich. → Es gibt so viel Verkehr, **dass** es für Kinder gefährlich **ist**.

Worked example

Listening Track 37 · Target grade 6

Noah is talking about his home town. What does he say?

Listen to the recording

> Die Stadt hat viel, aber nicht alles, was man braucht. Es freut mich, dass wir ein Kino haben, aber es wäre besser, wenn wir auch ein Theater hätten.

Listen to the recording and complete the following tables **in English**.

You do not need to write in full sentences.

(a)

Something good the town has
It has a cinema

(b)

Something that would make the town better
A theatre

(2 marks)

Conditional statements

H only

Grammar page 117

This is a way of saying what would happen if something else happened.

Es **wäre** besser, wenn wir mehr Geschäfte **hätten**.

It would be better if we had more shops.

Now try this

Writing · Target grade 2-5

Translate the following sentences **into German**.

(a) I like my town.
(b) There is lots to see.
(c) We have a lovely park with a lake.
(d) You can visit the castle and the museum.
(e) Last week I went to the cinema with friends.

(10 marks)

Digital resources

Finding the way

Nach dem Weg fragen

Gibt es hier in der Nähe einen / eine / ein …?	Is there a … near here?
Ich suche …	I'm looking for …
Können Sie mir helfen?	Can you help me?
Entschuldigung	Excuse me
Wie komme ich zu …?	How do I get to …?
Wo ist / sind …?	Where is / are …?

Which case?

Grammar page 96

After wo ist / sind use the **nominative**.	Wo ist der Bahnhof?
After suchen or es gibt use the **accusative**.	Gibt es hier in der Nähe einen Bahnhof, bitte?
After zu use the **dative**.	Wie komme ich zum Bahnhof?

Giving directions

Gehen Sie … Go … (on foot)
Fahren Sie … Drive

- geradeaus – straight on
- links um die Ecke – left at the corner
- am Ende der Straße – at the end of the street
- an der Ecke – at the corner
- bis zu – up to, as far as
- diese Straße entlang – along this street
- über die Brücke – over the bridge
- über den Fluss – over the river
- nach links – left
- nach rechts – right
- auf der rechten Seite – on the right
- auf der linken Seite – on the left

Worked example

LISTENING TRACK 38 | Target grade 3-4 | Listen to the recording

You are getting some directions to the pharmacy. What are you told?
Listen to the recording and complete the sentences by putting a cross ✗ in the correct box for each question.

Gehen Sie zuerst hier geradeaus und dann am Ende der Straße gehen Sie nach links. Dann an der Ecke gehen Sie nach rechts und die Apotheke ist auf der linken Seite.

(a) First of all …

☐	**A** turn right.
☐	**B** turn left.
☒	**C** go straight on.

(b) At the end of the street …

☐	**A** turn right.
☒	**B** turn left.
☐	**C** go straight on.

(c) At the corner …

☒	**A** turn right.
☐	**B** turn left.
☐	**C** go straight on.

(3 marks)

Now try this

WRITING | Target grade 1-5

Describe the photo. Write four short sentences **in German**.

(8 marks)

The word for 'street map' is **Straßenplan (m)**.

Shops and shopping

Digital resources

Einkaufen gehen

Dach (nt)	roof
Einkaufszentrum (nt)	shopping centre
Geschäft (nt)	shop
Laden (m)	shop
entfernt	away, distant
kaufen	to buy
einkaufen	to shop
einkaufen gehen	to go shopping

At Foundation tier, you only need the imperfect for **sein** and **haben** – ich war, ich hatte, etc.

In meiner Freizeit besuche ich gerne das Einkaufszentrum. Es ist nicht weit entfernt und hat meine Lieblingsläden und ein riesiges Dach aus Glas.

I like to visit the shopping centre in my free time. It is not far away and has my favourite shops and a huge roof made of glass.

Shopping in different time frames

Grammar pages 106, 113–117

Present

Heute kaufe ich Blumen, weil meine Mutter Geburtstag hat.

I'm buying flowers today, as it's my mother's birthday.

Perfect

Ich habe letzten Monat einen neuen Laptop gekauft, weil mein alter Laptop kaputt war.

I bought a new laptop last month because my old one was broken.

Imperfect

Als ich ein Kind war, kaufte ich immer Schokolade.

When I was a child, I was always buying chocolate.

Future

Nächste Woche werde ich mit meiner Freundin einkaufen gehen, um Geschenke zu kaufen.

Next week I'm going to go shopping with my friend to buy presents.

Conditional (H ONLY)

Wenn ich das Geld hätte, würde ich gern ein neues Handy haben, aber ich muss dafür sparen.

If I had the money, I would like to have a new phone, but I have to save for that.

Worked example

LISTENING TRACK 39 — Target grade 6-7 — Listen to the recording

Listen to the advert for a shopping centre. Which items are mentioned?

Listen to the recording and put a cross ✗ in each one of the **three** correct boxes.

Von Modegeschäften mit der neuesten Designerkleidung bis zur Sportausrüstung, hier gibt es alles! 83 Geschäfte, 12 Restaurants und eine tolle Auswahl an Einkaufsmöglichkeiten – egal, ob Sie einen Computer, eine Handtasche, ein Geschenk, ein Hemd oder elektrische Geräte brauchen.

✗	**A** clothing
✗	**B** sports kit
	C perfume
✗	**D** electrical appliances
	E children's toys
	F books

(3 marks)

Now try this

LISTENING TRACK 40 — Target grade 4-5 — Listen to the recording

Listen to the advert for a new shopping centre. What do you learn?

Listen to the recording and put a cross ✗ in each one of the **three** correct boxes.

The shopping centre …

	A has 156 shops.
	B has a large car park.
	C has two chemist shops.
	D has gift shops.
	E has a shoe shop.
	F is open until 9 pm.

(3 marks)

Digital resources

At the market

Worked example

WRITING — Target grade 2-5

Describe the photo. Write four short sentences **in German**. **(8 marks)**

1 Es gibt eine schöne Frau.
2 Sie ist auf dem Markt.
3 Sie kauft Gemüse und Obst.
4 Sie hat eine gelbe Tasche.

For this task, your answers only need to be brief, BUT they must be in complete sentences (with a verb) to score two marks each. For example, **auf dem Markt** on its own would score one mark, as there is no verb.

Worked example

SPEAKING TRACK 41 — Target grade 5-9

Describe the picture.

Your description must cover:

- people
- location
- activity.

Listen to the recording

(8 marks)

Auf dem Foto gibt es zwei Mädchen, die auf dem Markt einkaufen. Sie sehen Kleidung an. Ein Mädchen hat blonde Haare, und das andere hat braune Haare und eine Sonnenbrille. Sie sind glücklich.

When you have finished your description, your teacher will ask you two questions relating to the picture. You are expected to say a few words or a short phrase or sentence in response to each question. One-word answers will not be sufficient to gain full marks.

Questions:

(a) Wie oft gehst du einkaufen? **(2 marks)**

Ich gehe jeden Samstag mit meinem Freund einkaufen. Das macht immer Spaß.

(b) Was hast du neulich auf dem Markt gekauft? **(2 marks)**

Ich habe letzte Woche Obst und Gemüse gekauft.

Keep your answers to the follow-up questions quite brief. Just answer the question!
Remember that the second follow-up question will be in the past tense.

Don't worry if you haven't been to a market recently. Make something up that shows off the vocabulary you know.

Exam alert

In the exam you will have a choice of two pictures. Choose the one for which you can find most to say.

Try to develop your initial description of the picture as much as you can, giving details of the people, place and activity.

Now try this

LISTENING TRACK 42 — Target grade 3-5

Dictation

Listen to the recording

You are going to hear someone talking about the local market.

Sentences 1–3: write down the missing words in the gaps provided. In each gap, you will write one word **in German**.

Sentences 4–6: write down the full sentences that you hear in the spaces provided, **in German**.

1 Der ____________ ist am ____________ .
2 Ich gehe ____________ ____________ .
3 Man ____________ Obst und ____________ kaufen.
4 ________________________________ .
5 ________________________________ .
6 ________________________________ .

(10 marks)

Transport

Digital resources

Verkehrsmittel

mit dem Auto / Wagen

mit der Bahn / mit dem Zug

mit dem Boot / Schiff

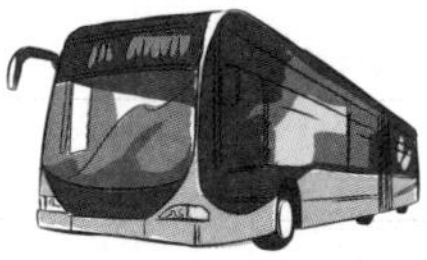
mit dem Bus

mit dem Rad (Fahrrad)

mit dem Flugzeug

mit der U-Bahn

zu Fuß

mit der Straßenbahn

Wie kommt man hin? – How do you get there?
öffentliche Verkehrsmittel (nt, pl) – public transport
fahren – to go / travel (in a vehicle)
gehen – to go / walk (on foot)

Worked example

READING — Target grade 4-5

Read these comments on the pros and cons of local transport.

Ardi: Ich finde es praktisch, mit dem Auto zu fahren, aber Autofahren ist jetzt teuer, und es ist umweltfreundlicher, mit dem Bus zu fahren. Es gibt oft einen Bus, den ich benutzen kann, aber die Busse sind manchmal schmutzig.

Paula: Ich gehe meistens zu Fuß. Das ist gesund, aber wenn es regnet, ist es nicht so schön. Die U-Bahn ist sehr schnell, aber es ist oft sehr heiß und es sind zu viele Leute drin.

Answer the following questions **in English**. You do not need to write in full sentences.

(a) What does Ardi thinks of driving? (**2** details)
Driving is practical but expensive

(b) What is Ardi's opinion of buses? (**3** details)
Buses are frequent / come often, are environmentally friendly but are dirty

(c) What does Paula think about walking? (**2** details)
Walking is good as it's healthy, but not good when it rains

(d) What is Paula's opinion of the underground? (**3** details)
The underground is fast, but hot and crowded / full of people

(10 marks)

Time – Manner – Place

Grammar page 103

In German, adverbs have to be in the order: Time – Manner – Place

All means of transport are Manner (how) expressions, so they come between Time and Place.

Ich fahre jeden Tag mit der U-Bahn zur Schule.
Every day I go to school by underground.

Ich gehe immer zu Fuß in die Stadt.
I always go to town on foot / walk to town.

Gestern sind wir mit dem Auto nach London gefahren.
Yesterday we went to London by car / we drove to London.

Nächste Woche wird er mit dem Flugzeug nach Berlin fliegen.
Next week he is going to Berlin by plane.

Now try this

LISTENING — TRACK 43 — Target grade 2-5

Dictation

You are going to hear someone talking about transport. Write down the missing words in the gaps provided. In each gap, you will write one word **in German**.

Listen to the recording

1 Ich ________ jeden Tag mit dem ________ .
2 Das ist ________ und gut für die ________ .
3 Mein ________ findet sein Auto schnell und ________ .

(6 marks)

Digital resources

Buying tickets for travel

Fahrkarten kaufen

Abfahrt (f)	departure
Ankunft (f)	arrival
Fahrkarte (f)	ticket
Fahrt (f)	journey
Fenster (nt)	window
Platz (m)	seat
Rückfahrkarte (f)	return ticket
Unfall (m)	accident
einfach	single (ticket)
hin	there
spät	late
wohin?	where to?
zurück	back
ankommen	to arrive
bleiben	to stay
sitzen	to sit
warten	to wait

Am Bahnhof

Wohin wollen Sie fahren?	Where do you want to go?
Einfach oder hin und zurück?	Single or return?
Wo möchten Sie sitzen?	Where would you like to sit?
Fährt der Zug direkt?	Is it a direct train?

Leider kommt der Zug spät an.
Unfortunately, the train is arriving late.

Es hat einen Unfall gegeben.	There has been an accident.
Woher kommen Sie?	Where do you come from?

Wann **kommt** der Zug in Berlin **an**? When does the train arrive in Berlin?

Wann **fährt** der Zug nach Berlin **ab**? When does the train to Berlin leave?

ankommen (to arrive) and **abfahren** (to depart) have a separable prefix (**an-**/**ab-**).

Worked example

READING — Target grade 5-6

Read Malik's message about his travels. What does he say?

> Mein Zug kam spät, weil es einen Unfall gab, und ich musste eine halbe Stunde auf dem Bahnsteig warten. Dann gab es viele Leute und viel Gepäck und ich konnte meinen Platz nicht finden. Ich musste die ganze Strecke im Gang bleiben. Ich bin am Ende eine Stunde später, kurz vor zwei Uhr morgens, angekommen.

Put a cross ✗ next to each one of the **three** correct statements.

Malik …

☐	**A** was late reaching the station.
☒	**B** had to wait for his train.
☐	**C** had a lot of luggage.
☒	**D** spent the journey standing in the corridor.
☐	**E** arrived two hours later than expected.
☒	**F** arrived one hour later than expected.

(3 marks)

Now try this

LISTENING — TRACK 44 — Target grade 6

Listen to the station announcements. What do you learn?

Listen to the recording

Complete the gaps in the sentences using words or numbers from the box below. There are more words / numbers than gaps.

Cologne	Vienna	Berlin
13	30	33
9	2	8

(a) The fast train to ____________ is delayed by ____________ minutes.

(b) The restaurant is located in carriage number ____________ .

(c) The night train to Vienna leaves in ____________ minutes.

(4 marks)

Places of interest near me

Digital resources

Machen wir eine Stadttour?

Ausstellung (f)	exhibition
Bahn (f)	railway
Besucher (m)	visitor
Brücke (f)	bridge
Fluss (m)	river
Gegend (f)	area
Geschichte (f)	history
Kultur (f)	culture
Markt (m)	market
Museum (nt)	museum
Schloss (nt)	castle
Theater (nt)	theatre
verschieden	different / diverse
besichtigen	to visit / view

Aber or sondern?

H ONLY

Grammar page 104

You normally translate 'but' with aber.

Ich habe das Museum besucht, **aber** nicht das Schloss.

I visited the museum but not the castle.

Sondern is used after a negative when the meaning is 'but rather'.

Ich ging nicht ins Theater, **sondern** ins Kino.

I didn't go to the theatre but (rather) to the cinema.

You can use nicht nur … sondern auch to mean 'not only … but also'.

Der Bahnhof ist **nicht nur** berühmt, **sondern auch** praktisch.

The railway station is not only famous but also convenient.

Worked example

READING

Target grade 6

Read this text from a student's poster about his town.

Ich wohne in Edinburgh. Man kann mit dem Bus eine Rundfahrt durch die Stadt machen, die gar nicht teuer ist. Man kann nicht nur das Schloss, sondern auch den ***Palast*** und den historischen Marktplatz im alten Stadtteil besichtigen. Hier kann man einkaufen oder zu Mittag essen. Es gibt täglich verschiedene Abfahrtszeiten.

What do you learn? Put a cross ✗ next to each one of the **three** correct statements.

The city tour …

☐	**A** is on foot.
☒	**B** is reasonably priced.
☐	**C** includes an art gallery.
☒	**D** includes the castle.
☒	**E** includes shopping opportunities.
☐	**F** takes place once a day.

(3 marks)

Which of these is the best translation for the word ***Palast***? Put a cross ✗ in the correct box.

☐	**A** place
☐	**B** plaster
☒	**C** palace

(1 mark)

Read carefully – don't just skim for the words in the options. For example, you might see **teuer** and think that the tour is expensive, but reading carefully will allow you to understand that it is **gar nicht teuer**.

Now try this

LISTENING TRACK 45

Target grade 5

Listen to the recording

Yusuf and Katherina are speaking in a podcast. What do they say? Listen to the recording and complete the sentences by putting a cross ✗ in the correct box for each question.

(a) Yusuf says the film studio was …

☐	**A** a long way from London.
☐	**B** easy to get to.
☐	**C** not worth the trip.

(b) Katherina's aunt visited a castle and …

☐	**A** a church.
☐	**B** an art gallery.
☐	**C** a museum.

(2 marks)

Digital resources

The environment

Die Umwelt

Grund (m)	reason
Menge (f)	a lot of
Müll (m)	rubbish
Verschmutzung (f)	pollution
sauber	clean
schmutzig	dirty
umweltfreundlich	environmentally friendly
verantwortlich	responsible
aussehen	to look / appear
respektieren	to respect
sammeln	to collect
schützen	to protect
verbieten	to ban / forbid
verursachen	to cause
wegwerfen	to throw away

Kommentare über die Umwelt

Ich finde meine Stadt nicht sehr sauber.
I don't think my town is very clean.
Hier gibt es Industrie, die das Meer verschmutzt.
There's industry here which pollutes the sea.
Das schlimmste Problem ist die Luftverschmutzung.
The worst problem is air pollution.
Wenige Leute machen etwas Positives, um die Umwelt zu schützen.
Few people do anything positive to protect the environment.
Autos sollten in der Stadt verboten werden.
Cars should be banned in the town.
Viele Leute werfen Müll auf die Straße.
Lots of people throw rubbish on the street.

Listen to the recording

Worked example

SPEAKING TRACK 46 — Target grade 4-6

Describe the picture. Your description must cover:

- people
- location
- activity. **(8 marks)**

When you have finished your description, your teacher will ask you two questions relating to your chosen picture. You are expected to say a few words or a short phrase / sentence in response to each question. One-word answers will not be sufficient to gain full marks.

Auf dem Foto sehe ich einen Strand. Das Meer ist blau, und es ist ein schöner Tag im Sommer, aber der Strand hat viel Müll. Besucher haben Plastikflaschen weggeworfen, und der Strand sieht schmutzig aus. Ein Mann und ein Junge versuchen, den Strand sauber zu machen. Man soll die Natur respektieren und seinen Müll nach Hause nehmen.

Questions:

(a) Wie findest du die Umwelt in deiner Stadt? **(2 marks)**

In meiner Stadt gibt es immer Müll auf der Straße. Ich finde das schlimm.

(b) Was machst du, um die Umwelt zu schützen? **(2 marks)**

Ich recycle Papier und Plastik und ich sammle Müll am Strand.

Now try this

WRITING — Target grade 5

Write to someone you know about your environment. You **must** include the following points:

- what is good about the environment where you live
- an environmental problem where you live
- what you have done recently to be environmentally friendly
- what you will do in the future to help the environment.

Write your answer **in German**. You should aim to write between 80 and 90 words. **(18 marks)**

Environmental problems

Digital resources

Die Erde braucht unseren Schutz

Erde (f)	earth
Industrie (f)	industry
Insel (f)	island
Schutz (m)	protection
See (m)	lake
Temperatur (f)	temperature
trocken	dry
umweltfreundlich	environmentally friendly
schützen	to protect
sparen	to save
steigen	to rise / increase

Der Klimawandel nimmt zu

H ONLY

Boden (m)	ground / earth
Klima (nt)	climate
Klimawandel (m)	climate change
Knappheit (f)	shortage
Krise (f)	crisis
knapp	scarce / in short supply
verschwinden	to disappear
verursachen	to cause
weitergehen	to go on / continue
zunehmen	to increase

Die Meerestemperaturen steigen.
Sea temperatures are rising.

Worked example

READING — Target grade 6-7

Read the newspaper headlines.

Wasserknappheit in Afrika
Meerestemperaturen steigen weiter!
Waldbrand in Asien!
Boden wird immer trockener
Heute 47 Grad in Teilen Europas

Complete the gap in each sentence using a word from the box below.
There are more words than gaps.

America	Europe	Australia	Asia	Africa
wetter	drier	higher	colder	warmer

(a) It's currently very hot in ......Europe......
(b) Wildfires rage across ......Asia......
(c) There is a water shortage in ......Africa......
(d) The ground is getting ......drier......
(e) The seas are getting even ......warmer......

(9 marks)

Now try this

SPEAKING — Target grade 5-9

Read aloud

Mohammed, your friend, has sent you some comments about environmental issues.
Read out the text below.

Der Klimawandel verursacht weltweit viele ernste Probleme, die wir noch nicht gelöst haben.
Die Erde wird wärmer, und die Meerestemperaturen steigen jedes Jahr weiter an.
In einigen Ländern wird es bald nicht mehr möglich sein, genug Wasser für die Bevölkerung zu finden.
Tausende von Tierarten werden durch den Klimawandel bedroht und können nicht mehr überleben.

(10 marks)

Digital resources

The dangers of pollution

Umweltkrise

Initiative (f)	initiative
Krise (f)	crisis
Umgebung (f)	surroundings
Windkraft (f)	wind power
erneuerbar	renewable
gefährlich	dangerous
nachhaltig	sustainable
unglaublich	incredible
beitragen (zu)	to contribute (to)
enthalten	to contain
entwickeln	to develop
retten	to save
schaden	to harm
schützen	to protect
sich sorgen (um)	to care (about)
überleben	to survive
verändern	to change
Experten warnen	experts warn

Adjective endings with no article

Grammar page 100

	masculine	feminine	neuter	plural
nominative	klein**er**	klein**e**	klein**es**	klein**e**
accusative	klein**en**	klein**e**	klein**es**	klein**e**
dative	klein**em**	klein**er**	klein**em**	klein**en**

Plastik enthält gefährlich**e** Produkte, die zur Umweltverschmutzung beitragen.
Plastic contains dangerous products that contribute to pollution.

Wir müssen neu**e** Wege entwickeln, erneuerbar**e** und nachhaltig**e** Energie zu produzieren.
We must develop new ways to produce renewable and sustainable energy.

Worked example

READING — Target grade 8-9

Read this extract from an article in a school magazine.

> Mein Bruder verbrachte einen Monat mit einer Initiative in Südamerika. Sie retteten verletzte Tiere und machten die Strände sauber. Er sagt, dass die Umweltverschmutzung in der Umgebung allen Tieren schadet. Er fand die Erfahrung unglaublich wichtig, weil unsere Welt in einer schlimmen Krise steckt. Er sagte, der Klimawandel könnte unsere Welt so verändern, dass einige Tierarten vielleicht nicht überleben. Wir sollten unsere Welt besser schützen.

Complete the sentences below. Put a cross ✗ in the correct box for each question.

(a) The brother rescued …

☒	**A** injured animals.
☐	**B** lost animals.
☐	**C** harmful animals.

(b) He found the experience …

☐	**A** uninteresting.
☒	**B** important.
☐	**C** too rainy.

(c) He said that climate change could change the world so that some animal species …

☒	**A** may not survive.
☐	**B** may live somewhere else.
☐	**C** may start to look different.

(3 marks)

Now try this

LISTENING TRACK 47 — Target grade 5

Listen to the recording

Mohammed is talking about his school. What does he say?
Listen to the recording and answer the following questions **in English**.

(a) What is special about the lights in school?
(b) How do Mohammed's friends get to school?

(2 marks)

The natural world

Digital resources

Die Natur

Baum (m)	tree	Zeichen (nt)	sign
Blatt (nt)	leaf	bunt	colourful
Blume (f)	flower	leise	quiet
Erde (f)	earth	nass	wet
Feld (nt)	field	rein	pure / clean
Fluss (m)	river	ruhig	peaceful
Geräusch (nt)	noise	trocken	dry
Landschaft (f)	landscape	unglaublich	unbelievably
Mauer (f)	wall	aussehen	to appear
Pferd (nt)	horse	riechen	to smell
Pflanze (f)	plant	(sich) verstecken	to hide
See (m)	lake		
Szene (f)	scene	wandern	to hike
Tier (nt)	animal		
Wald (m)	wood / forest		

am Meer	by the sea
an der Küste	on the coast
auf dem Land	in the countryside
in den Bergen	in the mountains
in der Natur	in nature / the country
um die Stadt	round the town

Worked example

READING — Target grade 6

Read this extract from a story.

> Auf dem Land sieht die Landschaft ruhig aus. Die einzigen Lebenszeichen sind die leisen Geräusche der versteckten Tiere. Ich kann die bunten Blumen riechen. Die Luft ist rein und der Regen macht die trockene Erde nass.

Answer the following questions **in English**. You do not need to write in full sentences.

(a) How does the landscape seem?

calm

(b) What are the flowers like?

colourful / they smell

(c) What is the air like?

pure / clean **(3 marks)**

Die Wälder und Felder sind so grün.
The woods and fields are so green.

Worked example

READING — Target grade 6

Read Noah's description of his village.

> Mein Dorf ist klein und ruhig. Ich wohne mit meiner Mutter und unserem Hund zusammen. Ich gehe gerne in der Natur rund um unser Haus wandern. Manchmal kaufe ich frische Milch, die direkt von den ***Kühen*** kommt, die auf den Feldern leben.

Complete the sentences below. Put a cross ✗ in the correct box for each question.

(a) Noah's village is …

☐	**A** big.
☐	**B** boring.
☒	**C** peaceful.

(b) He likes to …

☒	**A** hike.
☐	**B** cycle.
☐	**C** play football.

(c) Which of these is the best translation for the word ***Kühen***?

☒	**A** cows
☐	**B** birds
☐	**C** pigs

This word will be one that is not on the vocabulary list. Work it out from the context – they live in fields and Noah gets milk from them.

(3 marks)

Now try this

LISTENING — TRACK 48 — Target grade 5

Listen to the recording

Lena is describing where she lives. What does she like and dislike?

Listen to the recording and complete the following tables **in English**. You do not need to write in full sentences.

(a) Lena

likes ______________________.
because ______________________.

(b) She

dislikes ______________________.
because ______________________.

(4 marks)

Digital resources

Individual actions for the environment

Wie kann man Energie sparen?

Einzelperson (f)	individual person
Initiative (f)	initiative
Recyclingpapier (nt)	recycled paper
Recyclingprodukte (pl)	recycled goods
einzel	single / individual
nachhaltig	sustainable
beitragen zu	to contribute to
recyceln	to recycle
retten	to save (rescue)
sparen	to save (not to spend / waste)
trennen	to sort / separate
vermeiden	to avoid

Man kann Recyclingprodukte kaufen.
You can buy recycled products.

Was kann man tun, um die Umwelt zu schützen?

Man kann kein Auto benutzen.
You can not use a car.

Man kann den Müll trennen und nicht so viel wegwerfen.
You can sort the rubbish and throw less away.

Man kann Wasser sparen.
You can save water.

Man kann weniger Strom benutzen.
You can use less electricity.

Man kann wenn möglich zu Fuß gehen.
You can go on foot when possible.

Die Zeit wird **knapp**, um die Umwelt zu retten.
Time is becoming short to save the environment.

Worked example

LISTENING TRACK 49 — Target grade 3-4

Samira is talking about being green. Which actions does she mention? Listen to the recording and put a cross ✗ in each one of the **three** correct boxes.

Listen to the recording

Als Einzelne kann man etwas für die Umwelt tun. Zu Hause recyceln wir Papier, Glas und Plastik. Wir benutzen die öffentlichen Verkehrsmittel und haben kein Auto. Ich versuche, Recyclingprodukte zu kaufen und ich dusche* mich schnell, um Wasser zu sparen.

**sich duschen* – to shower

✗	**A** sorts the rubbish at home
☐	**B** does not buy plastic
✗	**C** uses public transport
☐	**D** goes everywhere on foot
☐	**E** saves electricity
✗	**F** has a quick shower

(3 marks)

Talking about negatives

Use kein (not a / none), nicht (not), wenig (little), knapp (scarce / short).

In der Schule gibt es **keine** Recycling-Initiativen.
In school there are no recycling initiatives.

Ich versuche, **nicht** viel zu fliegen.
I try not to fly much.

Wir müssen **weniger** zum Klimawandel beitragen.
We must contribute less to climate change.

Now try this

WRITING — Target grade 2-5

Describe the photo. Write four short sentences **in German**. **(8 marks)**

When answering this question, remember to mention the people, the place and the activity!

How to recycle

Digital resources

Wie sollen wir recyceln?

Energie (f)	energy
Müll (m)	rubbish
Mülltrennung (f)	sorting rubbish
Verschmutzung (f)	pollution
weg	away
recyceln	to recycle
reduzieren	to reduce
trennen	to separate / sort
vermeiden	to avoid
werfen	to throw

Using man

H ONLY

The term man can be used impersonally to say what 'you' can do.

Wenn man Müll trennt, ist es einfacher zu recyceln.
When you sort rubbish, it is easier to recycle.

Durch Recycling kann man das Wegwerfen reduzieren.
You can throw less away through recycling.

In Deutschland recycelt man fast 70% des Mülls.
In Germany almost 70% of rubbish is recycled.

Man sollte den Müll trennen.
You should separate rubbish.

Das Recycling von Computern und elektronischen Geräten reduziert die Umweltverschmutzung.
Recycling of computers and electronic devices reduces environmental pollution.

Worked example

LISTENING TRACK 50 — Target grade 6-8

You hear on the radio some guidelines about separating rubbish. What sort of rubbish goes in the yellow container?

Listen to the recording and put a cross ✗ in each one of the **three** correct boxes.

Listen to the recording

> In den gelben Müllcontainer kommen Plastiktüten, Plastikflaschen, Getränkedosen und Kaffeetüten. Papier, Flaschen aus Glas, alte Zeitungen und kaputte. Teller gehören entweder in den Restmüll oder in den blauen Müllcontainer.

✗	**A** plastic bottles
☐	**B** glass bottles
✗	**C** drinks cans
☐	**D** newspaper
✗	**E** bags for coffee
☐	**F** plates

(3 marks)

Now try this

LISTENING TRACK 51 — Target grade 1-5

Dictation

You are going to hear someone talking about recycling.

Listen to the recording

Sentences 1–3: write down the missing words in the gaps provided. In each gap, you will write one word **in German**.

Sentences 4–6: write down the full sentences that you hear in the spaces provided, **in German**.

1 Zu Hause ______________ wir fast ______________ .

2 Der ______________ Müllcontainer ist für ______________ .

3 ______________ kommt in den ______________ Müllcontainer.

4 ______________________________ .

5 ______________________________ .

6 ______________________________ .

(10 marks)

My school

Digital resources

Meine Schule

Bibliothek (f)	library
Gebäude (nt)	building
Schwimmbad (nt)	swimming pool
Sportplatz (m)	playing field
Tennisplatz (m)	tennis court
außerhalb	outside (of)
etwa	approximately
liegen	to be situated

Die Gebäude sind sehr modern.
The buildings are very modern.

Dative and accusative prepositions

Grammar pages 96 and 97

Dative and accusative	
an	on, to, at
auf	on, to
hinter	behind
in	in, into
neben	next to, beside
über	over, above
unter	under
vor	before, in front of
zwischen	between

These prepositions use the **dative** case when there is **no movement** of the subject.
Ich bin in der Schule.
I am in the school.
But they use the **accusative** case when there is **movement towards** something.
Ich gehe **in die** Schule.
I go into the school.

Meine Schule liegt **in der** Stadt.
My school is in the town.
Ich besuche eine kleine Schule **auf dem** Land.
I go to a small school in the countryside.
Es gibt zwei Tausend Schülerinnen und Schüler **an meiner** Schule.
There are two thousand pupils at my school.

Worked example

READING — Target grade 3

Matteo is writing about his school.

> Meine Schule ist nicht zu groß. Sie liegt in der Stadtmitte. Die Schule ist nicht modern, aber die Klassenzimmer sind groß und hell, und wir haben eine neue Bibliothek, die toll ist. Es gibt auch ein Schwimmbad und drei Tennisplätze.

What does he say?
Put a cross ✗ in each one of the **three** correct boxes.
Matteo's school …

☒	**A** is in the town centre.
☐	**B** is a modern building.
☒	**C** has large classrooms.
☒	**D** has a great library.
☐	**E** has no swimming pool.
☐	**F** has two tennis courts.

(3 marks)

Now try this

WRITING — Target grade 5-9

Write to an Austrian friend about your school. You **must** include the following points:

- where your school is
- your opinion of the buildings
- what your last school was like
- what your dream school of the future would be like.

Write your answer **in German**. You should aim to write between 80 and 90 words. **(18 marks)**

School subjects

Digital resources

Schulfächer

Englisch | Deutsch | Geschichte

Kunst | Mathe | Musik

Religion | Sport | Theater | Wissenschaft

Fach (nt)	subject	fleißig	hard-working
Fehler (m)	mistake	kompliziert	complicated
Kenntnis (f)	knowledge	nützlich	useful
Sprache (f)	language	praktisch	practical
Stunde (f)	lesson	schwierig / schwer	difficult
Unterricht (m)	lesson		
Wahlfach (nt)	optional subject	schwach	weak, not good at
einfach	easy	stark	strong, good at

Denn and weil

Grammar page 104

These both mean 'because', so can be used to explain your opinions.

- Weil sends the verb to the end.
  Ich mag Deutschunterricht, **weil** ich stark in Sprachen **bin**.
  I like German lessons because I am good at languages.
- With denn, the verb stays in the same place.
  Ich bin schwach in Geschichte, **denn** ich **mache** immer Fehler.
  I'm not good at history because I always make mistakes.

Note the use here of **schwach** and **stark** – their main meanings are 'weak' and 'strong', but they are also used to say 'good at / not good at' when talking about school subjects.

Worked example

LISTENING TRACK 52 — Target grade 3-4

Mia is talking about school. What does she say?

Listen to the recording and complete the following tables **in English**. You do not need to write in full sentences.

Listen to the recording

> Ich mag Mathe sehr, denn ich finde es ziemlich einfach, und die Stunden sind interessant. Englisch ist langweilig, denn ich lese nicht gern. Kunst ist mein Lieblingsfach, weil es praktisch ist.

(a)

Why she likes maths (**2** details)
She finds it quite easy and the lessons are interesting.

(b)

What she thinks of English (**2** details)
It is boring because she doesn't like reading.

(c)

What she thinks of art (**2** details)
It's her favourite subject because it's practical.

(6 marks)

Now try this

LISTENING TRACK 53 — Target grade 6-7

Yusuf is talking about school subjects. What does he say? Listen to the recording and put a cross ✗ in each one of the **three** correct boxes.

Listen to the recording

☐	**A** Yusuf likes a lot of his subjects.
☐	**B** German is a compulsory subject.
☐	**C** He has difficulty with science subjects.
☐	**D** Languages are his best subjects.
☐	**E** Yusuf says he makes lots of mistakes.
☐	**F** He thinks English is an important subject.

(3 marks)

Digital resources

My teachers

Meine Lehrer

Hilfe (f)	help
Prüfung (f)	exam
Ziel (nt)	destination / goal
beliebt	popular
bereit	prepared (to)
böse	angry / cross
ehrlich	honest
freundlich	friendly
locker	relaxed
negativ	negative
positiv	positive
stolz (auf)	proud (of)
streng	strict
verrückt	crazy
begeistern	to inspire
bestehen	to pass (an exam)

Obwohl

Grammar page 104

Obwohl (although) is a conjunction which, like weil, sends the verb to the end of the clause.

Obwohl der Lehrer locker **war**, **war** er auch sehr effektiv.

Although the teacher was relaxed, he was also very effective.

Obwohl die Lehrerin streng **war**, **war** sie bereit, uns zu helfen.

Although the teacher was strict, she was willing to help us.

Obwohl es schwierig **war**, **haben** wir unsere Prüfungen bestanden.
Although it was difficult, we passed our exams.

Worked example

READING — Target grade 6-7

Read this internet article about what makes a good teacher. Which qualities are mentioned?

> Gute Lehrer lieben das Fach, das sie unterrichten, sind fleißig und haben viel Energie. Sie haben klare Lernziele, die die Klasse versteht. Sie wollen jeder Schülerin und jedem Schüler die Chance geben, erfolgreich zu sein. Sie sind immer bereit, Hilfe zu geben, wo Hilfe gebraucht wird. Obwohl sie viel zu tun haben, haben sie auch immer Zeit, über Schwierigkeiten zu diskutieren. Sie verstehen, dass ihre Schüler verschieden sind.

Put a cross ✗ next to each one of the **three** correct statements.

A good teacher …

✗	**A** sets clear targets for the class.
☐	**B** has time to check homework.
✗	**C** wants everyone to do well.
✗	**D** is there to help.
☐	**E** works very long hours.
☐	**F** marks work thoroughly.

(3 marks)

Worked example

LISTENING TRACK 54 — Target grade 1-5

Listen to the recording

You are going to hear someone talking about teachers.

Write down the missing words in the gaps provided. In each gap, you will write one word **in German**.

1 Der Mathelehrer ......kann...... oft ......böse...... sein.

2 Meine Deutschlehrerin ist ......energisch...... und sehr ......beliebt...... .

3 Die Kunstlehrerin ist ......cool...... und ist immer ......geduldig...... .

(6 marks)

Now try this

WRITING — Target grade 2-5

Write a response to a survey about teachers.

You **must** include the following points:

- what your best teacher is like
- your opinion of a teacher who is not good
- whether you would like to be a teacher in the future.

Write your answer **in German**. You should aim to write between 40 and 50 words. **(14 marks)**

The school day

Digital resources

Der Schultag

Club / Klub (m)	club
Doppelstunde (f)	double lesson
Mittagspause (f)	lunch break
Pause (f)	break
Stundenplan (m)	timetable
anfangen	to start
beginnen	to begin
dauern	to last
enden	to end
dann / danach	then, after that
die erste / zweite / letzte Stunde	the first / second / last lesson
nach der Pause / Mittagspause	after break / lunch break

Which day?

Montag	Monday
Dienstag	Tuesday
Mittwoch	Wednesday
Donnerstag	Thursday
Freitag	Friday
Samstag	Saturday
Sonntag	Sunday

Am Montag hebe ich eine Prüfung.
On Monday I have an exam.

Montags hebe ich Geschichte.
On Mondays I have history.

Montags suggests that it happens **every** Monday. You can also add an -s to times of day.

Morgens kommen wir um 8:45 an.
In the mornings we arrive at 8:45.

In der Mittagspause gibt es einen Computerclub.
In lunch break there is a computer club.

Worked example

LISTENING TRACK 55 — Target grade 3

Listen to the recording

Mia is talking about her timetable. Listen to the recording and complete the gap in each sentence using a word from the box.
There are more words than gaps.

> Am Montag in der ersten Stunde habe ich Englisch, dann Deutsch und in der dritten Stunde Wissenschaft en. Am Ende des Morgens in der vierten Stunde gibt es Sport. Nach der Mittagspause habe ich um 13:30 Uhr eine Doppelstunde Kunst, und die Schule endet um 15:30 Uhr.

fourth first third second
science German English sport history
art 12:30 13:30 15:30 4 pm

(a) The ....first.......... lesson is English.
(b) The second lesson is ....German.......... .
(c) She has ....sport.......... in the fourth lesson.
(d) Mia's last lesson is ....art.......... .
(e) Afternoon school starts at ....13:30.......... .
(f) School finishes at ....15:30.......... **(6 marks)**

Now try this

LISTENING TRACK 56 — Target grade 6-7

Listen to the recording

Noah is talking about his timetable. What do you learn?
Listen to the recording and complete the sentences by putting a cross ✗ in the correct box.

(a) Noah has a full timetable due to …

☐	**A** subject choices.
☐	**B** exams.
☐	**C** extra maths lessons.

(b) The maths lesson lasts …

☐	**A** an hour.
☐	**B** an hour and a half.
☐	**C** two hours.

(2 marks)

Digital resources

School uniform

Die Schuluniform

Farbe (f)	colour
Hemd (nt)	shirt
Hose (f)	trousers
Jacke (f)	jacket
Kleid (nt)	dress
Kleidung (f)	clothes
Krawatte (f)	tie
Pullover (m)	jumper
Schuhe (m, pl)	shoes
altmodisch	old-fashioned
bequem	comfortable
eng	tight
locker	loose
modisch	fashionable
teuer	expensive
unbequem	uncomfortable
anziehen	to get dressed / put on

Adjective endings (der, die, das)

Grammar page 100

Masculine nouns

nom	acc	dat	
der blaue	den blauen	dem blauen	Pullover

Feminine nouns

nom / acc	dat	
die blaue	der blauen	Hose

Neuter nouns

nom / acc	dat	
das blaue	dem blauen	Hemd

Plural nouns

nom / acc	dat
die blauen Schuhe	den blauen Schuhen

Worked example

LISTENING TRACK 57 — Target grade 3

Samira is talking about school uniform. What does she say? Listen to the recording and complete the sentences by putting a cross ✗ in the correct box for each question.

Die Uniform ist nicht immer praktisch, weil sie oft unbequem ist, besonders im Sommer, wenn es mir zu warm wird. Die Farbe ist zu dunkel, und ich mag helle Farben. Warum grau und nicht rosarot? Noch ein Nachteil – eine Uniform kann viel Geld kosten.

Listen to the recording

(a) Samira says the uniform …

☐	**A** is impractical.
☒	**B** is not always practical.
☐	**C** is very practical.

(b) She dislikes the colour because …

☐	**A** it's too bright.
☐	**B** it's too old-fashioned.
☒	**C** it's too dark.

(c) She would prefer the uniform to be …

☒	**A** pink.
☐	**B** red.
☐	**C** grey.

(3 marks)

Ich mag unsere traditionelle Uniform, denn ich muss mich morgens nicht entscheiden, was ich anziehen soll.

I like our traditional uniform because I don't have to decide what to wear in the morning.

Now try this

LISTENING TRACK 58 — Target grade 7

Jonas is talking about school uniform. What are the disadvantages and advantages? Listen to the recording and complete the following table **in English**.

Listen to the recording

You do not need to write in full sentences.

(a) Disadvantage (**1** detail)	**(b)** Advantages (**2** details)

(3 marks)

School rules

Digital resources

Die Schulregeln

Gang (m)	corridor
Mobbing (nt)	bullying
Regel (f)	rule
Unfall (m)	accident
verboten	forbidden / banned
ankommen	to arrive
dürfen	to be allowed to
erlauben	to allow
führen	to lead
laufen	to run
rauchen	to smoke
respektieren	to respect

Don't confuse the German word **will** (want to) with the English 'will'.

You can also use **möchte** (would like):
Ich **möchte** später in die Schule kommen.
I would like to come into school later.

Modal verbs

Grammar page 112

These are used in the second position with an infinitive at the end.

- Können (to be able to)
  Laufen in der Schule **kann** zu Unfällen führen.
  Running in school can lead to accidents.
- Müssen (to have to / must)
  Wir **müssen** unsere Hausaufgaben machen.
  We must do our homework.
- Wollen (to want to)
  Sie **will** die Regeln respektieren.
  She wants to respect the rules.
- Dürfen (to be allowed to)
  Man **darf** nicht laufen.
  You are not allowed to run.
- Sollen (to be supposed to)

Wir **sollen** nicht durch die Gänge laufen.
We are not supposed to run through the corridors.

Worked example

LISTENING TRACK 59 — Target grade 3 — Listen to the recording

Leon is talking about school rules.
Which rules does he approve of? Listen to the recording and put a cross ✗ in each one of the **three** correct boxes.

Ich finde es normal, dass es verboten ist, in den Schulstunden zu essen, aber ich möchte meine Jacke und meinen Hut tragen. In dem Gang darf man nicht laufen – ja, klar, das kann gefährlich sein. Kein Handy im Unterricht ist auch OK, aber warum muss man in der Pause in der Schule bleiben? Ich möchte rausgehen. Die schlimmste Regel ist die Uniform, die wir tragen müssen …

✗	**A** no eating in class
	B no jackets in class
	C no smoking in school
✗	**D** no running in corridors
✗	**E** no mobiles in class
	F no leaving school premises

(3 marks)

Now try this

WRITING — Target grade 5-9

Translate the paragraph **into German**.

I think some school rules are necessary because they make school life safe. For example, running in the corridor is forbidden in order to avoid accidents, and of course, no one is allowed to smoke. Yesterday, a girl in my class used her mobile phone in a lesson and took a video.

(10 marks)

Digital resources

School clubs

Schulklubs / Clubs

Film (m)	film	Musik (f)	music
Handball (m)	handball	Tanz (m)	dance
Instrument (nt)	instrument	Team (nt)	team
Kochen (nt)	cookery	Trainer (m) / Trainerin (f)	trainer / coach
Kunst (f)	art	Verein (m)	club / association
Mannschaft (f)	team	üben	to practise
Mitglied (nt)	member		

Worked example

LISTENING TRACK 60 — Target grade 3 — Listen to the recording

There is an announcement about after-school clubs. What can you do and when?

Listen to the recording and complete the sentences by putting a cross ✗ in the correct box for each question.

Möchtest du nach dem Unterricht etwas anderes machen? Wir haben ein Angebot mit vielen neuen Aktivitäten! Montags gibt es Tanzklub, der immer beliebt ist und nicht nur bei Mädchen … Dienstags ist Sport – entweder Handball, Fußball, Leichtathletik oder Tennis … Mittwochs kannst du von 15 bis 17 Uhr mit dem Umweltteam arbeiten … Donnerstags ist Musik – komm doch mit und spiel ein Instrument oder singe mit anderen. Freitags ist wie immer Kunstklub … nächste Woche gehen wir zum Kunstmuseum …

(a) Monday's dance club is …

☐	**A** for girls only.
☐	**B** for boys only.
☒	**C** always popular.

(b) At sports club there is a choice of …

☐	**A** two activities.
☐	**B** three activities.
☒	**C** four activities.

(c) Environment club starts at …

☒	**A** 3 pm.
☐	**B** 4 pm.
☐	**C** 5 pm.

(d) Friday's activity is for those who like …

☐	**A** music.
☒	**B** art.
☐	**C** history.

(4 marks)

Useful phrases

Im Musikklub kann man ein Instrument lernen.
At music club you can learn an instrument.
Ich würde gern in den Kochklub gehen, um Kochen zu lernen.
I'd like to go to the cookery club to learn how to cook.
Donnerstags gibt es den Tanzklub – das macht Spaß und die Lehrerin ist toll.
On Thursdays there's dance club – it's fun and the teacher is great.

Notice the short way to say 'every Thursday / every Wednesday': donnerstags / mittwochs

Now try this

LISTENING TRACK 61 — Target grade 6-9 — Listen to the recording

In the exam there will be more sentences for you to write.

Dictation

You are going to hear someone talking about school clubs.

Write down the full sentences that you hear in the spaces provided, **in German**.

1 ______________________________ . **2** ______________________________ . **(4 marks)**

School trips

Digital resources

Die Schulreise

Ausflug (m)	trip / outing
Austausch (m)	exchange
Fahrt (f)	trip / journey
Reise (f)	trip / journey
Schulausflug (m)	school outing
Schulfahrt (f)	school trip / journey
Schulreise (f)	school trip / journey
mit der Bahn	by rail
mit dem Reisebus	by coach
mit dem Zug	by train

Remember the order:
Time – Manner – Place.

Talking about the past

Grammar pages 113 – 114

time expression	perfect tense		
Vor zwei Jahren Vor drei Monaten Letztes Jahr Letzten Monat Letzte Woche	haben / sind wir	+	past participle (at the end)

Vor drei Jahren haben wir ein Theaterstück **gesehen**.
Three years ago we saw a play.

Letztes Jahr sind wir mit dem Zug nach Cambridge **gefahren**.
Last year we travelled to Cambridge by train.

Worked example

READING — Target grade 3

Read these comments about school trips.

Joel: Ich habe letztes Jahr einen Austausch gemacht. Wir sind mit dem Reisebus gefahren. Das war lang, aber toll. Mein deutscher Austauschpartner Matteo ist jetzt ein guter Freund.

Bente: Letzten Monat habe ich mit meiner Musikklasse eine Schulreise mit dem Zug nach London gemacht, um ein Musical und eine Tanzshow zu sehen. Das hat Spaß gemacht!

Anna: Vor vier Monaten bin ich mit meiner Fußballmannschaft für drei Wochen nach Amerika geflogen, um zu trainieren.

Who did what? Choose the correct answers.
Put a cross ✗ in the correct column for each question.

	Who …	Joel	Bente	Anna
(a)	… went on a trip last month?		✗	
(b)	… got on well with their exchange partner?	✗		
(c)	… was away for three weeks?			✗
(d)	… took part in training?			✗
(e)	… travelled by train?		✗	
(f)	… travelled by coach?	✗		

(6 marks)

Now try this

WRITING — Target grade 2-5

Write a response to a survey about school trips.
You **must** include the following points:

- what sort of school trips you like
- why school trips are a good thing
- where you will go on your next school trip.

Write your answer **in German**. You should aim to write between 40 and 50 words. **(14 marks)**

Wir haben einen Ausflug gemacht.
We went on a trip.

Digital resources

Homework

Hausaufgaben

Leistung (f)	performance / achievement
Note (f)	mark / grade
Prüfung (f)	exam
kriegen	to get / receive
schaffen	to manage
sich beschweren	to complain
(sich) konzentrieren (auf)	to concentrate (on)
üben	to practise
verbessern	to improve
verstehen	to understand
wiederholen	to repeat / revise
täglich	daily
manchmal	sometimes

Key adverbs

Grammar page 101

äußerst	extremely
damit	so that / in order that
deshalb	therefore
durchschnittlich	on average
eigentlich	actually
häufig	often
normalerweise	usually
sicherlich	certainly
ungefähr	about
unbedingt	absolutely
wohl	probably

Abends mache ich durchschnittlich zwei Stunden Hausaufgaben.
I do on average two hours of homework in the evening.

Worked example

READING Target grade 3

Read the comments on the pros and cons of homework.

Mia: Hausaufgaben sind nötig, damit wir besser verstehen, aber es ist manchmal schwierig.

Yusuf: Ich muss täglich zwei lange Stunden zu Hause arbeiten, was schlimm ist, aber das gibt mir die Chance zu üben, was ich im Unterricht gelernt habe.

Complete the tables **in English**. You do not need to write in full sentences.

(a) Mia

One good thing about homework
She can understand better.

One bad thing about homework
It is difficult.

(b) Yusuf

One bad thing about homework
It takes two hours every day.

One good thing about homework
It lets him practise what he learned in class.

(4 marks)

Now try this

LISTENING TRACK 62 Target grade 7

Listen to the recording

Mila is talking about homework. What does she say?

Listen to the recording and put a cross ✗ in each one of the **three** correct boxes.

Mila thinks …

☐	**A**	homework is not vital if you work hard at school.
☐	**B**	there's too little time to learn everything in class.
☐	**C**	students should be responsible for their own learning.
☐	**D**	students are often unwilling to do homework.
☐	**E**	exams mean that less homework should be set.
☐	**F**	you should take time off from schoolwork.

(3 marks)

Ein Vorteil ist, dass wir mehr lernen. Ein Nachteil ist, dass wir müde sind.
An advantage is that we learn more. A disadvantage is that we are tired.

Stress at school

Digital resources

Der Schulstress

Druck (m)	pressure
Elternsprechabend (m)	parents' evening
Gefühl (nt)	feeling
Gespräch (nt)	conversation
Leistung (f)	achievement
Lösung (f)	solution
Ruhe (f)	silence / peace
Stimmung (f)	mood / atmosphere
geistig	mental / psychological
gestresst	stressed
schwer / schwierig	hard / difficult
Angst haben	to be scared
vermeiden	to avoid

Stress (m) is a cognate meaning 'stress'.

Bist du gestresst?

Ich habe oft Kopfschmerzen. I often have a headache.
Ich kann nicht schlafen. I can't sleep.
Ich habe keine Lust zu essen. I don't feel like eating.
Ich verbringe viel Zeit allein.
I spend a lot of time on my own.
Ich bin immer müde. I'm always tired.
Ich habe keine Energie. I have no energy.
Ich habe Angst, dass meine Noten nicht gut genug sind.
I'm afraid my grades are not good enough.
Ich spreche sehr schnell. I talk very quickly.
Ich bin zur Schule gegangen, obwohl ich Bauchschmerzen hatte.
I went to school although I had a stomach ache.

obwohl (although) sends the verb to the end of the clause, like **weil**.

Worked example

READING — Target grade 3

Read what Johanna says about school stress.

> Ich bin immer fleißig, aber ich habe das Gefühl, dass ich nicht genug mache. Ich arbeite lange Stunden zu Hause, esse nicht mehr mit der Familie, denn ich habe nie Hunger und gehe samstags nicht mehr mit Freundinnen aus. Mein Herz schlägt* manchmal zu schnell. Ich gehe spät ins Bett, aber schlafe nicht gut und bin am Morgen noch müde.

* *schlagen* – to beat

Put a cross ✗ in each one of the **three** correct boxes.

Johanna …

☐	**A** used to be less hard-working.
☒	**B** feels she's not doing enough.
☐	**C** spends time with her family every evening.
☒	**D** has lost her appetite.
☒	**E** doesn't go out on Saturdays.
☐	**F** always sleeps well.

(3 marks)

Die Lehrer fehlen oft, weil sie gestresst sind. The teachers are often absent because they are stressed.

Note: **nicht mehr** = no longer.

Now try this

LISTENING — TRACK 63 — Target grade 6-7

Lena is talking to a doctor about stress. Which problems does she mention? Listen to the recording and put a cross ✗ in each one of the **three** correct boxes.

Listen to the recording

☐	**A** tiredness
☐	**B** lack of concentration
☐	**C** sadness
☐	**D** lack of sleep
☐	**E** overwork
☐	**F** drinking alcohol

(3 marks)

Digital resources

Preparing for exams

Wir bereiten uns auf die Prüfungen vor!

Erfolg (m)	success
Oberstufe (f)	sixth form
Raum (m)	space / room
Weise (f)	way
Ziel (nt)	destination / goal
länger	longer
regelmäßig	regularly
unmöglich	impossible
organisieren	to organise
stattfinden	to take place
üben	to practise
unterstützen	to support
vorbereiten	to prepare

Lernen ist harte Arbeit!
Learning is hard work!

Separable verbs

Grammar page 107

Separable verbs break into two parts: main verb and prefix.

For example: **statt**finden, **vor**bereiten, **an**kommen and **aus**gehen.

Make sure you can use separable verbs:

- in the present tense.
  Schulprüfungen **finden** immer im Sommer **statt**.
  School exams always take place in summer.
- in the past tense.
  Unsere Lehrer haben uns gut auf die Prüfungen **vorbereitet**.
  Our teachers have prepared us well for the exams.
- in the future tense.
  Ich werde früher in der Schule **ankommen**.
  I will get to school earlier.
- with zu.
  Vor den Prüfungen habe ich keine Zeit mit Freunden **auszugehen**.
  Before the exams, I have no time to go out with friends.

H ONLY

Useful phrases

Es ist unmöglich, alles in letzter Minute zu lernen.
It's impossible to learn everything at the last minute.
Man braucht eine längere Zeit, um sich vorzubereiten.
You need a longer time (in order) to prepare.

Worked example

READING — Target grade 6

Read the extract from an online advice page.

- Jeden Tag feste Ziele haben.
- Handy und Musik immer ausmachen.
- Manchmal nicht allein, sondern mit einer Lerngruppe lernen.
- In einem stillen Raum arbeiten.
- Nach 90 Minuten Arbeit eine Viertelstunde Pause machen.
- Genug essen und Wasser trinken.

Complete the gap in each sentence using a word from the box below. There are more words than gaps.

group firm quiet warm
hour and a half quarter of an hour half hour

(a) Set ....firm.......... goals.
(b) Work in a ....quiet.......... room.
(c) Take breaks every ....hour and a half..........

(3 marks)

Now try this

LISTENING — TRACK 64 — Target grade 3

Sofie is talking about exam preparation. What does she mention? Listen to the recording and put a cross ✗ in each one of the **three** correct boxes.

Listen to the recording

☐	**A** asking her teachers	☐	**D** a break to eat
☐	**B** two hours' work after school	☐	**E** working with her family
☐	**C** getting to school early	☐	**F** going to bed early

(3 marks)

My ideal school

Digital resources

Conditional

H ONLY

Grammar page 117

Use the conditional to say how you **would** like things to be if you could choose.
To form it, use part of würde (would) + sentence + infinitive at the end.

ich würde du würdest er / sie / es / man würde wir würden ihr würdet Sie / sie würden	+ infinitive

Die Schule **würde** erst um 10 Uhr **beginnen**.
School would only begin at 10 am.

Some frequently used conditional verbs have shortened forms:

würde sein → wäre
würde haben → hätte
würde können → könnte
würde mögen → möchte
würde sollen → sollte

Wir **sollten** eine modische Uniform **tragen**.
We should wear a fashionable uniform.
Wir **könnten** mehr Sport **treiben**.
We could do more sports.

Ich würde lieber …
I would prefer …

Worked example

WRITING

Target grade 6-9

Write to a friend about your current and your ideal school.
You **must** include the following points:

- what your current school is like
- what you think should be improved
- what you did yesterday in school
- what your ideal school would be like.

Write your answer **in German**. You should aim to write between 80 and 90 words. **(18 marks)**

Einerseits ist meine Schule gar nicht schlecht, weil wir tolle Lehrer haben, die gut unterrichten. Andererseits ist das Schulgebäude sehr alt und nicht sehr praktisch.

Meiner Meinung nach brauchen wir unbedingt neue Gebäude, die heller und wärmer wären, sowie eine saubere Kantine mit genug Platz für alle.

Gestern konnte ich mittags kein Essen kaufen, weil es zu viele Schüler gab, die essen wollten.

In meiner idealen Schule wäre die Kantine groß und hätte eine tolle Auswahl an Gerichten. Die Klassenzimmer wären modern und bequem, und wir hätten auch einen neuen Computerraum.

This student uses their language effectively to cover each of the bullet points.
A first opinion (**Einerseits**) with an explanation using **weil**.
A relative clause (**tolle Lehrer haben, die …**) with the verb at the end.
Andererseits (on the other hand) introduces a different opinion.
Meine Meinung nach … clearly indicates an opinion. Remember to invert the verb.
Unbedingt (absolutely) is a useful intensifier.
A second relative clause (**Gebäude, die … wären**).
The time expression **gestern** indicates the past tense, along with three verbs in the imperfect tense.
Verbs in the conditional / subjunctive (**wäre, hätte**).

Although **Kantine** is not on the Edexcel vocabulary list, this student has used it effectively.

Now try this

WRITING

Target grade 1-5

Translate the following sentences **into German**.

(a) My school is very old.
(b) The classrooms are cold and dark.
(c) I don't like the uniform.
(d) Our teachers are good but sometimes strict.
(e) I would like to have more sports lessons.

(10 marks)

Digital resources

Plans for next year

Future time frame

Grammar page 116

To talk about next year, you need a future time frame.
You can do this with:

- future tense ... (with werden)
  Ich **werde** in die Oberstufe **gehen**. I'll go into the sixth form.
- future time marker + present tense
  Nächstes Jahr suche ich einen Job. Next year I'll look for a job.
- ich möchte + infinitive
  Ich **möchte** nach Europa **fahren**. I would like to travel to Europe.
- ich will + Infinitive
  Ich **will** nächstes Jahr in der Schule **bleiben**.
  I want to stay at school next year.
- ich hoffe + zu + infinitive
  Ich **hoffe**, in London **zu wohnen**. I hope to live in London.
- ich könnte + infinitive
  Ich **könnte** nächstes Jahr nach Amerika **fahren**.
  I could go to America next year.
- es wäre gut / es würde gut sein + zu + infinitive
  Es **wäre** perfekt, in dieser Schule **zu bleiben**.
  It would be perfect to stay at this school.

Ich **möchte** meine Sprachen **üben**.
I would like to practise my languages.

Worked example

WRITING — Target grade 4-5

Translate the following five sentences **into German**.

(a) Next year I want to stay at school.
Nächstes Jahr will ich in der Schule bleiben.

(b) I would like to learn languages.
Ich möchte Sprachen lernen.

(c) If it is possible, I hope to travel to Europe.
Wenn es möglich ist, hoffe ich, nach Europa zu reisen.

(d) Then I want to find a job.
Dann will ich eine Arbeit / einen Job finden.

(e) Last year I learned German.
Letztes Jahr habe ich Deutsch gelernt. **(10 marks)**

Ich **will** mit meinen Freunden in dieser Schule **bleiben**.
I want to stay in this school with my friends.

Remember that when you use **wenn**, the verb goes to the end of the clause or sentence and the next verb is inverted – look out for the sequence **verb – comma – verb**.

Now try this

LISTENING TRACK 65 — Target grade 7-8

Listen to the recording

Layla is talking about her plans for next year.
Which possibilities does she mention? Listen to the recording and put a cross ✗ in each one of the **three** correct boxes.

☐	**A** going into the sixth form	☐	**D** learning a new language
☐	**B** helping in her parents' business	☐	**E** doing voluntary work
☐	**C** finding a paid job	☐	**F** going travelling

(3 marks)

Future studies

Digital resources

Weiterbildung

Ausbildung (f)	education / training
Gelegenheit (f)	opportunity
Hochschulbildung (f)	higher education
Hochschule (f)	college / uni
Kosten (pl)	costs
Medizin (f)	medicine (subject)
Student (m) / Studentin (f)	student
Studium (nt)	studies
Uni(versität) (f)	university
Zukunftspläne (m, pl)	future plans
studieren	to study (at university)

Sich freuen auf + accusative

Grammar page 96

Use this reflexive verb to talk about something you are looking forward to.

Ich freue mich auf die Zukunft.
I'm looking forward to the future.
Ich freue mich darauf, auf die Uni zu gehen.
I'm looking forward to going to university.
Ich freue mich nicht auf den Druck.
I'm not looking forward to the pressure.

If you want to use **sich freuen auf** followed by a **zu** clause, note that **auf** adds **dar** to the front – **Ich freue mich darauf** … = I'm looking forward to it …

Worked example

LISTENING TRACK 66 — Target grade 3-5

Jana is talking about her future plans.

What does she plan to do? Listen to the recording and put a cross ✗ in each one of the **three** correct boxes.

Listen to the recording

> Ich habe keine Lust, auf die Uni zu gehen, denn es ist zu teuer und ich will nicht weit weg von zu Hause sein. Ich werde an der Hochschule in meiner Stadt studieren und möchte dort einen Kochkurs machen. Das wird schön sein.

☐	**A** study at university
☒	**B** stay near to home
☐	**C** move to another town
☒	**D** go to college
☒	**E** study cookery
☐	**F** study beauty therapy

(3 marks)

Ich habe Lust / ich habe keine Lust are used to say what you wish / do not wish to do.

Worked example

SPEAKING TRACK 67 — Target grade 5-9

Read aloud

Max has sent you some information about his future plans.

Read out the text below.

Listen to the recording

> Meiner Meinung nach ist es wichtig, eine gute Ausbildung zu haben.
> Wenn meine Noten gut genug sind, möchte ich auf der Uni Medizin studieren.
> Ein Nachteil ist, dass die Kosten eines Studiums so hoch sind.
> Ich denke, das Studentenleben wird viel Spaß machen, obwohl die Arbeit schwierig ist.

(8 marks)

Flexible phrases

Ich freue mich darauf.
I'm looking forward to it.
Es wird eine tolle Erfahrung sein.
It will be a great experience.

Now try this

WRITING — Target grade 5

Write to a friend about your thoughts on future studies.

You **must** include the following points:

- the advantages of continuing to study
- the disadvantages of future study
- something interesting you have learned in class recently
- whether you plan to go to university / college.

Write your answer **in German**. You should aim to write between 80 and 90 words. **(18 marks)**

Digital resources

Future career

Was willst du später werden?

Bereich (m)	area / sphere of work
Beruf (m)	career
Firma (f)	firm / company
Karriere (f)	career
gut bezahlt	well paid
bezahlen	to pay
gelingen	to succeed
gründen	to found / set up
verdienen	to earn
werden	to become

Arzt (m) / Ärztin (f)	doctor
Chef (m) / Chefin (f)	boss
Kollege (m) / Kollegin (f)	colleague
Künstler (m) / Künstlerin (f)	artist
Manager (m) / Managerin (f)	manager
Polizist (m) / Polizistin (f)	police officer
Schauspieler (m) / Schauspielerin (f)	actor / actress
Schriftsteller (m) / Schriftstellerin (f)	writer / author
Tierarzt (m) / Tierärztin (f)	vet
Zahnarzt (m) / Zahnärztin (f)	dentist

Ich möchte Polizistin werden.
I want to be a police officer.

Many masculine words for people are made feminine by adding **-in**. Some add an umlaut too: **Arzt / Ärztin**.

There is no article in front of job names, e.g. **Ich will Arzt sein**, unless there's an adjective with it, e.g. **Ich will ein guter Arzt sein.**

Worked example

LISTENING TRACK 68 — Target grade 3-5

Listen to the recording

Yasmin is talking about her future career. What does she say? Listen to the recording and complete the sentences by putting a cross ✗ in the correct box for each question.

Ich möchte später Polizistin sein. Die Arbeit ist nicht sehr gut bezahlt, aber der Kontakt zu anderen Menschen interessiert mich. Meine Eltern, die Lehrer sind, denken, ich soll Ärztin sein, um viel Geld zu verdienen, aber in diesem Beruf hat man sehr lange Arbeitszeiten … lieber nicht!

(a) Yasmin wants to …

☐	**A** earn a lot of money.
☒	**B** work with people.
☐	**C** work with animals.

(b) Her parents think she should …

☐	**A** be a police officer.
☒	**B** be a doctor.
☐	**C** be a teacher.

(2 marks)

Travelling for work

Most countries and cities are used without an article.
Use nach to say you are **travelling** there.
Ich reise nach Afrika. I am travelling to Africa.
Use in if you are **staying** there.
Ich arbeite in Amerika. I'm working in America.

Some countries are used with an article – for example die Schweiz, die Türkei.
Then you use in, and change the case of the article:
movement → accusative no movement → dative
Movement: Ich reise in die Türkei. I'm travelling to Turkey.
No movement: Ich arbeite in der Türkei. I'm working in Turkey.

Now try this

WRITING — Target grade 5-9

Translate the following paragraph **into German**.

In the future I would like to become a dentist, although the training is long. It's important to me to earn a lot of money, and dentists are well paid. I hope to work in nice surroundings and have friendly colleagues. My mum is a dentist and loves her job.

(10 marks)

Pros and cons of some jobs

Digital resources

Was sind die Vor- und Nachteile?

gefährlich	dangerous
nützlich	useful
spannend	exciting
unmöglich	impossible
zufrieden	happy / content
beitragen zu	to contribute to
gelingen	to succeed
mitbringen	to bring (with it)
sitzen	to sit
teilnehmen an	to take part in
verdienen	to earn
vorhaben	to plan, intend

Worked example

LISTENING TRACK 69 — Target grade 4-5

Arda is talking about possible future jobs.

Which pros and cons does he mention?

Listen to the recording and put a cross ✗ in each one of the **three** correct boxes.

Listen to the recording

Polizist sein ist ein spannender Job, aber kann auch gefährlich sein. Lehrer sein ist eine harte Arbeit, aber man hat lange Ferien. Ich will nie in einem Büro arbeiten. Es ist langweilig, immer vor dem Computer zu sitzen. Arzt sein ist ein nützlicher Beruf, denn man hilft anderen, aber die Arbeitszeiten sind lang.

✗	**A** boring	☐	**D** interesting
✗	**B** exciting	✗	**E** useful
☐	**C** easy	☐	**F** well paid

(3 marks)

Worked example

WRITING — Target grade 2-5

Translate the following five sentences **into German**.

(a) I want to be a teacher.

Ich will Lehrer / Lehrerin sein.

(b) I think it is a good job.

Ich denke, es ist ein guter Job.

(c) Teachers have long holidays.

Lehrer haben lange Ferien.

(d) I would like to work with young people.

Ich möchte mit jungen Leuten arbeiten.

(e) It is important to be happy at work.

Es ist wichtig, bei der Arbeit zufrieden zu sein.

(10 marks)

Remember: no article before a job name!

Ich möchte sends the infinitive **arbeiten** to the end.

bei der Arbeit – at work

Ich möchte Lehrerin werden, weil es Spaß macht, mit Kindern zu arbeiten.
I would like to be a teacher because it is fun to work with children.

Now try this

LISTENING TRACK 70 — Target grade 6-8

Listen to the recording

Paul is talking about a possible career choice.

What are the advantages and disadvantages?

Listen to the recording and complete the following tables **in English**.

You do not need to write in full sentences.

(a) Advantages (**2** details)

(b) Disadvantages (**2** details)

(4 marks)

My dream job

Mein Traumberuf

Bildung (f)	education
Einkommen (nt)	income / pay
Erfolg (m)	success / achievement
Fähigkeit (f)	skill / ability
Mitarbeiter (m) / Mitarbeiterin (f)	employee
Ziel (nt)	destination / goal
ermüdend	tiring
heiraten	to get married

Ich möchte ... werden

Arzt (m) / Ärztin (f)	doctor
Banker (m) / Bankerin (f)	banker
Direktor (m) / Direktorin (f)	director / head teacher
Künstler (m) / Künstlerin (f)	artist
Lehrer (m) / Lehrerin (f)	teacher
Polizist (m) / Polizistin (f)	policeman / policewoman
Tierarzt (m) / Tierärztin (f)	vet
Übersetzer (m) / Übersetzerin (f)	translator
Wissenschaftler (m) / Wissenschaftlerin (f)	scientist

This / these, that / those, every, which

Grammar page 99

dieser	this / these
jener	that / those
jeder	every
welcher?	which?

These follow the pattern of der, die, das.

	masc.	fem.	neuter	plural
nominative	dies**er**	dies**e**	dies**es**	dies**e**
accusative	dies**en**	dies**e**	dies**es**	dies**e**
dative	dies**em**	dies**er**	dies**em**	dies**en**

Welchen Job würdest du lieber machen?
Which job would you prefer to do?
Ich finde **jede** Arbeit ermüdend.
I find every job tiring.
Ich möchte in **diesem** Restaurant arbeiten.
I would like to work in this restaurant.

Mein Traumberuf wäre eine Karriere in der Modeindustrie.
My dream job would be a career in the fashion industry.

Worked example

SPEAKING TRACK 71 | Target grade 1-5

Listen to the recording

Describe the picture. Your description must cover:

- people
- location
- activity. **(8 marks)**

Auf dem Foto gibt es zwei Frauen in einem Büro. Eine Frau trägt eine graue Jacke und eine Frau trägt eine schwarze Jacke. Sie tragen weiße Hemden. Sie lächeln und reden. Ich denke, sie machen ein Interview. Die Frau stellt vielleicht eine Frage. Es gibt ein großes Fenster und die Sonne scheint.

Now try this

SPEAKING TRACK 72 | Target grade 1-5

Listen to the recording

Listen to the recording of two questions relating to the picture above.
You are expected to say a few words or a short phrase / sentence in response to each question. One-word answers will not be sufficient to gain full marks. **(4 marks)**

Gap year

Digital resources

Ein Gap Year

Ausland (nt)	abroad
Auslandsjahr (nt)	year abroad
Gelegenheit (f)	opportunity
Möglichkeit (f)	possibility
direkt	directly / straight
nützlich	useful
bauen	to build
erlauben	to allow
helfen	to help
verbringen	to spend (time)
verlassen	to leave

Intensifiers

Intensifiers

- auf jeden Fall – definitely
- natürlich – naturally
- äußerst – extremely
- sicherlich – certainly
- unbedingt – absolutely
- völlig – completely
- echt / wirklich – really
- total – totally
- besonders – particularly
- sehr – very

Note the ways that you can talk / write about future intentions: **ich möchte … / ich würde gern … / ich werde …**

Useful phrases

Wenn ich die Schule verlasse …
When I leave school …
… werde ich nicht direkt auf die Uni gehen.
… I won't go straight to university.
… möchte ich unbedingt ein Auslandsjahr machen.
… I would absolutely like to have a year abroad.
… würde ich gern anderen Menschen helfen.
… I would like to help others.

Worked example

READING

Target grade 6-7

Read these comments on a blog.

Elif: Ich will ein Auslandsjahr in einem Dorf in Afrika verbringen, wo man eine Schule baut.

Paul: Vor der Uni möchte ich etwas Nützliches tun. Ich werde bei einer Umweltorganisation arbeiten.

Yannie: Wenn ich die Schule verlasse, werde ich für sechs Monate mit Leuten in meiner Stadt arbeiten, die auf der Straße leben.

Who says what? Choose the correct answers. Put a cross ✗ in the correct column for each question.

	Who plans to …	Elif	Paul	Yannie
(a)	… work with the homeless?			✗
(b)	… do ecological work?		✗	
(c)	… work overseas?	✗		

(3 marks)

Flexible phrases

Das ist wirklich eine gute Gelegenheit, etwas Positives zu tun.
It's really a good opportunity to do something positive.

Now try this

LISTENING TRACK 73

Target grade 1-5

Dictation

You are going to hear someone talking about future plans.

Write down the full sentences that you hear in the spaces provided, **in German**.

Listen to the recording

1 ______________________________.

2 ______________________________.

3 ______________________________.

(6 marks)

Equality and helping others

Digital resources

Menschenrechte

Diskriminierung (f)	discrimination
Flüchtling (m)	refugee
Frieden (m)	peace
Gesellschaft (f)	society
Gesetz (nt)	law
Heimat (f)	home country
Krankenhaus (nt)	hospital
Opfer (nt)	victim
Vergangenheit (f)	past
Ziel (nt)	goal
schwul	gay
unabhängig	independent
erfahren	to experience
erhalten	to receive
erreichen	to reach
kämpfen	to fight
pflegen	to care
verbieten	to forbid
verlassen	to leave
zeigen	to show

Using adjectives

Grammar page 101

Adjectives can add interest and are a good way to express opinions.

beliebt	popular
ernst	serious
möglich	possible
notwendig	necessary
schlimm	bad, serious
verschieden	different, diverse

You can also make adjectives comparative, often just by adding -er to the end (schlimm**er** – 'more serious'), and superlatives by adding -st- (schlimm**ste** – 'most serious').

There are some exceptions, such as gut – besser – best-, and some which add an umlaut: groß – größer – größt-.

You can even make adjectives into neuter nouns, so **das Beste** = 'the best thing'.

Worked example

READING — Target grade 8-9

Read this extract from a student project.

> Deutschland ist eines der beliebtesten Ziele für Flüchtlinge, die aufgrund von Konflikten und Kämpfen ihr Heimatland verlassen, um Frieden zu suchen. Viele stammen aus Syrien oder der Ukraine*. In Deutschland gibt es eine Willkommenskultur, und Flüchtlinge erhalten Unterkunft** und Essen, sowie Pflege, im Krankenhaus, wenn sie verletzt sind. Man liest jedoch, dass viele Flüchtlinge Diskriminierung erfahren.

* *aus Syrien oder der Ukraine* – from Syria or Ukraine

** *Unterkunft* – accommodation / shelter

What do they say? Put a cross ✗ next to each one of the **two** correct statements.

☐	**A** Not many refugees go to Germany.
☐	**B** Many refugees are denied food and shelter.
☒	**C** Injured people are cared for in hospital.
☒	**D** Many refugees experience discrimination.

(2 marks)

Nach dem Zweiten Weltkrieg war ein Grenzübergang ein Ort, wo man zwischen Ost und West gehen konnte.

After World War II, a border crossing checkpoint was a place where people could go between East and West.

Now try this

LISTENING — TRACK 74 — Target grade 6-7

Ben is talking about a recent visit. Listen to the recording and answer the following questions **in English**. You do not need to write in full sentences.

Listen to the recording

(a) Where did Ben go?
(b) Why was this place important?
(c) Until which year was Germany divided?
(d) What did Ben find sad? **(4 marks)**

Holiday activities

Digital resources

Ferienaktivitäten

Ferien (pl)	holidays
Ferienwohnung (f)	holiday apartment
Schwimmbad (nt)	swimming pool
Urlaub (m)	holiday
Wagen (m)	car / carriage
an der Küste	at the coast
auf dem Land	in the country
in den Bergen	in the mountains
in der Stadt	in the town
übernachten	to stay overnight
verbringen	to spend time

Key question words

Wann?	When?	Wer?	Who?
Warum?	Why?	Wie?	How?
Was?	What?	Wo (hin / her)?	Where (to / from)?

Was machst du in den Ferien? What do you do in the holidays?

Wann besuchen Sie Ihre Familie? When do you visit your family?

Wohin fährst du mit deinem Wohnwagen?
Where do you go to in your caravan?

Useful phrases

Wir verbringen eine Woche bei meiner Tante auf dem Land.
We spend a week in the country at my aunt's house.

Ich bleibe zu Hause und mache einen Ferienkurs in Fußball.
I stay at home and do a holiday course in football.

Mein Großvater hat einen Wohnwagen an der Küste.
My grandfather has a caravan at the coast.

Ich mache einen Musikkurs in meiner Stadt.
I'm doing a music course in my town.

Ferienaktivitäten machen Spaß.
Holiday activities are fun.

Ich gehe wandern.
I go hiking.

Worked example

READING — Target grade 3-4

Read these blog posts.

Mika: Ich mag es, in den Ferien meine Cousinen zu sehen und verbringe im Sommer vierzehn Tage bei meinem Onkel in seinem Wohnwagen in den Bergen. Es ist toll, an der frischen Luft zu sein und wandern zu gehen.

Elif: Wir bleiben meistens in den Ferien zu Hause. Ich mache oft einen Malkurs in den Ferien, weil ich später Künstlerin sein will.

Who says what? Choose the correct answers. Put a cross ✗ in the correct column for each question.

	Who …	Mika	Elif
(a)	… has an educational holiday?		✗
(b)	… likes to see family?	✗	
(c)	… enjoys the outdoors?	✗	
(d)	… spends two weeks away?	✗	

(4 marks)

Now try this

SPEAKING — Target grade 5-9

During the conversation task, you will be asked questions in the present, past and future tenses like those below.

(a) Was machst du in den Ferien?
(b) Warum sind die Ferien für dich wichtig?
(c) Was wirst du diesen Sommer machen?
(d) Was hast du letztes Jahr gemacht?

(16 marks)

Digital resources

Camping

Camping

Campingplatz (m)	campsite
Feuer (nt)	fire
Fluss (m)	river
Frühstück (nt)	breakfast
Insel (f)	island
Schwimmbad (nt)	swimming pool
See (m)	lake
Sonne (f)	sun
Tennisplatz (m)	tennis court
Wald (m)	forest
Zelt (nt)	tent
zelten	to go camping

Wir haben auf dem Land gezeltet. Der See **war** schön.
We camped in the countryside. The lake was beautiful.

Imperfect tense

Grammar page 115

present			imperfect	
ist	is	→	war	was
hat	has	→	hatte	had
geht	goes	→	ging	went
fährt	drives	→	fuhr	drove
sieht	sees	→	sah	saw
es gibt	there is	→	es gab	there was
macht	do	→	machte	did
kann	can	→	konnte	was able to

Der Campingplatz **war** neben einem See.
The campsite was beside a lake.
Man **konnte** zu der Insel schwimmen.
You could swim to the island.
Es **gab** einen Wald in der Nähe.
There was a forest nearby.
Der Campingplatz **hatte** ein Café, wo man essen **konnte**.
The campsite had a cafe where you could eat.

Worked example

LISTENING TRACK 75 — Target grade 3-4

Listen to the recording

Matteo is talking about a camping trip. What does he mention? Listen to the recording and complete the sentences by putting a cross ✗ in the correct box for each question.

Im Frühling waren wir auf einem Campingplatz in den Bergen. Es war schön, aber nicht sehr warm. Wir waren fünf in der Gruppe und hatten ein neues Zelt mit Platz für sechs Personen. An einem Abend machten wir ein Feuer und haben gekocht und gesungen. Das war aber lustig!

(a) They went camping …

☐	**A** at Easter.
☐	**B** in summer.
☒	**C** in spring.

(b) There were … of them.

☐	**A** four
☒	**B** five
☐	**C** six

(2 marks)

Now try this

SPEAKING — Target grade 5-9

Read aloud

Leon, your friend, has sent you some information about camping holidays. Read out the text below.

Zelten kann viel Spaß machen, aber nur, wenn es nicht regnet oder kalt und windig ist. Ich mag es am besten, wenn der Campingplatz entweder auf dem Land oder in den Bergen liegt, wo es ruhig ist. Wir fahren besonders gern mit dem Zug in den Urlaub nach Österreich. Letztes Jahr waren wir in unserem Zelt auf einer kleinen Insel.

(8 marks)

Holiday accommodation

Digital resources

Wo sollen wir übernachten?

Garten (m)	garden
Lage (f)	location
Wohnung (f)	flat
bequem	comfortable
bieten	to offer
entfernt	away
kostenlos	free of charge
liegen	to be situated
mieten	to rent
übernachten	to spend the night, stay
verbringen	to spend time

Adjective endings (after ein, eine, ein)

	masculine	feminine	neuter	plural
nominative	ein schön**er** Garten	eine schön**e** Wohnung	ein schön**es** Haus	keine schön**en** Häuser
accusative	einen schön**en** Garten	eine schön**e** Wohnung	ein schön**es** Haus	keine schön**en** Häuser
dative	einem schön**en** Garten	einer schön**en** Wohnung	einem schön**en** Haus	keinen schön**en** Häusern

Worked example

READING

Target grade 6-7

Read these advertisements from a holiday brochure.

Übernachten Sie im Sonnenhaus!

Ein riesiges Ferienhaus erwartet Sie direkt am sauberen Strand und bietet auch Ruhe in einem schönen Garten.

Spaß im Wald!

Dieses Ferienhaus für zwei Personen bietet eine fantastische Terrasse, Grillmöglichkeiten und liegt mitten im Wald. Sie können an den spannenden Aktivitäten teilnehmen und in einem tiefen See schwimmen.

Modisch in Berlin!

Diese eleganten Ferienwohnungen mit Hotelservice liegen in zentraler Lage Berlins, nur 1 km von einem wunderbaren Marktplatz und Einkaufszentrum entfernt.

Which place is it? Put a cross ✗ in the correct column for each question.

	Which place …	Sonnenhaus	Spaß im Wald!	Modisch in Berlin!
(a)	… is close to the shops?			✗
(b)	… has a barbecue?		✗	
(c)	… has a garden?	✗		
(d)	… has a terrace?		✗	
(e)	… is close to a beach?	✗		

(5 marks)

Now try this

READING

Target grade 5-9

Translate the following paragraph **into English**.

Als ich jünger war, blieben wir in den Sommerferien immer zu Hause, aber in den letzten Jahren haben wir oft unseren Urlaub in der Schweiz verbracht. Letztes Jahr waren wir in einem Ferienhaus direkt am Strand, was toll war, weil ich mit meinem Rollstuhl einfach zum See fahren konnte.

(10 marks)

Digital resources

Other holiday accommodation

Andere Übernachtungsmöglichkeiten

Auto (n)	car
Badezimmer (n)	bathroom
Berg (m)	mountain
Wettbewerb (m)	competition
genießen	to enjoy
sich unterhalten	to chat / amuse oneself
teilen	to share

Es gibt ...

Grammar page 96

Use es gibt (there is / are ...) + accusative in different tenses to help improve your work.

Present	**Es gibt** einen Parkplatz. There is a parking space.
Imperfect	**Es gab** ein Schwimmbad. There was a swimming pool.
Future	**Es wird** viel Schnee **geben**. There will be lots of snow.

Worked example

READING · Target grade 3-5

Read the following advertisement.

Bequemes Ferienhaus in den Alpen für sechs Gäste mit Badezimmer. Es gibt Parkplätze für zwei Autos. Tolle Terrasse, auf der man sitzen und die schöne ***Aussicht*** auf den Schnee und die Berge genießen kann.

Which of these is the best translation for the word ***Aussicht***?
Put a cross ✗ in the correct box.

✗	**A** view
☐	**B** ski lift
☐	**C** valley

(1 mark)

This type of question asks you to infer the meaning of a word which is not on the Edexcel vocabulary list. You need to read the words around the word to work out the correct option.
Here, you are told that it is something you can enjoy from the terrace over the snow and the mountains – so it must be the view.

Worked example

LISTENING TRACK 76 · Target grade 5-7

Listen to the recording

Yasmin is talking about her last holiday. What does she mention? Listen to the recording and put a cross ✗ in each one of the **three** correct boxes.

Mein Bruder hat letztes Jahr bei einem Wettbewerb als Preis einen Winterurlaub gewonnen, und wir sind in die Schweiz geflogen. Das Haus war klein und in den Bergen, und überall lag Schnee, weil es Dezember war. Es war lustig, weil es nur zwei Schlafzimmer gab und ich ein Schlafzimmer mit meinen Schwestern teilen musste. Wir unterhielten uns bis spät in die Nacht! Das Essen war etwas anders, aber es hat sehr gut geschmeckt.

✗	**A** weather	☐	**D** skating
☐	**B** wine	✗	**E** food
✗	**C** bedrooms	☐	**F** neighbours

(3 marks)

Now try this

WRITING · Target grade 1-5

Describe the photo. Write four short sentences **in German**. **(8 marks)**

Making a complaint

Digital resources

Ich bin nicht zufrieden

Koffer (m)	suitcase	langsam	slow
Manager (m) / Managerin (f)	manager	laut	loud
		leider	unfortunately
Messer (nt)	knife	schmutzig	dirty
Teller (m)	plate	sofort	immediately
WLAN (nt)	Wi-Fi	zufrieden	content
frisch	fresh	funktionieren	to work
hell	bright / light	riechen	to smell
kalt	cold	sich beschweren	to complain
kaputt	broken	(über)	(about)

Seit + present tense (H ONLY)

Use this to say how long you **have been doing** something.

Ich **warte seit** einer halben Stunde.
I've been waiting for half an hour.

Seit is followed by the **dative** case.

Seit eine**r** Stunde.
Seit zwei Tage**n**.

Dative plurals add -n.

Worked example (READING, Target grade 4-5)

Read Helmut's review of a hotel.

> Das Hotelgebäude hat mir gefallen. Das Schwimmbad war auch schön. Unser Zimmer war aber etwas schmutzig und es gab keinen Platz für unsere Koffer.

Complete the tables **in English**. You do not need to write in full sentences.

(a) Helmut

Two things he likes
the hotel building the pool

(b)

Two things he dislikes about the room
dirty no room for suitcases

(4 marks)

Worked example (LISTENING, TRACK 77, Target grade 5)

You hear this conversation in a restaurant. Which problems does the customer complain about?

> Ich habe Fisch bestellt und Sie haben mir Fleisch gebracht, das ich nicht essen kann. Mein Glas ist schmutzig, und mein Mann hat bis jetzt nichts zu essen bekommen. Er wartet schon eine Stunde auf das Essen. Wo ist der Manager? Ich will mit ihm sprechen!

Put a cross ✗ in each one of the **three** correct boxes.

Listen to the recording

✗	**A** wrong meal served
	B missing cutlery
✗	**C** dirty glass
	D cold food
✗	**E** long wait
	F noisy surroundings

(3 marks)

Now try this (LISTENING, TRACK 78, Target grade 7-9)

Listen to the recording

Dictation

You are going to hear someone complaining in a restaurant. Write down the missing words in the gaps provided. In each gap, you will write one word **in German**.

1 Ich habe keine __________ mehr. Ich __________ jetzt __________ vierzig Minuten.
2 Wir haben die __________ mit __________ und __________ bestellt.

(6 marks)

In the dictation exercise, you may hear words you are not familiar with. Try to work out the spelling from your knowledge of other German words and sounds.

Pros and cons of travelling

Digital resources

Reisen: Vor- und Nachteile

Alltag (m)	everyday life
Aspekt (m)	aspect
Eindruck (m)	impression
Freiheit (f)	freedom
Grenze (f)	border / frontier
Kontakt (m)	contact
Kultur (f)	culture
Nachteil (m)	disadvantage
Sprache (f)	language
Tradition (f)	tradition
Verständnis (nt)	understanding
Vorteil (m)	advantage
Ziel (nt)	destination / goal
ausbilden	to educate / train
bedeuten	to mean
erfahren / erleben	to experience

Useful phrases

Reisen bildet.
Travel educates.

This is a well-known German saying.

Fliegen ist schlecht für die Umwelt.
Flying is bad for the environment.

Wenn man reist, lernt man immer etwas Neues.
Whenever you travel, you always learn something new.

Touristen bringen nicht nur Vorteile.
Tourists don't just bring advantages.

Es ist mein Traum zu reisen, um die Kulturen anderer Länder kennenzulernen.
It is my dream to travel, in order to get to know the cultures of other countries.

Worked example

LISTENING TRACK 79 — Target grade 7-8 — Listen to the recording

Listen to this item about travel.

Man sagt oft, dass Reisen eine Art Ausbildung für das Leben ist, dass wenn wir andere Kulturen erleben, wir mehr Verständnis für Leute haben, die außerhalb unserer Landesgrenzen anders leben. Wenn man Fremdsprachen lernt, hat man die Gelegenheit, direkt ins Gespräch mit anderen Menschen zu kommen … über den Alltag und die Traditionen. Wir leben in einer globalen Welt – und sollen als Ziel haben, nicht nur in der Sonne zu liegen, sondern auch internationale Freundschaften aufzubauen.

Which views are mentioned? Complete the sentences by putting a cross ✗ in the correct box for each question.

(a) It is often said that travel is …

☐	**A** a problem for the environment.
☒	**B** an education for life.
☐	**C** an expensive activity.

(b) Experiencing other cultures means …

☐	**A** we appreciate our own life more.
☒	**B** we understand other ways of life.
☐	**C** we contribute to other economies.

(2 marks)

Now try this

LISTENING TRACK 80 — Target grade 4-5 — Listen to the recording

Max is talking about travel. Which activities does he mention? Listen to the recording and put a cross ✗ in each one of the **three** correct boxes.

☐	**A** flying	☐	**D** eating
☐	**B** swimming	☐	**E** playing
☐	**C** learning	☐	**F** buying

(3 marks)

Plans for next summer

Digital resources

Ich plane ...

Angst haben	to be afraid
brauchen	to need
empfehlen	to recommend
entscheiden	to decide
hoffen	to hope
organisieren	to organise
planen	to plan
reservieren	to book
sparen	to save
teilnehmen an	to take part in
überraschen	to surprise
überzeugen	to convince
vorhaben	to intend
wagen	to dare
wollen	to want
wünschen	to wish

Using wenn

Develop your language by linking clauses together using wenn. Remember to put the verb at the end of the clause.

Wir werden in den Urlaub fahren. Es ist möglich. → Wir **werden** in den Urlaub fahren, **wenn** es möglich **ist**.

We will go on holiday. It is possible. → We will go on holiday, if it is possible.

wenn es möglich ist	if it's possible
wenn das Wetter gut ist	if the weather is good
wenn meine Eltern *ja* sagen	if my parents agree

wenn meine Freunde mitkommen wollen
if my friends want to come with me

wenn ich die Gelegenheit habe if I have the opportunity

Ich habe vor, Spaß mit meiner Familie zu haben.
I intend to have fun with my family.

Worked example

READING — Target grade 3-4

Read these travel plans from a social media discussion. Complete the tables **in English**. You do not need to write in full sentences.

Malik: Ich werde eine Reise mit dem Fahrrad machen, wenn meine Freunde mitkommen wollen.

Layla: Ich möchte in einem Hotel in London übernachten, wenn ich das Geld habe.

(a) Malik

Something he would like to do	a cycle trip
If	his friends want to go with him

(b) Layla

Something she would like to do	stay in a hotel in London
If	she has the money

(4 marks)

Now try this

LISTENING — TRACK 81 — Target grade 7-8

Listen to the recording

Anna and Lukas are talking about summer holiday plans.

Listen to the recording and complete the sentences by putting a cross ✗ in the correct box for each question.

(a) Anna would like to …

☐	**A** see her grandparents.
☐	**B** go swimming.
☐	**C** have a week away.

(b) Her parents don't want her to …

☐	**A** be away from home.
☐	**B** travel by herself.
☐	**C** make long journeys.

(c) Lukas's family can't go away because …

☐	**A** his parents have to work.
☐	**B** his brother is unwell.
☐	**C** his mum had an accident.

(3 marks)

Past holidays

Digital resources

Ferien in der Vergangenheit

Perfect tense

Ich bin nach ... gefahren.
I went to ...

Ich habe das Essen ... gefunden.
I thought the food was ...

Ich habe ... gekauft. I bought ...

Wir haben zwei Wochen an der Küste verbracht.
We spent two weeks at the coast.

Imperfect tense

Ich war in ...	I was in ...
Die Reise war ...	The journey was ...
Die Leute waren ...	The people were ...
Der Strand war ...	The beach was ...

Unser Urlaub dauerte zwei Wochen.
Our holiday lasted two weeks.

You can also use **time markers:**
letztes Jahr
last year
vor zwei Jahren
two years ago
früher
previously
in der Vergangenheit
in the past

Er war von den Lichtern begeistert.
He was thrilled by the lights.

Flexible phrases

Ich erinnere mich gut daran.
I remember it well.

Es war eine Erfahrung, die ich nie vergessen werde.
It was an experience I will never forget.

Worked example

READING — Target grade 3-4

Read this comment about holidays last year.

Yusuf: Wir waren letztes Jahr in der Schweiz. Die Gegend war fantastisch, aber ich habe das Essen schlecht gefunden. Ich mag keinen Käse, und im Hotel gab es zu viel davon.

Complete the table **in English**. You do not need to write in full sentences.

Yusuf

One thing he liked	the area / region
One thing he disliked	the food

(2 marks)

Now try this

LISTENING — TRACK 82 — Target grade 5-9 — Listen to the recording

Dictation

You are going to hear someone talking about a past holiday.

Sentences 1–2: write down the missing words in the gaps provided. In each gap, you will write one word **in German**.

1 Wir ____________ in den ____________ in ____________ .

2 Ich ____________ ein paar ____________ in der alten ____________ gekauft.

Sentences 3–6: write down the full sentences that you hear in the spaces provided, **in German**.

3 ____ .

4 ____ .

5 ____ .

6 ____ . **(10 marks)**

Holiday problems

Digital resources

Urlaubsprobleme

Fahrkarte (f)	ticket
Flug (m)	flight
Flughafen (m)	airport
Flugzeug (nt)	plane
Gepäck (nt)	luggage
Pass (m)	passport
neblig	foggy
vergessen	to forget
verlieren	to lose
verpassen	to miss

Unusual past participles

Grammar pages 108–109

Verbs starting with be- or ver- do not add ge- to form the past participle.

Ich habe ein neues Ticket **bezahlt**.
I paid for a new ticket.

Wir haben den Bus **verpasst**.
We missed the bus.

Wir haben unsere Pässe **vergessen**.
We have forgotten our passports.

Worked example

SPEAKING TRACK 83 — Target grade 5-9

Listen to the recording

Describe the picture.

Your description must cover:

- people
- location
- activity. **(8 marks)**

Auf dem Foto gibt es viele Leute an einem Flughafen. Alle warten auf einen Flug. Der Flughafen ist groß und modern. Im Vordergrund ist eine Frau. Sie hat einen Koffer und sieht müde und traurig aus. Sie muss vielleicht lange auf ihren Flug warten.

Now listen to the recording of the sample response.

Worked example

LISTENING TRACK 84 — Target grade 4-5

Lena is talking about a recent family holiday. What did they have problems with? Listen to the recording and put a cross ✗ in each one of the **three** correct boxes.

Zuerst hat mein Bruder seinen Pass vergessen und er musste ihn holen. Deshalb haben wir den Zug verpasst. Als wir endlich am Flughafen angekommen sind, war es neblig, und alle Flugzeuge kamen spät an. Die Hotelzimmer haben uns alle gefallen, aber leider war das Schwimmbad geschlossen.

☐	**A**	train ticket
☒	**B**	travel document
☒	**C**	weather
☐	**D**	food
☐	**E**	hotel room
☒	**F**	use of a hotel facility

Listen to the recording

(3 marks)

Now try this

LISTENING TRACK 85 — Target grade 6-7

Listen to the recording

Listen to Arda talking about his last holiday. What happened? Listen to the recording and complete the sentences by putting a cross ✗ in the correct box for each question.

(a) Arda was travelling …

☐	**A**	early in the morning.
☐	**B**	in the afternoon.
☐	**C**	at night.

(b) He had trouble …

☐	**A**	carrying his luggage.
☐	**B**	finding his seat.
☐	**C**	getting to sleep.

(2 marks)

Lost property

Digital resources

Ich kann es nicht finden!

Geld (nt)	money
Handtasche (f)	handbag
Handy (nt)	mobile phone
Koffer (m)	suitcase
Laptop (m/nt)	laptop
Polizei (f)	police
jemand	someone
anrufen	to call / phone
nehmen	to take
vergessen	to forget
verlassen	to leave
verlieren	to lose

Useful phrases

Ich habe meine Handtasche verloren.
I've lost my handbag.
Jemand hat mein Geld genommen.
Someone has taken my money.
Ich habe meinen Laptop im Zug verlassen.
I left my laptop on the train.
Ich habe meinen Pullover im Bus vergessen.
I left my sweater on the bus.
Jemand hat mein Fahrrad genommen.
Someone has taken my bike.
Ich habe meinen Pass nicht mehr.
I don't have my passport anymore.

Wir können unseren Koffer nicht finden.
We can't find our suitcase.

Read the introduction carefully, as it may help you. Here, you will be listening for things that people have left on a train. So they will be small physical things they can carry with them. The other words are times or days, as they are answering 'when?' This helps to narrow down the options.

Worked example

LISTENING TRACK 86 — Target grade 3-4

These people have left something on a train. What have they left and when? Listen to the recording and complete the following tables **in English**. You do not need to write in full sentences.

Listen to the recording

Man: Ich habe meine neue Jacke im Zug vergessen. Das war gestern Abend.
Woman: Ich kann meinen Koffer nicht finden! Habe ich ihn im Zug vergessen? Ich bin heute Morgen gefahren.

(a) The man has lost …

what?	his new jacket
when?	yesterday evening

(b) The woman has lost …

what?	her suitcase
when?	this morning

(4 marks)

When you hear an unfamiliar word, think about the rules about German sounds you know. Use the first listen to note down what you think you hear, the second to refine your notes and the third to double-check that what you have written matches what you heard. Check the number of syllables too!

Now try this

LISTENING TRACK 87 — Target grade 5-6

Dictation

You are going to hear someone talking about lost property. Write down the missing words in the gaps provided. In each gap, you will write one word **in German**.

Listen to the recording

1 Ich kann ________ gestern ________ meinen Pass und meinen ________ nicht finden.
2 Ich brauche ________ meinen Pass, weil ich morgen ________ nach ________ fliege.

(6 marks)

Places to visit

Digital resources

Tagesausflüge

Attraktion (f)	attraction / ride
Ausflug (m)	trip
Freizeit (f)	leisure / free time
Freizeitpark (m)	theme park
Park (m)	park

Am liebsten gehe ich in den Freizeitpark.
I like going to the theme park the best.

Using adjectives

Grammar page 101

Adjectives add colour and interest to what you say and write, and are a good way to express opinions.

bunt	colourful	schön	beautiful
fantastisch	fantastic	spannend	exciting
hoch	high	toll	great

You can also make adjectives comparative, often just by adding -er to the end (schön**er** – 'more beautiful'), and superlatives by adding -st- (schön**ste** – 'most beautiful').

There are some exceptions, such as gut – besser – best-, and some which add an umlaut: groß – größer – größt-.

You can even make adjectives into neuter nouns, so **das Beste** = 'the best thing'. H ONLY

You only need to know superlatives at Higher tier.

Worked example

READING — Target grade 6-7

Read about Lena's visit to a theme park.

> Europa-Park in Rust* ist der größte Freizeitpark Deutschlands. Ich war im Winter da, und die Stimmung war so schön – ein Winterwunderland mit Schnee, bunten Lichtern in den hohen Bäumen und Musik überall! Ich habe eine tolle Flussfahrt gemacht und viele spannende Attraktionen probiert, aber die fantastische Eisshow war das Beste. Als Souvenir habe ich eine ***Wollmütze*** gekauft, weil es schneite und ich kalte Ohren hatte!

*Rust is a town in Germany.

Don't be put off by long words like **Winterwunderland**. Remember that you can form compound words in German. Spot the words you know – **Winter**, **Wunder**, **Land** – to work out what it means.

Complete the sentences below. Put a cross ✗ in the correct box for each question.

(a) Lena admired …

☐	**A**	the buildings.
☒	**B**	the atmosphere.
☐	**C**	the refreshments.

(b) During her visit she went …

☒	**A**	on a boat trip.
☐	**B**	ice skating.
☐	**C**	skiing.

(c) Which of these is the best translation for the word ***Wollmütze***? Put a cross ✗ in the correct box.

☐	**A**	gloves
☐	**B**	sweater
☒	**C**	woolly hat

(3 marks)

Now try this

WRITING — Target grade 5-8

Translate the paragraph **into German**.

> I live in an area which is popular with tourists. Every year many people come to see the historic buildings and the beautiful old town. The streets are narrow and there are great shops and restaurants everywhere. Last weekend the weather was good and we had a walk along the river.

(10 marks)

Digital resources

Holiday jobs

Ferienjobs

Beruf (m)	job
Büro (nt)	office
Erfahrung (f)	experience
Kenntnis (f)	knowledge / skill
Konkurrenz (f)	competition
Stelle (f)	position
nützlich	useful
ausgeben	to spend
helfen	to help
kennenlernen	to get to know
verbessern	to improve
verbringen	to spend (time)
verdienen	to earn
wöchentlich	every week

Talking about jobs

In den Ferien habe ich versucht, etwas Nützliches zu machen.
In the holidays I tried to do something useful.

Ich habe Berufserfahrung in einem Krankenhaus gesammelt, weil ich gerne Arzt werden möchte.
I did work experience in a hospital because I would like to become a doctor.

Ich habe viele nette Leute kennengelernt.
I get to know lots of nice people.

Ich musste Geld verdienen, weil ich für ein neues Handy spare.
I had to earn money because I am saving for a new phone.

You can use adjectives as nouns with **etwas** and **nichts**. Just add **-es** and a capital letter: **nichts Neues** / **etwas Nützliches**. (H ONLY)

Verbs which have an inseparable prefix like **be-** and **ver-** don't use **ge-** in the past participle.
Ich habe **versucht**.

Ich habe wöchentlich in einer Küche gearbeitet, um meine Kochkenntnisse zu verbessern.
I worked in a kitchen every week to improve my cookery skills.

Worked example

LISTENING TRACK 88 | Target grade 4-5

Listen to the recording

Noah is talking about what he did in the summer. What does he mention? Listen to the recording and put a cross ✗ in each one of the **three** correct boxes.

☒	**A** doing something positive
☐	**B** gaining experience
☐	**C** looking after stray cats
☒	**D** preparing food for the animals
☐	**E** having great fun
☒	**F** meeting new people

(3 marks)

Ich wollte etwas Positives machen und habe sechs Wochen in einem Tierzentrum gearbeitet, aber nicht um Geld zu verdienen – ich wollte den Hunden helfen, die kein Zuhause* haben. Ich habe ihr Essen gemacht und Zeit mit ihnen verbracht. Es war nicht einfach und manchmal traurig, aber ich habe jetzt viele neue Freundinnen und Freunde unter meinen Kolleginnen und Kollegen.

* *Zuhause* – home

Now try this

READING | Target grade 7-8

Translate the following paragraph **into English**.

Dieses Jahr habe ich beschlossen, die Sommerferien anders zu verbringen. Ich wollte ein bisschen Geld verdienen, denn ich spare, um mein eigenes Auto zu kaufen. Arbeitsplätze sind nicht einfach zu finden, trotzdem habe ich am Ende Glück gehabt und einen Job in einem Sportgeschäft gefunden, wo einer der Verkäufer im Urlaub war.

(10 marks)

Buying gifts and souvenirs

Digital resources

Geschenke aus dem Urlaub

Bild (nt)	picture
Brille (f)	glasses
Erinnerung (f)	memory
Geschenk (nt)	present
Hut (m)	hat
Markt (m)	market
Produkt (nt)	product
Tasche (f)	bag
Teller (m)	plate
sich erinnern an	to remember
vergessen	to forget

Reflexive verbs

Grammar page 107

Reflexive verbs need a reflexive pronoun – mich, dich, etc.

sich erinnern an – to remember	
ich erinnere **mich**	wir erinnern **uns**
du erinnerst **dich**	ihr erinnert **euch**
er / sie / es erinnert **sich**	Sie / sie erinnern **sich**

Vocabulary in action

Wo hast du Souvenirs gekauft?
Where did you buy souvenirs?

Auf dem Markt gab es tolle Produkte aus der Gegend.
There were great local products at the market.

Ich habe ein T-Shirt für meinen Bruder gekauft.
I bought my brother a T-shirt.

Ich habe ein Bild von dem Strand gekauft.
I bought a picture of the beach.

Ich habe eine gelbe Sonnenbrille gekauft. Wenn ich sie trage, erinnere ich **mich** an meinen Urlaub.
I bought yellow sunglasses. When I wear them, I remember my holiday.

Worked example

LISTENING TRACK 89 · Target grade 5 · Listen to the recording

Johanna is talking about souvenirs. Which items did she buy? Listen to the recording and put a cross ✗ in each one of the **three** correct boxes.

Ich wollte kleine Geschenke für meine Freunde und Familie mit nach Hause bringen. Auf dem Markt habe ich eine rote Tasche gefunden – perfekt für meine Schwester. Ich wollte für meinen Bruder eine Uhr kaufen, aber sie war teuer, also kaufte ich ihm eine Krawatte. Und einen Sonnenhut für meinen Großvater, weil er gern draußen sitzt. Mein Vater bekommt einen Kuli mit einem Bild von dem Hotel darauf. Ich habe mir ein blaues Sommerkleid gekauft.

☒	**A** bag	☒	**D** tie
☐	**B** book	☒	**E** pen
☐	**C** clock	☐	**F** picture

(3 marks)

Note that you can use the dative case to say 'for him / for her / for me' rather than using **für**. (See page 97.)
Ich habe ihm ein Geschenk gekauft. I bought him a present.
Ich kaufe mir ein Kleid. I'm buying myself a dress.

Now try this

WRITING · Target grade 7-9

Translate the paragraph **into German**.

When I am on holiday, I always bring back presents for my friends and family. They are not expensive things and have to be small as my suitcase is not big. Last year I was in Switzerland. I bought a clock for my grandparents and chocolate for my best friend.

(10 marks)

Digital resources

Weather

It's useful to be able to describe weather in speaking and writing, especially for image-based tasks.

Wie ist das Wetter?

Es ist kalt. It's cold.	Es ist warm. It's warm.	Es ist heiß. It's hot.
Es ist windig. It's windy.	Es ist sonnig. It's sunny.	Es ist neblig. It's foggy.
Es regnet. It's raining.	Es schneit. It's snowing.	

Himmel **(m)** sky Schnee **(m)** snow
Regen **(m)** rain Sonne **(f)** sun

The weather in different tenses

Grammar pages 113 – 116

Future	Es wird kalt sein. Es wird regnen. Es wird sonnig sein.	It will be cold. It will rain. It will be sunny.
Imperfect	Es war warm. Es war neblig. Es regnete.	It was warm. It was foggy. It was raining.
Perfect	Es hat geregnet. Es hat geschneit.	It rained. It snowed.

Remember the words **Norden / Süden / Osten / Westen** (m), which are often used in weather forecasts.

Worked example

READING Target grade 4-5

Read the weather report.

> Gestern hat es im Osten den ganzen Tag geregnet, aber heute wird es weniger Regen geben, und die Temperaturen werden höher sein. Im Westen wird es wieder kalt sein mit einem starken Wind aus dem Norden und Temperaturen bei 9 Grad. Im Norden des Lands wird es nicht so kalt sein, aber es wird am Nachmittag immer weniger blauen Himmel und immer mehr dicke ***Wolken*** geben. Abends wird es neblig werden, besonders an der Küste.

Complete the sentences below. Put a cross ✗ in the correct box for each question.

(a) Yesterday in the east it was …

☐	**A** windy.
☒	**B** wet.
☐	**C** foggy.

(b) Today in the west it will be …

☐	**A** warm.
☒	**B** windy.
☐	**C** sunny.

(c) In the north the evening will be …

☐	**A** windy.
☒	**B** foggy.
☐	**C** wet.

(d) Which of these is the best translation for the word ***Wolken***?

☐	**A** heatwave
☒	**B** clouds
☐	**C** frost

(4 marks)

Now try this

READING Target grade 7-9

Translate the following paragraph **into English**.

> Morgen früh wird es im Norden kalt bleiben mit einem leichten Wind aus dem Osten. Es wird während des Tages noch kälter werden mit Temperaturen am Abend bei 7 Grad. In den nächsten zwei Tagen wird sich die Situation verbessern, und am Wochenende wird es wärmer sein, mit Sonnenschein in allen Regionen.

(10 marks)

Tourism and the environment

Digital resources

Touristen und die Umwelt

Faktor (m)	factor
Flug (m)	flight
Flugzeug (nt)	aeroplane
Industrie (f)	industry
Klima (nt)	climate
Klimawandel (m)	climate change
Verschmutzung (f)	pollution
global	global
verantwortlich	responsible
wärmer	warmer
fliegen	to fly
vermeiden	to avoid
verursachen	to cause

Useful phrases

Fliegen ist ein wichtiger Faktor im Klimawandel.
Flying is an important factor in climate change.

Jeder Flug verursacht Luftverschmutzung.
Every flight causes air pollution.

Die Industrie ist verantwortlich für 5% der globalen Erwärmung.
The industry is responsible for 5% of global warming.

You won't meet this word in the exam, but you can use it in your own writing or speaking.

Flexible phrases

Zusammen können wir einen Unterschied machen.
Together we can make a difference.

Worked example

LISTENING TRACK 90 — Target grade 4

Jan is talking about climate change. What does he mention?

Listen to the recording and put a cross ✗ in each one of the **two** correct boxes.

Listen to the recording

Warum wollen so viele Leute mit dem Flugzeug in den Urlaub fahren? Es ist nicht nötig. Sie denken nur an sich selbst und vergessen unsere Welt. Wissen sie nicht, wie Fliegen die Umwelt verschmutzt? Sie sollen daran denken!

✗	**A** too many people fly too often
☐	**B** flying is expensive
✗	**C** people who fly think only of themselves
☐	**D** people should travel by train

(2 marks)

Immer mehr Leute fliegen – die Zahl wird in den nächsten 20 Jahren doppelt so hoch sein.
More and more people are flying. The number will double in the next 20 years.

Worked example

LISTENING TRACK 91 — Target grade 2-5

Dictation

Listen to the recording

You are going to hear someone talking about their journey.

Sentences 1–3: write down the missing words in the gaps provided. In each gap you will write one word **in German**.

1 Der ....Flug..... ist ....lang...... .

2 Ich ....trage..... einen ....Mantel..... .

3 Ich ....trinke..... eine ....Tasse..... Kaffee.

Sentences 4–6: write down the full sentences that you hear in the spaces provided, **in German**.

4 Die Leute sind immer glücklich.

5 Der Flughafen ist sehr groß.

6 Jeder Koffer ist schwer.

(10 marks)

Now try this

LISTENING TRACK 92 — Target grade 7

Jonas and Samira are talking about holiday plans.

Listen to the recording

Listen to the recording and answer the following questions **in English**. You do not need to write in full sentences.

(a) What sort of holiday does Jonas want?
(b) What does Samira say they should not do?
(c) What reasons does she give? Give **two** details.
(d) What solution does she suggest? **(5 marks)**

Digital resources

Paper 1: Speaking

Overview

Task 1: Read aloud and follow-up questions
Task 2: Role play
Task 3: Picture, follow-up questions and conversation
Timing: Preparation – 15 mins before exam; Foundation exam – 7–9 mins; Higher exam – 10–12 mins
Marks: 50 marks; 25% of the exam total

Cans and Cannots:

✓ You **can** make notes on an A4 sheet of paper.
✓ You **can** write on the read aloud passage.
✓ You **can** use the notes during the exam.
✓ You **can** use any vocabulary, whether it comes from the prescribed vocabulary list or not.
✗ You **cannot** use a dictionary.
✗ You **cannot** write on the role play or picture card.

Using the preparation time

- Start with the **read aloud** task. Read it through in your head, getting an understanding of the meaning. Make notes on the card itself of any pauses or tricky pronunciation.
- Turn to the **role play**. Check the scenario, read the full task and write your responses on the paper provided. Just prepare what you are asked for – no developments or extras are needed.
- Next, look at the **picture task**. Decide which photo to talk about, jot down ideas and vocabulary about the picture, remembering 'people, location, activity'.
- Think about the **conversation**. Look at the thematic context and jot down notes about vocabulary or phrases you might want to include. Don't write everything down or try to learn something by heart.

This is **one** recommendation for how to prepare. See what works best for you when you get the chance to practise.

Task 1: The read aloud task – what to expect

All the words in the read aloud passage come from Edexcel's prescribed lists.

In the last one minute of the preparation time, you have the chance to read parts or all of it out loud to practise, if you wish.

Your teacher will tell you when the preparation time is up and will ask you to read the card.

After your reading, there are two follow-up questions on the same topic as the passage, in the present tense at both Foundation and Higher levels. These are not printed on the card.

Answers that are relevant and totally clear are awarded 2 marks, those with some ambiguity receive 1 mark. If the message is not communicated – no marks.

The read aloud task: tips for success

- Take time to understand the passage during the preparation period – your intonation will improve if you know what you are saying.
- You can write on the read aloud text, so make any notes you want to remind you of pauses and particular pronunciations.
- Read the text steadily and clearly. You will not sound 'more German' if you try to read fast – it will just prevent the examiner from hearing your pronunciation.

Answer each follow-up question with a short sentence. Revise phrases like **Ich mag … / Ich finde es toll / wunderbar / schlecht / langweilig / gefährlich / spannend** (and other adjectives).

Worked example

This student has underlined the letters where they need to take special care with pronunciation and included written notes to remind themselves about pronunciation.

Ich mag meine Schule.
Jeden Tag haben wir fünf Stunden.
Mein Lieblingsfach dieses Jahr ist Geschichte.
In der Mittagspause esse ich Brot mit Käse.
Zweimal in der Woche gehe ich nach der Schule zu dem Filmklub.

The follow-up questions will not be printed on the card but will be asked by your teacher. After this example, the questions might be:
Q1 **Was lernst du gern dieses Jahr?**
Q2 **Wie findest du die Klubs an deiner Schule?**

Paper 1: Speaking

Digital resources

Task 2: Role play – what to expect

- You will be given a card with a setting, a scenario and instructions in English.
- The role play consists of 5 bullet points (five things to say), with a total of 10 marks.
- Foundation level: you will need to ask one question. Higher level: you will need to ask two.
- All the situations will be 'transactional', such as in a café, buying tickets, etc.
- At Foundation level, all bullet points can be tackled using the present tense or ich möchte. At Higher level, one bullet point will require a future time frame.
- Each response is awarded 2 marks if the message is relevant and clear, 1 mark if there is some lack of clarity and 0 marks if the message does not come across. Keep your answers short and clear.

You cannot write on the role play card or the picture task, but you can make notes on the paper provided.

Setting: Train Station

Scenario:

- You are at a train station in Austria.
- The teacher will play the part of an employee and will speak first.
- Your teacher will ask questions in German, and you must answer in German.
- You are expected to say a few words or a short phrase / sentence in response to each prompt. One-word answers will not be sufficient to gain full marks.

Task:

1 Say where you want to go.
2 Say why you want to go.
3 Say who you are travelling with.
4 Tell the employee what you think about the town.
5 Ask a question about the next train.

Role play – tips for success

- ✓ You can address your teacher as Sie or du, but don't change between the two.
- ✓ If you can't think of a word, think of another way of saying it.
- ✓ Keep to language you know.

Task 3: Picture task – what to expect

Describing the picture – 8 marks

Two weeks before the exam, you will be given a choice of two thematic contexts, and you will choose one. In the exam, you will be given a card with two photos on the context you have chosen, and from these you will select one photo to describe.

You always need to describe the **people**, the **location** and the **activity** that you see in the picture.

Two follow-up questions – 4 marks

Answer each question clearly and accurately in a short sentence with a verb.

Broader conversation – 16 marks

The conversation has a lot of marks available.

- Keep your answers relevant – answer the question!
- Develop some of your answers to give more detail – show your teacher what you know.
- Answer in the appropriate tense and show that you can use past and future tenses as well as the present.
- Aim to use more complex structures, for example weil and obwohl, and a range of vocabulary.

Describe ONE of these pictures. You will tell your teacher which one you have chosen to describe.
Your description must cover:

- people
- location
- activity.

When you have finished your description, your teacher will ask you two questions relating to your chosen picture. You are expected to say a few words or a short phrase / sentence in response to each question. One-word answers will not be sufficient to gain full marks.
You will then move on to a conversation on the broader thematic context of 'Studying and my future'. During the conversation, your teacher will ask you questions in the present, past and future tenses. Your responses should be as full and detailed as possible.

Digital resources

Paper 2: Listening

Overview

Section A: Listening comprehension.
Section B: Dictation.
Timing: Foundation – 45 minutes; Higher – 1 hour.
Marks: 50, including 10 marks for the dictation.

- There are between 9 and 11 questions plus 6 sentences for dictation in section B.
- There is a reading time of five minutes before the recording begins. Use it to familiarise yourself with the paper and perhaps jot down the German word for some of the English options. Remember, you might hear a synonym. For example, Fahrt instead of the option Reise.
- Questions appear in the same order as the recording.
- You will hear the recordings three times. There are pauses to give you time to think and write.
- There is a gradual increase in difficulty throughout the paper.
- Use the marks in brackets on the papers to guide you. One mark usually means one detail.

Multiple choice questions

Ich habe am Montag eine Geschichtsprüfung.

On Monday Yannie has ...

☐ **A** a PE lesson.
☐ **B** a history exam.
☐ **C** an English trip.

You must select one of three given options for 1 mark. If you make a mistake, put a single line through the box ☒ and put your cross in the correct place.

Mein bester Freund ist lustig.

Lina's best friend is ...

☐ **A** funny.
☐ **B** sad.
☐ **C** ill.

Sometimes you may not hear the exact word (here, **lustig** = 'funny') but need to work it out.

Multiple response questions

These are questions where you listen to a slightly longer recording and select three from six options for 3 marks.

Mika is talking about school.
What does she mention?

Mathe ist interessant, aber mein Lieblingsfach ist Englisch, weil ich darin gut bin und immer gute Noten bekomme. Aber Sport mag ich nicht, weil die Lehrer zu streng sind und wir oft draußen spielen müssen. Ich finde den Unterricht in Wissenschaft sehr schwierig, obwohl es ein wichtiges Fach ist.

Listen to the recording and put a cross ✗ in each one of the **three** correct boxes.

☐	**A** finding maths interesting
☒	**B** doing well in English
☐	**C** getting good grades in maths
☒	**D** disliking sports lessons
☒	**E** finding science difficult
☐	**F** enjoying art lessons

Word clouds

These questions require you to complete sentences using a word from a box.

The possible answers for each question can all be found on the same line. There are more words than gaps.

All the possible answers for question (a) are on the first line of the word box.

Samira is talking about school. What does she say? Complete the gap in each sentence using a word or phrase from the box below.
There are more words / phrases than gaps.

bus	train	bike	car
tie	jacket	shirt	uniform
playing tennis		playing basketball	
swimming			

a Samira goes to school by ____________. **(1)**
b She dislikes wearing a blue ____________. **(1)**
c After school she likes ____________ with her friends. **(1)**

Paper 2: Listening

Digital resources

Questions to answer in English

These questions require short responses in English. Pauses are inserted into the recording to allow you time to write.

You might need to fill in a table.

Wir müssen schnell hingehen, denn das Museum schließt um halb drei.

Closing time of museum
..........2:30.......... (1)

Or you might need to answer a question with a short phrase.

Um fit zu bleiben, macht es meiner Meinung nach mehr Spaß, Mannschaftssport zu treiben.

(a) What does Johanna like to do to keep fit?

..........play team sports..........

Answers in the recording come in the same order as the questions.

A good opportunity for this is when the audio is spoken in short groups of words.

General Listening tips

- You can make notes as you listen (ensuring you leave your answer area clear). For the dictation, you can jot down words in the first listen that you can then check and refine into sentences.
- Ensure you read the question introductions, titles and instructions. They give important information such as the context and number of correct answers.
- Do not give two alternative answers when only one is required.
- Move on when the audio moves on, so you don't miss marks from later questions.
- When answering in English, don't waste time giving long responses when a short phrase is all that is needed to give a clear answer.

Closing time of museum
....2:30....

This answer is quicker to write than 'The museum closes at half past two.'

- If you are not sure, try to work out meanings from the context. If, on the third listen, you still don't know, make a guess. Don't leave blanks.
- Use the third listen to check your answers.

Dictation

You will listen to a recording and write down what you hear in German for a total of 10 marks.

There will be an introductory sentence explaining the general subject of the dictation (e.g. Music), to help you decide on the words you hear.

Some sentences will need you to fill in gaps with the words you hear.

You are going to hear someone talking about school.
Sentences 1–3: write down the missing words in the gaps provided.
In each gap, you will write one word **in German**.

1 Mein ______________ ist ______________.

2 Ich ______________ oft ______________.

3 Ich ______________ immer ______________.

Sentences 4–6: write down the full sentences that you hear in the spaces provided, **in German**.

4 ______________________________

5 ______________________________

6 ______________________________

Others will need you to write down whole sentences that you hear.

At Higher level, there are two gapped sentences and four whole sentences to complete.

Dictation – points to remember

- The dictation will test your spelling of the typical sounds in the German language.
- Remember that German words sometimes have different sounds. For example, wir starts with an English *v* sound and stehen has a *sh* sound at the beginning and a *y* (as in the English *yacht*) in the middle.
- Small errors may not lose you marks unless the meaning of the sentence is lost.
- There will be two words in Foundation and three in Higher which are not from Edexcel's prescribed list. Don't worry! Try to work out how they might be spelt from your knowledge of other German words.

All names (people, countries and cities) are taken from the specification and prescribed lists.

Digital resources

Paper 3: Reading

Overview

Section A: Reading comprehension
Section B: Translation
Timing: Foundation – 45 mins; Higher – 1 hour.

Marks: 50 (including 10 for the translation into English); 25% exam total

Tips for Reading tasks

- All answers will either be in English or as a cross by a letter, so there will be no German to write.
- Pay attention to the number of marks given, as this is often a good indicator of how much detail you should give and how long you should spend on that answer.
- Watch out for small words that can modify answers. For example, if a passage says Ich habe genug Geld and you are asked what a person has, you might need to write *enough money* rather than just *money*.
- The tasks will include formal contexts such as newspaper articles and informal contexts such as emails from friends.
- The exam will use only names of people listed in the specification.
- You may meet **cognates** in the Reading paper. These are German words which look the same, or almost the same, in English and have the same meaning in both languages, for example das Baby.

Questions will increase in difficulty as you work through the paper.

Section A: Reading comprehension

Most questions come in the order of the text, so if you can find the answers to Questions 1 and 3 but not 2, you should be able to locate the section of the passage in which to find the missing answer. These questions follow a similar format to the Listening paper questions (pages 88–89).

This question type asks you to select one option on each row to complete the sentence. This is the only question style where the answers do **not** appear in the same order as the questions.

Who says what? Choose the correct answers.

Put a cross ✗ in the correct column for each question.

Elif	Mein Lieblingsfach ist Deutsch, weil ich gerne Bücher lese. Ab und zu machen wir Schulausflüge ins Theater.
Finn	Ich mag Geschichte, weil der Unterricht interessant ist und der Lehrer Spaß macht.
Bente	Kunst ist der beste Unterricht, weil man während der Arbeit kreativ sein und mit seinen Freunden reden kann.

	Who …	**Elif**	**Finn**	**Bente**
(a)	… goes to the theatre?	✗		
(b)	… finds history interesting?		✗	
(c)	… likes to chat with their friends?			✗
(d)	… finds the teacher fun?		✗	
(e)	… likes reading?	✗		
(f)	… likes German?	✗		

Gestern bin ich ins Schwimmbad gegangen, aber morgen gehe ich Rad fahren und normalerweise schaue ich zu Hause fern.

Yesterday he …

☐ **A** watched TV.
☐ **B** went cycling.
☒ **C** went swimming.

Look out for tenses or time frames to help you answer questions. In this case, the tense is important as all three activities are mentioned in the passage, but only one, C *went swimming*, is in the past. Clues are **ich bin gegangen** (*I went* in the perfect tense) and **gestern** (*yesterday*).

Paper 3: Reading

Digital resources

Section A: Reading comprehension – example

Kite festival in Germany

Read this online article about a kite festival in Germany.

Eine beliebte Veranstaltung in Deutschland ist das Drachenfest* auf einem Feld in der Nähe von Berlin, zu dem viele Touristen kommen, um teilzunehmen.

Das Festival findet normalerweise im September statt. Viele Menschen treffen sich im Feld, um ihre Drachen in Aktion zu zeigen. Es gibt oft wunderbare Formen wie Tiere und Monster.

Es gibt viele kostenlose Aktivitäten für Kinder, bei denen sie ihre eigenen Drachen bauen können. Am Abend, wenn der Himmel dunkel wird, gibt es ein schönes Feuerwerk, das bunt und oft laut ist.

* *Drachenfest* – kite festival

(a) Complete the sentences below. Put a cross ✗ in the correct box for each question.

i. The festival takes place …

☐	on the beach.
☒	in a field near a city.
☐	on a cliff.

ii. The festival is normally …

☐	in the middle of winter.
☐	in early spring.
☒	in late summer.

iii. The activities for children are …

☒	free.
☐	clean.
☐	expensive.

(b) Which of these is the best translation for the word ***Feuerwerk***? Put a cross ✗ in the correct box.

☐	**A** windmills
☒	**B** fireworks
☐	**C** banquets

Glossing may be used for words outside the vocabulary list.

Questions follow the order of the text (the answer to Question (i) will always come in the text before the answer to Question (ii)).

Real exam questions may look slightly different – this one is just to show you some of the features you might meet.

Images are often used to help you understand the text, but they will not contain clues to the answers!

There may be cognates (German words that look like, and mean the same as, the English words).

You will be asked to infer (work out) the meaning of a new term. Look at the context, as there will be clues. Here, the words am Abend, schön, laut and Himmel are clues to the term Feuerwerk.

Section B: Translation

- This section is a translation from German into English.
- At Foundation level, there are five sentences to translate. At Higher level, there is a paragraph. Both are worth 10 marks.
- Read through the text to ensure you understand.
- Make sure you consider each word in your translation, taking care not to miss anything.
- There is often more than one possible correct translation. The key thing is for the same meaning to be communicated into English.
- At Foundation level, the meaning needs to be 'appropriately transferred'. So if you don't know an exact translation, you can still get marks for something similar. For example, you could put *I want to go to Africa* for sentence (b) here. However, always try to be as accurate as you can.
- Read through your work at the end to ensure it makes sense.
- If there is a word you don't know, don't panic or leave a blank, but work out something which makes sense in the context.

Translation

Holidays

Translate the following sentences **into English**.

(a) Ich mag Abenteuerurlaube.

I like adventure holidays.

(b) Ich möchte Afrika besuchen.

I would like to visit Africa.

(c) Es ist ein idealer Ort für einen Familienurlaub.

It is an ideal place for a family holiday.

(d) Letztes Jahr bin ich mit meiner Schwester in die Schweiz gefahren.

Last year I went to Switzerland with my sister.

(e) Nächstes Jahr werde ich während der Schulferien in England bleiben.

Next year I will stay in England during the school holidays.

Although you must consider each word, not every German word will have a direct translation into English. The translation of this sentence is likely to be *Last year I went to Switzerland with my sister* (not 'in the Switzerland').

Digital resources

Paper 4: Writing

Overview

The Writing paper comprises:

- Writing tasks (3 at Foundation tier; 2 at Higher tier).
- A translation task.

Timing: Foundation – 1 hour 15 minutes; Higher – 1 hour 20 minutes.
Marks: 50, including 10 marks for the translation into German.

Foundation tier: Question 1 (8 marks)

- This question asks you to describe a photo in four short sentences. It appears only on the Foundation paper.
- Keep your sentences short (but make sure they **are** sentences – include a verb!). Stick to words you know.
- You can use sentence starters like Es gibt. It is fine to repeat yourself in this task. You could, if you wanted, start each sentence with Es gibt.
- You can describe the people in the picture using hair, eyes, height, clothes and colours.
- You can describe where they are or what they are doing. If there is more than one person, you can describe just one of them if you prefer to use the singular rather than the plural form of the verb. Here, you could write Die Frau trinkt einen Kaffee.
- You can write about the weather if it is visible.
- There are only marks for correct communication of relevant information, so ensure that your answer is relevant (you are describing something in the photo), correct (your German is accurate) and you communicate a point. There are no marks for elaborating on your answer in this question.

1 Describe the photo. Write four short sentences **in German**.

Es gibt zwei Personen. (2)
Der Mann sitzt in einem Rollstuhl. (2)
Die Frau hat dunkle Haare. (2)
Sie trinken Kaffee. (2)

Make sure you describe the picture. For example, the sentence **Ich sehe einen Hund** in response to this picture would not receive any marks, even though the German is correct, as there is no dog in the photo!

Longer writing tasks

There are two open-response questions per level: Foundation level – Q2 formal text (40–50 words, 14 marks) and Q3 informal text (80–90 words, 18 marks); Higher level – Q1 informal text (80–90 words, 18 marks) and Q2 formal text (130–150 words, 22 marks).

- You **must** write about **all** of the bullet points given in the question, although you can write more about one than another, if you like. Ensure you respond to the points using the time frames indicated by the bullet points.
- You are given an expected number of words to write. Try to stick to this – the quality rather than the quantity of your writing is key here, as everything you write will be marked.
- Think hard:
  - o What relevant vocabulary do you know?
  - o Can you use conjunctions like aber or deshalb?
  - o Can you give an opinion using Meiner Meinung nach or Ich glaube?
  - o Can you give reasons using denn or weil?

  Revise these beforehand, so they come to you more quickly when you are in the exam.
- Even if the context is formal, you can use du if you prefer.
- Check your answer at the end to make sure your answer is:
  - ✓ accurate – correct any mistakes you see.
  - ✓ clear – ensure it makes sense.
  - ✓ relevant – double-check that you have covered all the bullets – this is very important!
  - ✓ developed – make sure your ideas include a variety of vocabulary and structures.

Paper 4: Writing

Digital resources

Examples of longer writing tasks

You have a choice of two tasks for each question – (a) or (b). Put a cross in the box of the question that you choose.

Read the bullet points carefully. Remember, you **must** cover **all** of them in your answer.

The bullet points may require you to write in the present, future or past form. Make sure you do this.

Choose either Question 1 (a) or Question 1 (b).

If you answer Question 1 (a), put a cross in the box ☒.

1 (a) Write an email to your exchange partner about your town.

You **must** include the following points:

- a description of a place in your town
- your opinion of your chosen place
- what you did the last time you went there
- what you will do the next time you go there.

Write your answer **in German**. You should aim to write between 80 and 90 words. **(18)**

Use vocabulary, grammar and phrases that you know, but try to vary your language, so you can show off the German you can use correctly to develop your ideas. Remember – what you write does not need to be true.

Write in German, aiming for the number of words stated. Although this is a guideline, it helps you achieve enough variety to score highly without making too many errors or running out of time.

Always read back your answer to ensure it makes sense.

This question could appear as Question 1 on a Higher tier paper or as Question 3 on a Foundation tier paper.
Other longer writing questions look similar, but always read the contexts, bullets and word count guidelines carefully, as they differ for different questions.

Translation into German

- At Foundation tier, there are five sentences to translate; at Higher tier, there is a short passage.
- Look out for different tenses – make sure you translate them accurately.
- There are 6 marks for how closely you translate the meaning from English to German and 4 marks for accuracy.
- Think about word order rules like inversion (Gestern habe ich ...), Time – Manner – Place (Ich fahre / morgen / mit dem Bus / zur Schule) and when to move the verb to the end of the clause (Ich kann ihn nicht sehen).
- There is often more than one possible correct translation.
- If there is a word you don't know, try using a similar word. Don't leave a blank.
- A minor error might still receive some marks – for example Es gibt zu viel Touristen ✗ (instead of viele ✓) – as the meaning is clear. But Es gibt grobes Touristen ✗ will lose marks because the meaning is unclear.
- Read through your work at the end to ensure it makes sense.

Translate the following five sentences **into German**. **(10)**

(a) I love nature.
Ich liebe die Natur.

(b) I live in the countryside.
Ich wohne auf dem Land.

(c) In the town there are too many tourists.
Es gibt zu viele Touristen in der Stadt.

(d) Yesterday I recycled paper and glass at school.
Gestern habe ich in der Schule Glas und Papier recycelt.

(e) Tomorrow I am going to school by bus because it is good for the environment.
Ich fahre morgen mit dem Bus zur Schule, weil das gut für die Umwelt ist.

Digital resources

Gender and plurals

When you learn a new noun, learn it with the correct word for 'the' – this word shows its gender. All German nouns are masculine (m), feminine (f) or neuter (nt).

Der, die, das (singular) and die (plural) – 'the'

Der Junge ist sportlich.
The boy is sporty.
Die Frau ist groß.
The woman is tall.
Das Mädchen ist müde.
The girl is tired.
Die Fische sind rot.
The fish are red.

Most male people are masculine nouns.

Most female people are feminine nouns.

-chen / -lein endings are always neuter nouns.

These examples are in the nominative case.

A very few nouns have a spelling change and a different ending when they are plural.
Stadion ➡ Stadi**en**
Museum ➡ Muse**en**

	masc	fem	neut	plural
nominative	der	die	das	die

You have to learn the gender of a word, but there are some 'rules' that can help you.

- **Masculine** nouns include days, months, seasons, nouns ending in -ling, many nouns ending in -en: Montag, Dezember, Winter, Zwilling, Morgen.
  Feminine nouns include most fruits, nouns ending in -ung, -heit, -keit, -schaft, -ei, -in, many nouns ending in -e: Banane, Rechnung, Freiheit, Schwierigkeit, Freundschaft, Bäckerei, Apothekerin, Kantine.
- **Neuter** nouns are all the infinitives used as nouns (e.g. Lesen, Essen, Schwimmen) and diminutive nouns ending in -lein and -chen (e.g. Mädchen, Fräulein, Brötchen).

The subject

Der (m), die (f), das (nt) and die (pl) are the definite articles (meaning 'the') which are used when the noun is the subject of the sentence, so doing the action of the verb.
This is the **nominative** case.

Der Mann geht aus.	The man goes out.
Das Mädchen arbeitet.	The girl is working.
Die Kinder spielen.	The children are playing.
Die Lehrerin spricht.	The teacher is speaking.

You can make a masculine noun feminine by adding -in: Schüler ➡ Schüler**in**.

Compound nouns

Compound nouns, made from putting together two or more nouns, take the gender of the last word, and this word determines their plural form too.
Klassenzimmer is neuter because Zimmer is neuter.
Marktplatz is masculine because Platz is masculine.

Plurals

German nouns form their plurals in several ways. When you learn a new noun, you should try to learn its plural as well as its gender. You can check a plural form you don't know in a dictionary. Here are some examples.

noun	add for plural		plural form
der Mann	+ umlaut + **-er**	➡	**die** M**ä**nn**er**
die Frau	+ **-en**	➡	**die** Frau**en**
das Kind	+ **-er**	➡	**die** Kind**er**

Some nouns do not change in the plural:
das Mädchen – the girl ➡ **die** Mädchen – the girls
das Zimmer – the room ➡ **die** Zimmer – the rooms.
Some nouns are always plural:
Eltern (parents), Ferien (holidays) and Geschwister (siblings).

Now try this

Give the correct definite article for these words (**der**, **die** or **das**). Then find the plural of each noun.

(a) Tier
(b) Pause
(c) Bus
(d) Wohnung
(e) Buch
(f) Glas
(g) Reise
(h) See (= 'lake')
(i) Supermarkt

Indefinite articles and possessives

Digital resources

The indefinite article is needed to say 'a / an' and possessives tell us to whom something belongs.

Indefinite articles

The indefinite articles are ein (m), eine (f) and ein (nt), and replace der, die, das when you say 'a / an'.

Ein Bus kommt bald. A bus is coming soon.
Eine Frau wartet. A woman is waiting.
Ein Eis, bitte! An ice cream, please!

Ein, eine, ein are only used in the **singular** (not plural), because they mean 'a / an' or 'one'.

Saying 'no' / 'not a / an'

The negative of ein / eine / ein is kein / keine / kein and has the plural form keine.
It means 'no' or 'not a / an'.

Das ist **kein** spannender Film.
That's not an exciting film.
Sie ist **keine** gute Lehrerin.
She is not a good teacher.
Kein Flugzeug kommt heute.
No plane is coming today.
Keine Kinder sind in dem Klassenzimmer.
No children are in the classroom.

Possessives

Possessives follow the same pattern as ein / eine / ein and kein / keine / kein.

mein Buch my book
deine Schwester your sister

Here are their masculine, feminine and neuter forms (in the nominative case):

mein / meine / mein my
dein / deine / dein your (familiar singular)
sein / seine / sein his or its
ihr / ihre / ihr her
unser / unsere / unser our
euer / euere / euer your (familiar plural)
Ihr / Ihre / Ihr your (formal singular and plural)
ihr / ihre / ihr their

Das ist unser Bus!
That's our bus!

Mein Abendessen war lecker.
My dinner was delicious.

This compound noun is neuter because **Essen**, the final part, is neuter.

You can add **Lieblings**- to the front of a noun to say 'favourite …'.
Mein **Lieblings**fach ist Mathe.
My favourite subject is maths.
Ihre **Lieblings**aktivität ist Tennis.
Her favourite activity is tennis.

Now try this

1 Which is the correct indefinite article – **ein**, **eine** or **ein**?
(a) Mann
(b) Schule
(c) Haus
(d) Mädchen

2 Which is the correct negative article – **kein**, **keine** or **kein**?
(a) Hotel
(b) Hausaufgaben
(c) Kind
(d) Schwester

3 How would you say … ?
(a) my friends
(b) her brother
(c) their teachers
(d) your parents (familiar singular)

Digital resources

Nominative and accusative cases

Grasping the case system is a key part of being accurate in German. Once you understand it, your work will be much more impressive!

The nominative case

This is used for the **subject** of a sentence – the person / thing doing the action of the verb.

Der Lehrer arbeitet fleißig.
The teacher works hard.
Die Frau wartet auf den Zug.
The woman waits for the train.
Das Kind spielt im Garten.
The child is playing in the garden.
Ein Job ist wichtig für mich.
A job is important to me.
Keine Schüler machen genug Hausaufgaben.
No students do enough homework.
Mein Onkel wohnt in der Schweiz.
My uncle lives in Switzerland.

The accusative case

This is used for the **direct object** of a sentence. The *receiver of the action of the verb* is a way of understanding what this means.

These sentences have a **subject** and a **direct object**.

Meine Schwester hat eine Freundin.
My sister has a friend.
Der Junge findet den Fußball.
The boy finds the football.
Die Kinder essen kein Obst.
The children do not eat fruit / eat no fruit.
Seine Mutter hat ihr Handy verloren.
His mother has lost her mobile phone.
Mein Bruder sucht seinen Pullover.
My brother is looking for his sweater.

Not sure which is the subject? Who / what is doing the action of the verb? Who lives in Switzerland? My uncle, so he is the subject.

Not sure which is the direct object? What is the action of the verb? What has the action done to it? What is the boy looking for? The sweater, so that is the direct object.

Note that the question word **wer?** (who?) also changes in the accusative case: **Wen hast du gesehen?** Whom did you see?

Using sein and es gibt

- sein is **always** used with the **nominative** case: Wo ist **der** Hund? Where is the dog?
- es gibt (there is / there are) is **always** followed by an **accusative** case: Es gibt **einen** starken Wind. There's a strong wind.

You will notice that the words 'the', 'a', 'not a' and the possessives change in the masculine accusative case.

the

	m	f	nt	pl
nominative	der	die	das	die
accusative	**den**	die	das	die

a / not a possessives

	m	f	nt	pl
nominative	ein	eine	ein	keine
accusative	ein**en**	eine	ein	keine

Now try this

Choose the correct word to complete each sentence. There are examples of both nominative and accusative cases.

(a) In Manchester gibt es **ein / eine / einen** Bahnhof.
(b) **Der / Die / Das** Haus hat **ein / einen / eine** Garten.
(c) **Mein / Meine / Meinen** Bruder hat **den / das / die** Auto gekauft.
(d) Ich kann **mein / meine / meinen** Bücher nicht finden.
(e) Wo ist **der / die / das** Supermarkt?
(f) **Der / Die / Das** Mädchen kauft morgen **ein / eine / ein** Handy.
(g) Max sucht **seine / sein / seinen** Mathelehrer.

Other cases and prepositions

Digital resources

There are two other cases you need to know and how to use them with prepositions.

The case system

Different cases are used in different circumstances. The nominative (for the subject) and accusative (for the direct object) are covered on page 96.

You also need to know the dative and the genitive.

Use the **dative** to say 'to / for someone'. This is known as the **indirect object**.

Ich gebe das Buch meinem Freund. I give the book to my friend / I give my friend the book.

Use the **genitive** to express 'of' and belonging to / possession.

Ich gebe meinem Freund das Buch meiner Mutter. I give my mother's book to my friend / I give my friend my mother's book.

The genitive will only appear in Higher level Listening and Reading papers.

Some verbs are followed by a dative case, for example **geben** (to give (to)), **helfen** (to help) and **erklären** (to explain (to)): **Ich habe meiner** Mutter **geholfen.** I helped my mother.

Changes to 'the'

	masc	fem	neut	pl
nominative	der	die	das	die
accusative	den	die	das	die
dative	dem	der	dem	den
genitive	des	der	des	der

Changes to 'a'

	masc	fem	neut	pl
nominative	ein	eine	ein	keine
accusative	einen	eine	ein	keine
dative	einem	einer	einem	keinen
genitive	eines	einer	eines	keiner

Prepositions

Prepositions are words which precede nouns or pronouns. They are followed by a particular case.

Prepositions with the **accusative**:

für	for
um	around
durch	through
gegen	against
entlang	along (follows the noun)
bis	until / as far as
ohne	without

FUDGEBO = first letters of all accusative prepositions!

durch die Stadt
through the town
für meinen Freund
for my friend

Prepositions with the **dative**:

aus	out of
außer	except
bei	at / at the house of
gegenüber	opposite
mit	with / by (transport)
nach	after / to a town / country
seit	since
von	from
zu	to

aus dem Haus — out of the house
nach der Schule — after school
mit dem Bus — by bus
Er hat sich **beim** Fußballspielen verletzt.
He got injured playing football.

Prepositions with the **genitive**:

trotz	in spite of / despite
während	during
wegen	because of

während der Ferien
during the holidays

See page 98 for prepositions that can take either the accusative or the dative case.

The final example shows **bei dem** shortened to **beim**.

Now try this

Complete sentences (a)–(c) with the correct form of **der / die / das** and sentences (d)–(f) with the correct form of **ein / eine / ein**.

(a) Wir fahren durch ______ Wald.
(b) Der Hund läuft aus ______ Haus.
(c) Trotz ______ Wetters gehen wir wandern.
(d) Er geht ohne ______ Jacke aus.
(e) Ich bin seit ______ Stunde hier.
(f) Wegen ______ Unfalls kam der Zug spät an.

Digital resources

Prepositions with the accusative or dative

Some prepositions can use either the accusative (if there is movement) or dative (if there is no movement).

Dual case prepositions

an	on (vertically), at
auf	on (horizontally)
hinter	behind
in	in
neben	next to
über	over / above
unter	under / below
vor	in front of / before
zwischen	between

Movement towards something (accusative):
Ich gehe **in das** Klassenzimmer.
I go into the classroom.
Die Katze läuft **hinter die** Tür.
The cat runs behind the door.

Static position (dative):
Ich bin **in dem** Klassenzimmer.
I am in the classroom.
Die Katze schläft **hinter der** Tür.
The cat is sleeping behind the door.

Remember that you can shorten **in das** to **ins**, **in dem** to **im** and **an dem** to **am**.
Die Kinder laufen **ins** Klassenzimmer.
The children run into the classroom.
Wir sind **im** Klassenzimmer.
We are in the classroom.
Ich arbeite **am** Samstag.
I'm working on Saturday.

Note that if you want to say 'in it / on it / in front of it', etc. without using a specific noun, you can prefix the preposition with **da-** or **dar-** if it begins with a vowel: **darin** – 'in it'; **darauf** – 'on it'; **dahinter** – 'behind it'.

Useful phrases with prepositions in the accusative

Wir fahren im Sommer **ins Ausland**.
We are going abroad in the summer.
Gehst du heute Abend **ins Kino**?
Are you going to the cinema tonight?
Meine Freundin und ich gehen **in die Stadt**.
My friend and I are going into town.
Ich gehe früh **in die Schule**.
I go to school early.

Useful phrases with prepositions in the dative

Er wohnt **im Ausland**. He lives abroad.
Unser Dorf liegt **auf dem Land**.
Our village is in the countryside.
Wohnst du **in den Bergen**?
Do you live in the mountains?
Ich warte auf dich **vor dem Kino**.
I'll wait for you in front of the cinema.
Ich bin bis 14:00 Uhr **in der Schule**.
I'm at school until 2 pm.

Now try this

Complete the sentences with the correct form of the definite article ('the').

(a) Das Kino ist zwischen ______ Park und ______ Hauptstraße.
(b) Der Hund läuft unter ______ Tisch.
(c) Es gibt viele Bücher auf ______ Tisch.
(d) Wir fahren am Wochenende auf ______ Land.
(e) Wohnt er in ______ Stadt?
(f) Treffen wir uns vor ______ Café?
(g) Wollen wir in ______ Park gehen?
(h) Ich wohne an ______ Küste.
(i) Wir schwimmen in ______ Meer.

Dieser, jener and jeder

Digital resources

Dieser, jener and jeder are key words meaning 'this', 'that' and 'each / every'.

Using dieser, jener and jeder

These words follow exactly the same pattern as der / die / das.

Welcher (which), solcher (such) and mancher (some) also work in the same way.

	masc.	fem.	neut.	pl.
nom.	dieser	diese	dieses	diese
acc.	diese**n**	diese	dieses	diese
dat.	diese**m**	diese**r**	diese**m**	diese**n**
gen.	diese**s**	diese**r**	dieses	diese**r**

Note that **jener** is only needed in the Higher tier papers, as is **mancher**.

Ways to use these words

Auf diese Weise in this way

dieser … jener the former … the latter

Welches Buch möchten Sie?

Which book would you like?

Welchen Beruf hat er?

What profession does he have?

Mit welchem Zug wollen Sie fahren?

Which train do you want to travel on?

Manche Leute besuchen die Museen.

Some people visit the museums.

Solche Ideen sind falsch. Such ideas are wrong.

Ich habe solchen Hunger. I'm so hungry.

Jener Fluss ist sehr bekannt.

That river is very famous.

Time expressions using dieser and jeder

These two articles are often used in time expressions and are useful in speaking and writing tests.

When you make a statement of definite time, it is always in the accusative case. Check that you are familiar with all of these.

jeden tag	every day
jeden morgen	every morning
jeden nachmittag	every afternoon
jeden abend	every evening
jeden samstag / donnerstag	every Saturday / Thursday
jede woche	every week
jeden monat	every month
jedes jahr	every year
diese woche	this week
diesen monat	this month
dieses jahr	this year

Worked example

Choose the correct word to complete each sentence. Look carefully at the gender of the noun and the case needed.

(a) Ich fahre mit **dieser / diesen / diesem** Zug.

(b) Auf **welche / welcher / welches** Straße wohnen sie?

(c) **Welche / Welches / Welcher** Fach magst du am besten?

(d) Mit **diesem / dieser / diesen** Kuli kann ich besser schreiben.

(e) **Jener / Jene / Jenes** Schloss ist sehr bekannt.

Answers:
(a) diesem; (b) welcher; (c) Welches;
(d) diesem; (e) Jenes

Now try this

1 Translate these sentences **into English**.

(a) **Diese Woche** habe ich viel zu tun.
(b) **Welches Kleid** hast du gekauft?
(c) Mit **welchem Bus** fährt er?
(d) Wir haben **jedes Jahr** im Dezember eine Party.
(e) Kennst du **jenen Lehrer**?

2 Read the sentences again and note down which case is being used for the words in **bold**.

Digital resources

Adjective endings

You will only meet the genitive at Higher tier.

Adjectives after der / die / das

These are the adjective endings after der / die / das. Dieser, jener, jeder, welcher, solcher and mancher follow the same pattern. A good tip is to remember that all the dative singular, genitive singular, masculine accusative singular and plural adjective endings are -en (shaded blue in the table). The rest end in -e.

	masculine	feminine	neuter	plural
nominative	der alt**e** Mann	die alt**e** Frau	das alt**e** Haus	die alt**en** Häuser
accusative	den alt**en** Mann	die alt**e** Frau	das alt**e** Haus	die alt**en** Häuser
dative	dem alt**en** Mann	der alt**en** Frau	dem alt**en** Haus	den alt**en** Häusern
genitive	des alt**en** Mann**es**	der alt**en** Frau	des alt**en** Haus**es**	der alt**en** Häuser

You can make nouns from adjectives by giving them a capital letter, so **der Alte** = 'the old man' and die **Alte** = 'the old woman'. These nouns will have adjective endings according to the case.

Adjectives after ein / eine / ein

These are the adjective endings after ein / eine / ein, kein / keine / kein and all the possessives (mein / dein / sein / ihr / unser / euer / Ihr / ihr). Try to remember: all the dative singular, genitive singular, masculine accusative singular and plural adjective endings are -en (shaded blue in the table). The other endings (-er for the masculine nominative, -e for the feminine nominative and accusative, and -es for the neuter) reflect the gender of these nouns by reminding you of d**er** / di**e** / da**s**.

	masculine	feminine	neuter	plural
nominative	ein alt**er** Mann	eine alt**e** Frau	ein alt**es** Haus	keine alt**en** Häuser
accusative	einen alt**en** Mann	eine alt**e** Frau	ein alt**es** Haus	keine alt**en** Häuser
dative	einem alt**en** Mann	einer alt**en** Frau	einem alt**en** Haus	keinen alt**en** Häusern
genitive	eines alt**en** Mann**es**	einer alt**en** Frau	eines alt**en** Haus**es**	keiner alt**en** Häuser

Adjectives with no article

These are the adjective endings when there is **no article** preceding the adjective. See how the adjective endings, with a couple of exceptions in the genitive, look like the endings of the der / die / das case system. So gut**es** Wetter is neuter (and reminds you of da**s**).

	masculine	feminine	neuter	plural
nominative	schwarz**er** Kaffee	kalt**e** Milch	gut**es** Wetter	nett**e** Leute
accusative	schwarz**en** Kaffee	kalt**e** Milch	gut**es** Wetter	nett**e** Leute
dative	schwarz**em** Kaffee	kalt**er** Milch	gut**em** Wetter	nett**en** Leuten
genitive	schwarz**en** Kaffee**s**	kalt**er** Milch	gut**en** Wetter**s**	nett**er** Leute

These are the endings to use with **viele** (many), **einige** (some) and after numbers.

Now try this

Add the correct ending to each adjective.

(a) Der alt _____ Mann wohnt in dieser klein _____ Stadt.
(b) Mein best _____ Freund hat einen älter _____ Bruder.
(c) Ich habe heute unglücklich _____ Menschen in den Nachrichten gesehen.
(d) Ich möchte bitte schwarz _____ Tee.
(e) Wir waren mit nett _____ Leuten zusammen.

Note that if the adjective is a compound one, e.g. **dunkelblau**, or if it's negative, e.g. **unglücklich**, the endings are the same as for the simple (**blau**) and positive (**glücklich**) adjectives.

Comparative and superlative adjectives

Using comparative and superlative adjectives allows you to express more interesting opinions and adds to the complexity of the language you can demonstrate, especially in speaking and writing.

Forming comparative and superlative adjectives

To make a comparative, just add -er, as is often the case in English: schnell ➡ schnell**er**

Das Auto ist schnell. The car is fast.

Der Zug ist schnell**er**. The train is faster.

For a superlative add -(e)st ➡ schnell**st-**

Das Flugzeug ist das schnell**ste** Verkehrsmittel. The aeroplane is the fastest means of transport.

Irregular forms

Some adjectives add an umlaut or have a small spelling change in the comparative and superlative forms.

alt – **ä**lter – **ä**lteste — old – older – oldest

jung – j**ü**nger – j**ü**ngste — young – younger – youngest

H ONLY

gro**ß** – grö**ß**er – grö**ß**te — big – bigger – biggest

lang – l**ä**nger – l**ä**ngste — long – longer – longest

hoch – h**ö**her – h**ö**chste — high – higher – highest

Others are irregular and need to be learned:

gut – besser – beste — good – better – best

You can make superlatives into neuter nouns by giving them a capital letter:

das Beste – **'the best thing'**

das Schlimmste – **'the worst thing'**

You can also use **etwas / nichts** with adjectives and an initial capital letter + **-es** ending to say etwas Interessantes (**something interesting**) or nichts Gutes (**nothing good**).

H ONLY

Comparative and superlative adverbs

Adverbs describe verbs in almost exactly the same way as adjectives describe nouns.

Er läuft schnell. — He runs quickly.

Sie läuft schneller. — She runs more quickly.

Ich laufe am schnellsten. — I run the quickest.

Lea singt gut. — Lea sings well.

Joel singt besser als Lea.

Joel sings better than Lea.

Mika singt am besten. — Mika sings best.

Note how to say 'than' when making comparisons: besser **als** (better **than**), schöner als (more beautiful **than**).

Gern, lieber, am liebsten

These are great ways of expressing opinions and preferences.

Ich fahre **gern** Rad. ♥

I like cycling.

Ich schwimme **lieber**. ♥♥

I prefer swimming.

Am liebsten spiele ich Tennis. ♥♥♥

Most of all I like playing tennis.

It's usual to put **am liebsten** at the start of the sentence and invert the verb.

Note that to say 'best of all / fastest of all' you need **am** followed by the superlative adjective ending in **-en**: Mein Auto fährt **am** schnellst**en**. My car goes the fastest (of all).

H ONLY

Now try this

Complete each sentence with the comparative form of the adjective in brackets.

(a) Ist deine Schwester ________ als du? (*jung*)

(b) Dieses Video ist ________ als das letzte. (*gut*)

(c) Wir finden Englisch ________ als Musik. (*interessant*)

(d) Der Film dauert ________ als drei Stunden. (*lang*)

Digital resources

Personal pronouns

Personal pronouns – words referring back to named people and objects (e.g. 'she', 'her', 'it', 'us', 'they') – have different forms depending on the case.

Pronouns

nominative	accusative	dative
ich	mich	mir
du	dich	dir
er / sie / es	ihn / sie / es	ihm / ihr / ihm
wir	uns	uns
ihr	euch	euch
Sie	Sie	Ihnen
sie	sie	ihnen

The plural dative forms are only required at Higher tier.

Use the nominative case for the subject of the verb: **Er ist nett. He** is nice.

Use the accusative case for the direct object of the verb: **Wir haben ihn gestern gesehen.** We saw **him** yesterday.

Use the dative case with dative prepositions (mit **ihm** – 'with **him**') and after verbs taking the dative: **Ich helfe ihm**. I'm helping **him**.

Sie hat **ihm** ein Geschenk gegeben.
She gave **him** a present / She gave a present **to him**.

This is a more complex sentence with both a direct and an indirect object, which you may come across at Higher tier.

Using personal pronouns

Pronouns can give more fluency to your spoken and written German, because you avoid repeating yourself.

Wo ist **dein Bruder**? Ich habe **deinen Bruder** heute nicht gesehen.
Where's your brother? I haven't seen your brother today.

Wo ist **dein Bruder**? Ich habe **ihn** heute nicht gesehen.
Where's your brother? I haven't seen **him** today.

The second version is not only shorter but also sounds more natural.

Two useful indefinite pronouns, **jemand** (**someone**) and **niemand** (**no one**), can also add further variety to your German:
Wo ist dein Bruder? **Jemand / Niemand** hat ihn heute gesehen.
Where's your brother? Someone / No one has seen him today.

Useful phrases using pronouns

Es freut **mich**, dass … I'm happy that …
Es geht **mir** gut. I'm fine.
Wie geht es **dir**? How are you?
Das schmeckt **mir**.
It tastes good / I like the taste.
Mir ist kalt! I'm cold!
Es gelingt **uns**, … zu (+ infinitive).
We manage to …
Es tut **mir** leid. I'm sorry.
Es ist **mir** egal. I'm not bothered.
… gefällt **mir**. I like … (singular)
Deine Tasche gefällt **mir**. I like your bag.
… gefallen **mir**. I like … (plural)
Diese Jungen gefallen **mir** nicht.
I don't like these boys.

Now try this

Complete these sentences with the correct pronoun.

(a) Kannst du ________ helfen? (*me*)
(b) Hast du ________ gesehen? (*him*)
(c) Dieses T-Shirt gefällt ________ . (*her*)
(d) Es freut ________, dass du hier bist. (*me*)
(e) Wie geht es ________? (*him*)
(f) Er hat ________ Geld gegeben. (*us*)
(g) Ich wollte mit ________ gehen. (*them*)
(h) Gibt es am Freitag bei ________ eine Party? (*you,* familiar plural)

Word order 1

Digital resources

German word order has a few rules. If you follow them, your German will be more fluent!

Verb as second idea

1	2	3	
Er	**geht**	ins Kino.	
Subject	Verb	Rest of sentence	
Am Samstag	**geht**	**er**	ins Kino.
First idea	Verb	Subject	Rest of sentence

If a word or phrase is added to the start of a sentence, you invert the verb and subject (swap them around), so that the verb is back in second place.

A German sentence will only start with a verb if it's a 'yes / no' question or a command. **Magst** du Fußball? **Komm** schnell mit! Do you like football? Come with me quickly!

Perfect tense

The part of haben / sein is the main verb, so is in second position, and the past participle goes at the end.

1	2	3	4
Wir	**haben**	Handball	gespielt.
Gestern	**haben**	wir Handball	gespielt.

Future tense

The part of werden is the main verb, so is in second position, and the infinitive goes at the end.

1	2	3	4
Ich	**werde**	im Restaurant	essen.
Morgen	**werde**	ich im Restaurant	essen.

Modal verbs

The part of müssen / wollen / sollen / können, etc. is the main verb, so is in second position, and the infinitive is at the end.

1	2	3	4
Ich	**muss**	nach Hause	gehen.

Time – Manner – Place

Time – Manner – Place (TMP) is the order in which information should appear in a sentence.

	T	M	P
Er geht	heute	zu Fuß	in die Stadt.

Or:

T		M	P
Heute	geht er	zu Fuß	in die Stadt.

Negation

When you negate a sentence, you must put nicht in the correct position. Nicht will precede:

- an adjective at the end of a sentence
- an infinitive at the end of a sentence
- a past participle at the end of a sentence
- a separable prefix at the end of a sentence

or:

- it will be the last word.

Er ist nicht intelligent.	He is not intelligent.
Ich werde nicht heiraten.	I will not get married.
Wir haben nicht gegessen.	We have not eaten.
Er kommt nicht mit.	He's not coming with us.
Ich verstehe nicht.	I don't understand.

Now try this

Write the sentences in the correct order.

(a) mit seiner Familie / fährt / mein Freund / **Jeden Sommer** / in den Urlaub.
(b) ein spannendes Fußballspiel / wir / **Gestern** / gesehen / haben.
(c) auf die Uni / werde / **Ich** / gehen / in der Zukunft.
(d) zelten / ich / gegangen / auf dem Land / **Letztes Jahr** / bin.
(e) müssen / immer / machen / viele Hausaufgaben / **Wir**.
(f) du / **Kannst** / später / kommen / ins Kino / ?
(g) will / mit dem Zug / **Er** / fahren / nach Berlin.

Digital resources

Conjunctions

It's a good idea – especially for the Writing exam – to practise extending and developing basic sentences into longer and more complex statements. You can use conjunctions to do this.

Coordinating conjunctions

These are straightforward linking words that do not alter the word order.

aber	but
denn	because
oder	or
und	and

Ich sehe fern **oder** höre Musik.
I watch TV or listen to music.

Using sondern

H ONLY

Sondern is another word for 'but'. It is only used when:

- the two clauses have the same subject
- the first clause is negative
- the two clauses contradict each other.

Es ist nicht warm, sondern kalt.
It's not warm, but cold.

Sie kamen nicht früh, sondern spät.
They didn't come early, but late.

Use sondern when you could add 'but rather', meaning 'on the contrary ...'

Subordinating conjunctions

Words like weil send the verb to the end of the clause. Put a comma between the two clauses. Some of the conjunctions which do this are:

als	when (past)	während	while
bevor	before	warum	why
da	since / because	was	what
damit	so that	weil	because
nachdem	after	wenn	if / when (present / future)
obwohl	although	wie	how

Er geht wandern, **obwohl** es kalt ist.
He's going hiking, although it's cold.
Or:
Obwohl es kalt ist, geht er wandern.
Although it's cold, he's going hiking.

If you begin the sentence with the conjunction clause, the verb in the next clause inverts, so in the middle you should see **verb – comma – verb**.

Interrogatives (question words like wie / was / warum) also act as conjunctions, where an indirect question is implicit.

Ich verstehe nicht, **warum** sie böse ist.
I don't understand why she is angry.

Ihre Mutter weiß nicht, **wo** sie ist.
Her mother doesn't know where she is.

Ich will wissen, **wann** der Zug kommt.
I want to know when the train is coming.

Conjunctions and the perfect tense

H ONLY

Subordinating conjunctions (where the conjunction sends the verb to the end of the clause) can be used in the perfect tense. The part of sein / haben is sent right to the end of the clause, with the past participle just before it.

Weil ich meine Arbeit **gemacht habe**, gehe ich aus.
Because I've done my work, I'm going out.

Ich habe gegessen, **bevor** ich **ausgegangen bin**.
I ate before I went out.

Conjunctions and the future tense and with modal verbs

H ONLY

In the future tense, the part of werden goes last, with the dependent infinitive just before it.

With modal verbs, the part of the modal goes last with the infinitive just before it.

Da ich morgen nach London **fahren werde**, brauche ich meinen Koffer.

As I'm going to London tomorrow, I need my suitcase.

Ich weiß nicht, was ich **machen soll**.
I don't know what I should do.

Now try this

Link the sentences together using the conjunction in brackets.

(a) Wir haben auf dem Land gewohnt. Ich war jünger. (*als*)
(b) Er wird in der Schweiz leben. Er hat eine neue Arbeit gefunden. (*weil*)
(c) Ich habe Essen gekauft. Meine Mutter ist krank. (*da*)
(d) Ich verstehe nicht. Er hat das gesagt. (*warum*)
(e) Es freut mich. Meine Noten sind jetzt viel besser. (*dass*)

Word order 2

Digital resources

Here are a few more interesting structures you can use to enhance the quality of your spoken and written German. They are all good examples of complex language, which will help you aim for higher grades.

Um ... zu clauses

H ONLY

Um ... zu + infinitive is the way to say 'to' when you mean 'in order to'.

Er arbeitet samstags, **um** Geld **zu verdienen**.

He works on Saturdays, (in order) to earn money.

Add a comma before um and put zu + infinitive at the end of the clause.

Ich arbeite fleißig**, um** gute Noten **zu bekommen**.

I work hard (in order) to get good marks.

Sie geht aus**, um** neue Leute kennen**zu**lernen.

She goes out (in order) to get to know new people.

With separable verbs, **zu** goes between the prefix and the main verb as one complete word.

Other clauses with zu + infinitive

H ONLY

Some verbs need zu ... + infinitive after them to make sense. Use a comma, then put zu + infinitive at the end of the clause.

Ich **hoffe,** gute Noten **zu bekommen**.

I hope to get good grades.

Wir **versuchen,** früh ins Bett **zu gehen**.

We try to go to bed early.

Ich **habe begonnen,** gesünder **zu essen**.

I have started to eat more healthily.

Ich **habe vor,** auf die Uni **zu gehen**.

I intend / plan to go to university.

Other structures to try:

Es **macht Spaß,** ins Kino **zu gehen**.

It's fun to go to the cinema.

Es **ist nützlich,** Mathe **zu lernen**.

It's useful to learn maths.

Note also these structures with **zu** + infinitive: **ohne** ... **zu** + infinitive (without ...) and **statt** ... **zu** + infinitive (instead of ...).

Er ging nach Hause, **ohne** auf mich **zu** warten. He went home without waiting for me.

Relative clauses

You can add information to a sentence by adding a relative clause starting with 'which / who / whom / that', as follows.

- Start with the **main** clause, which can stand on its own: Der Lehrer ist toll. The teacher is great.
- Add the **relative** clause, which gives extra information but can't stand on its own:
  ... der uns Deutsch unterrichtet ... ... who teaches us German ...
- Together: Der Lehrer, **der** uns Deutsch unterrichtet, ist toll.
  The teacher **who** teaches us German is great.

When forming a sentence with a relative clause:

- put the verb at the end of the relative clause
- use a comma to divide the two clauses
- decide the case by looking at the relative clause itself.

At Foundation tier, you only need to know clauses with single-verb structures.

Ich habe das Buch gefunden, **das** du verloren hast. I found the book **which** you lost.
(nt, accusative – das Buch is the object of verloren)

Der Film, **den** wir gesehen haben, war sehr lang. The film **that** we saw was very long.
(m, accusative – den Film is the object of gesehen haben)

Now try this

Translate these sentences **into German** using the following structures.

Um ... zu	**(a)** I play sport, (in order) to be healthy. **(b)** We are going to the cinema, (in order) to see a new film.
Zu + infinitive	**(c)** I hope to find a job. **(d)** She tries to work hard.
Relative clauses	**(e)** The girl who has blonde hair is called Anna. **(f)** The people who live here are friendly.

Digital resources

The present tense

Verbs in the present tense can be regular, irregular (with a stem vowel change) or very irregular. The first two groups are explained on this page. For the very irregular verbs, see pages 108–109.

Regular verbs

Regular present tense verbs have different forms to match different people. To make them:

1. remove the -en ending from the infinitive to form the **stem**: spiel~~en~~ ➡ spiel
2. add the endings below to the stem.

ich	spiel**e**	I play / am playing
du	spiel**st**	you play / are playing
er / sie / es	spiel**t**	he / she / it plays
wir	spiel**en**	we play / are playing
ihr	spiel**t**	you play / are playing
Sie	spiel**en**	you play / are playing
sie	spiel**en**	they play / are playing

The indefinite pronoun **man** (one / you / people) uses the **er / sie / es** form.

- You can also use **present time expressions** like heute (today), jetzt (now), jeden Tag (every day), im Moment (at the moment), am Wochenende (at the weekend) to say what is happening now or regularly.
- You can also use the present with a **future time expression** to indicate future actions.
  Nächste Woche arbeite ich.
  I'm working / I'll be working next week.

Remember that **seit** + dative is used with a present tense verb to say how long something has been happening.
Ich **warte seit** einer Stunde! I've been waiting for (literally, 'since') an hour! H ONLY

Verbs with vowel changes

Some verbs change their vowel sound in the du and er / sie / es forms, but the endings stay the same.

fahren (to drive / travel) adds an umlaut:

ich	fahre		wir	fahren
du	fährst		ihr	fahrt
er / sie / es	fährt		Sie / sie	fahren

Laufen / schlafen / tragen also follow this pattern.

sehen (to see) adds a vowel:

ich	sehe		wir	sehen
du	siehst		ihr	seht
er / sie / es	sieht		Sie / sie	sehen

Lesen also follows this pattern.

Essen / helfen / sprechen / treffen / vergessen / werden / werfen also follow this pattern.

geben (to give) changes the vowel:

ich	gebe		wir	geben
du	gibst		ihr	gebt
er / sie / es	gibt		Sie / sie	geben

The imperative H ONLY

Use this to give an instruction / command.

- Sie form – invert the present tense verb and subject: Kommen Sie bitte mit! Please come with me!
- Ihr form – use the present tense verb form without the subject pronoun: Kommt mit! Come with me!
- Du form – use the present tense verb form without its -st ending and without du: Komm mit! Come with me!
- The du form may sometimes have an -e added: Spiele Basketball! Play basketball!
- Where an irregular verb has a vowel change, this is also in the du form imperative: Gib mir das Buch! Give me the book!
- Where an irregular verb has an umlaut added, this change disappears in the du form imperative: Schlaf gut! Sleep well!

Now try this

Complete each sentence with the present tense form of the verb in brackets.

(a) Ich ______ morgen nach Hause. (*fahren*)
(b) ______ du gern ein Instrument? (*spielen*)
(c) Mein Vater ______ mir oft Geschenke. (*geben*)
(d) Wir ______ in die Stadt. (*gehen*)
(e) Das Mädchen ______ krank aus. (*sehen*)
(f) Was ______ ihr am Wochenende? (*machen*)
(g) Wo ______ Sie, Frau Hecht? (*wohnen*)
(h) Die Klasse ______ klassische Musik. (*hören*)

Reflexive and separable verbs

Digital resources

Using these verbs in speaking and writing adds to the variety and complexity of your language.

Reflexive verbs

The verbs are used with a reflexive pronoun, which reflects the person doing the action.
Ich wasche **mich**. (literally, 'I wash myself.')

sich freuen (to be glad / happy)

ich freue mich	wir freuen uns
du freust dich	ihr freut euch
er / sie / es freut sich	Sie / sie freuen sich

The reflexive pronoun does not always have a literal equivalent in English.

Note this reciprocal use of the reflexive pronoun meaning 'each other'.

Some more reflexive verbs

sich anziehen	to get dressed
sich fühlen	to feel
sich interessieren für	to be interested in
sich konzentrieren	to concentrate
sich setzen	to sit down
sich treffen mit	to meet up with
sich kennen	to know each other
sich lieben	to love each other
sich sehen	to see each other

Reflexive verbs form the perfect tense with **haben** and the reflexive pronoun follows the part of **haben**:
Ich **habe mich gesetzt**. I sat down.

Separable verbs

These verbs have two parts, the prefix and the verb. When used in the present tense, these parts separate, with the prefix going to the end of the clause / sentence.
Ich **sehe** gern **fern**. I like watching television.
Er **zieht** sich schnell **an**. He gets dressed quickly.

This verb is reflexive and separable!

When you use these verbs in the perfect tense, the -ge- appears in the middle of the past participle.
Ich bin früh aufgestanden.
I got up early.
Wir haben das Licht ausgemacht.
We switched the light off.

Some useful separable verbs

anhaben	to have on / be wearing
ankommen	to arrive
ansehen	to watch
aufgeben	to give up
aufstehen	to get up
ausgehen	to go out
ausmachen	to switch off
fernsehen	to watch television
herunterladen	to download
teilnehmen an	to take part in
zurückkommen	to come back

Now try this

1 Complete each sentence with the correct reflexive pronoun.
(a) Interessierst du ______ für Mathe?
(b) Ich ziehe ______ an, bevor ich das Frühstück esse.
(c) Treffen wir ______ vor dem Kino?
(d) Die Frau setzt ______ in dem Büro hin.

2 Rewrite these sentences in the correct order. The first word is shown in bold.
(a) dein / **Wann** / an / Zug / kommt / ?
(b) auf / **Ich** / stehe / immer / früh
(c) **Meine** / zurück / morgen / Eltern / kommen
(d) lustigen / sieht / an / **Sie** / Film / einen

Irregular verb tables 1

Digital resources

The key parts of some common verbs are shown here.

* This means that the verb takes sein in the perfect tense.

Where (*) is shown in brackets, the verb can be used with either haben or sein. This depends on whether it has a direct object or not. Er hat sein neues Auto gefahren (Auto is the direct object) = 'He drove his new car'. Sie ist nach Köln gefahren (no direct object) = 'She drove / travelled to Cologne'.

infinitive / meaning		3rd person present sing.	3rd person imperfect sing.	past participle
beginnen	to begin	beginnt	begann	begonnen
bleiben	to stay	bleibt	blieb	geblieben *
brechen	to break	bricht	brach	gebrochen
bringen	to bring	bringt	brachte	gebracht
dürfen	to be allowed	darf	durfte	gedurft
essen	to eat	isst	aß	gegessen
fahren	to travel	fährt	fuhr	gefahren (*)
fallen	to fall	fällt	fiel	gefallen *
finden	to find	findet	fand	gefunden
geben	to give	gibt	gab	gegeben
gehen	to go	geht	ging	gegangen *
gewinnen	to win	gewinnt	gewann	gewonnen
haben	to have	hat	hatte	gehabt
halten	to hold / stop	hält	hielt	gehalten
helfen	to help	hilft	half	geholfen
kennen	to know	kennt	kannte	gekannt
kommen	to come	kommt	kam	gekommen *
können	to be able	kann	konnte	gekonnt
lassen	to allow / let	lässt	ließ	gelassen
laufen	to run	läuft	lief	gelaufen *
lesen	to read	liest	las	gelesen
mögen	to like	mag	mochte	gemocht
müssen	to have to	muss	musste	gemusst

Key: These verb forms should be familiar to both tiers. These are required at Higher tier only.

Non-highlighted verb forms are for information and are not required for the exam.

Irregular verb tables 2

Digital resources

The key parts of some common verbs are shown here. * This means that the verb takes sein in the perfect tense.

Where (*) is shown in brackets, the verb can be used with either haben or sein. This depends on whether it has a direct object or not.

infinitive / meaning		3rd person present sing.	3rd person imperfect sing.	past participle
nehmen	to take	nimmt	nahm	genommen
rufen	to call	ruft	rief	gerufen
scheinen	to shine	scheint	schien	geschienen
schließen	to shut	schließt	schloss	geschlossen
schreiben	to write	schreibt	schrieb	geschrieben
schwimmen	to swim	schwimmt	schwamm	geschwommen (*)
sehen	to see	sieht	sah	gesehen
sein	to be	ist	war	gewesen *
singen	to sing	singt	sang	gesungen
sitzen	to sit	sitzt	saß	gesessen
sollen	ought to	soll	sollte	gesollt
sprechen	to speak	spricht	sprach	gesprochen
stehen	to stand	steht	stand	gestanden *
steigen	to climb	steigt	stieg	gestiegen *
tragen	to carry	trägt	trug	getragen
treffen	to meet	trifft	traf	getroffen
treten	to step	tritt	trat	getreten
trinken	to drink	trinkt	trank	getrunken
vergessen	to forget	vergisst	vergaß	vergessen
werden	to become	wird	wurde	geworden *
wissen	to know	weiß	wusste	gewusst
wollen	to want to	will	wollte	gewollt
ziehen	to pull	zieht	zog	gezogen

Key: These verb forms should be familiar to both tiers. These are required at Higher tier only.
Non-highlighted verb forms are for information and are not required for the exam.

Digital resources

Using irregular verbs in different tenses

As verbs are such a fundamental part of any language, knowing something about irregular verb forms will boost your confidence in understanding and using German.

Irregular verbs in the present tense

In the irregular verb tables (see pages 108–109), column 2 shows what happens to the verb in the third person **present** tense singular form – the er / sie / es form. The same vowel change happens in the du form (just add the ending -st), but the rest of the verb follows a regular pattern.

This is the **er / sie / es** form in the present tense.

infinitive / meaning	3rd person present sing.	3rd person imperfect sing.	past participle
geben to give	gibt	gab	gegeben

sehen: Wo **siehst** du geme Filme an? – Where do you like watching films?
tragen: Mein Freund **trägt** ein rotes Hemd. – My friend is wearing a red shirt.
wollen: Was **willst** du heute machen? – What do you want to do today?

Irregular verbs in the imperfect tense

The **imperfect** form is shown in column 3 of the tables.
Remember that this shows both the er / sie / es and the ich form.

This is the **er / sie / es** form in the imperfect tense.

infinitive / meaning	3rd person present sing.	3rd person imperfect sing.	past participle
haben to give	hat	hatte	gehabt

sein: Ich **war** sehr glücklich. – I was very happy / lucky.
müssen: Er **musste** in die Stadt gehen. – He had to go to town.
beginnen: Der Film **begann** um 20:00 Uhr. – The film began at 8pm.

Irregular verbs in the perfect tense

The irregular **perfect** tense past participle is shown in column 4 of the tables. Note that most of these end in -en.

This is the past participle.

infinitive / meaning	3rd person present sing.	3rd person imperfect sing.	past participle
lesen to read	liest	las	gelesen

Ich habe das Buch **gelesen**. – I read the book.
Ich habe den Preis **gewonnen**. – I won the prize.
Ich habe das Gmüse **gegessen**. – I ate the vegtables.

Now try this

Complete these sentences with the past participle of the verb in brackets.

(a) Wir sind nach Wien ________ . (*fahren*)
(b) Hat er dir ________ ? (*helfen*)
(c) Wir haben über die Umwelt ________ . (*sprechen*)
(d) Ich habe meine Bücher ________ . (*vergessen*)
(e) Meine Freundin hat mir das Buch ________ . (*geben*)

Remember that verbs with an inseparable prefix like **ver-** do not add **ge-** in the past participle.

Sein and *haben*

Digital resources

The two most useful and frequent verbs you will need in every context are also among the most irregular.

Sein and haben in the present tense

person	sein	haben
ich	bin	habe
du	bist	hast
er / sie / es / man	ist	hat
wir	sind	haben
ihr	seid	habt
Sie	sind	haben
sie	sind	haben

Some expressions with haben

Angst haben	to be afraid
Durst haben	to be thirsty
Glück haben	to be lucky
Hunger haben	to be hungry
Lust haben	to want to / feel like (doing something)
Zeit haben	to have time to
Hab keine Angst!	Don't be afraid!
Hast du Hunger?	Are you hungry?
Ich habe Durst!	I'm thirsty!
Ich habe Lust, einen Film zu sehen.	I feel like seeing a film.

Sein and haben in the imperfect tense

The irregular verb tables on pages 108–109 show that war and hatte are the er / sie / es forms. They are also the ich forms. You simply need to add the correct endings to make the other forms (see page 115).

Ich war müde.	I was tired.	Er hatte Angst.	He was afraid.
Wir waren müde.	We were tired.	Wir hatten Angst, dass ...	We were afraid that ...
Warst du müde?	Were you tired?	Hattest du keine Angst?	Weren't you afraid?

Sein and haben in the perfect tense

The past participle of haben is gehabt, and for sein, it's gewesen. Sein forms its perfect tense with sein.

See page 114 for more details on the perfect tense with **sein**.

gewesen is not in the specification, but it is useful for you to know.

Ich **bin** krank **gewesen**.
I have been ill.

Now try this

1 Complete these sentences with the correct form of **haben** in the tense shown in brackets.
(a) Mein Bruder __________ heute keine Zeit. (*present*)
(b) Ich __________ gestern Kopfschmerzen. (*imperfect*)
(c) Wir __________ Glück __________ . (*perfect*)

2 Complete these sentences with the correct form of sein in the tense shown in brackets.
(a) Er __________ Arzt. (*present*)
(b) Als ich jünger __________, __________ ich sportlich. (*imperfect*)
(c) Meine Freundinnen __________ krank __________ . (*perfect*)

Digital resources

Modal verbs in the present tense

Modal verbs need the infinitive of another verb to complete their sense. This infinitive appears at the end of the clause or sentence.

Können (to be able to)

ich	kann
du	kannst
er / sie / es / man	kann
wir	können
ihr	könnt
Sie / sie	können

Kannst du Deutsch **sprechen**?
Can you speak German?

Müssen (to have to / must)

ich	muss
du	musst
er / sie / es / man	muss
wir	müssen
ihr	müsst
Sie / sie	müssen

Wie lange **muss** ich **warten**?
How long do I have to wait?

Wollen (to want to)

ich	will
du	willst
er / sie / es / man	will
wir	wollen
ihr	wollt
Sie / sie	wollen

Wir **wollen** heute **ankommen**.
We want to arrive today.

Dürfen (to be allowed to / may)

ich	darf
du	darfst
er / sie / es / man	darf
wir	dürfen
ihr	dürft
Sie / sie	dürfen

Er **darf** heute nicht **ausgehen**.
He's not allowed to go out today.

Sollen (ought to / should)

ich	soll
du	sollst
er / sie / es / man	soll
wir	sollen
ihr	sollt
Sie / sie	sollen

Man **soll** nicht so oft **fliegen**.
People should not fly so often.

Mögen (to like)

ich	mag
du	magst
er / sie / es / man	mag
wir	mögen
ihr	mögt
Sie / sie	mögen

Ich **mag fernsehen**. I like watching television.

One of the most useful forms of **mögen** is of course **ich möchte …** (**I would like …**).

Now try this

Rewrite each sentence with the correct form of the modal verb shown in brackets.
Example: Ich bewege mich mehr. (*sollen*) ➔ Ich **soll** mich mehr **bewegen**.

(a) Ich habe eine Geburtstagsparty. (*wollen*)
(b) Er geht nicht in die Bar in der Stadt. (*dürfen*)
(c) Man schützt die Umwelt. (*sollen*)
(d) Das machen wir nächste Woche. (*können*)
(e) Alle Schüler machen täglich Hausaufgaben. (*müssen*)
(f) Ich schwimme im Meer. (*mögen*)

Remember that the current verb will become an infinitive and move to the end.

The perfect tense with *haben*

Digital resources

The perfect tense

- is used to talk about past events
- can mean 'I played / I did play / I have played'
- has two parts:
  – the appropriate part of haben or, with certain verbs, sein (auxiliary verb)
  – the past participle of the verb you are using (at the end of the sentence).
  Ich **habe** Fußball **gespielt**. I played football.

To form a regular past participle:

- take the stem of the verb by removing -en
- add ge- to the front and -t to the end of the stem: spielen → **ge**spiel**t**
  hören → **ge**hör**t**
  machen → **ge**mach**t**
  kaufen → **ge**kauf**t**.

The perfect tense with haben

- Most verbs form their perfect tense with haben.
- All reflexive verbs form the perfect tense with haben.
- Regular past participles are formed as shown with spielen above.
- Irregular past participles don't follow a pattern, but often end in -en rather than -t. You can check these in the irregular verb tables.

See page 114 for more on verbs taking **sein**.
Revise the parts of **haben** on page 111.

Some common irregular past participles

Ich habe	*rest of sentence*	gebrochen.	I broke …
		gegessen.	I ate …
		gefunden.	I found …
		gegeben.	I gave …
		geholfen.	I helped …
		genommen.	I took …
		gesehen.	I saw …
		getragen.	I wore …
		getroffen.	I met …
		getrunken.	I drank …
		verstanden.	I understood …

Verbs with an inseparable prefix like **ver-** do not add **ge-** in the past participle.

Remember that the perfect also means 'I **have** broken', 'I **have** eaten', 'I **have** found', etc.

Word order in the perfect tense

The key rule is that the past participle is at the end of the clause / sentence.

If weil or another conjunction sends the verb to the end, the final verb is the part of haben / sein and the past participle immediately precedes it.

Ich **habe** am Wochenende Handball **gespielt**.

Am Wochenende **habe** ich mit Freunden Handball **gespielt**.

Ich bin müde, **weil** ich am Wochenende Handball **gespielt habe**.

Normal perfect tense word order.

Inversion after time expression.

weil sends **habe** to the end, after the past participle.

Some other examples of verbs with inseparable prefixes are bekommen ('to receive', past participle bekommen), empfehlen ('to recommend', past participle empfohlen).

Ich habe seine E-Mail **bekommen**. I got his email.

Er hat den Film **empfohlen**.
He recommended the film.

Now try this

Complete the sentences with the correct part of haben and the past participle of the verb in brackets.

(a) Er ______ seine Hausaufgaben schon ______ . (*machen*)
(b) Wo ______ du gestern Abend ______ . (*essen*)
(c) Wir ______ unsere Freunde ______ . (*treffen*)
(d) ______ ihr diesen Film ______? (*sehen*)
(e) Mein Bruder ______ ein neues Auto ______ . (*kaufen*)

Digital resources

The perfect tense with *sein*

Some verbs form their perfect tense with sein instead of haben.

Verbs with sein in the perfect tense

- denote movement from one place to another:

ankommen	to arrive
fahren	to travel / drive
fliegen	to fly
gehen	to go / walk
kommen	to come
laufen	to run

- describe a state (what / the way something is):

bleiben	to stay / remain
sein	to be

- describe a change of state:

werden	to become

- mean 'to happen':

geschehen	to happen
passieren	to happen

Most of these verbs are irregular and have past participles ending in **-en**, e.g. **gekommen**, **gelaufen**, **geblieben**.
When you use the past participle of a separable verb, the **-ge-** appears between the prefix and the past participle: **Ich bin früh angekommen. I came early.**

You can check how to form the parts of **sein** on page 111 and revise irregular past participles on pages 108–109.

Verbs ending in **-ieren** are all regular and never add **ge-** to the past participle.
Was ist passiert? What happened?

Bear in mind that verbs **without** direct objects are used with **sein**. If the verb has a direct object, its perfect tense is formed with **haben**.
Mein Bruder hat sein Flugzeug geflogen.
My brother flew his plane.
Mein Bruder ist mit dem Flugzeug gereist.
My brother travelled by plane.

Word order in the perfect tense

The same rules apply as for verbs with haben.

Ich **bin** letzte Woche nach Berlin **geflogen**.
I flew to Berlin last week.

Normal perfect tense word order with **bin** in second place and the past participle at the end.

Letzte Woche **bin** ich mit dem Zug nach Berlin **gefahren**.
Last week I went to Berlin by train.

Past participle at the end but inversion of **ich bin** after time expression, so the verb remains in second place.

Das Flugzeug war schmutzig, als ich gestern nach Berlin **geflogen bin**.
The plane was dirty when I flew to Berlin yesterday.

After the conjunction **als**, **bin** moves right to the end, with the past participle immediately preceding it.

Als ich nach Berlin **geflogen bin**, bin ich krank geworden.
When I flew to Berlin, I became ill.

When the **als** clause comes first, the verb in the second clause inverts. Remember the verb – comma – verb rule.

Now try this

Complete the sentences with the correct part of sein and the past participle of the verb in brackets.

(a) Wann ______ er gestern ______ (*ankommen*)
(b) Der Unfall ______ gestern ______ . (*passieren*)
(c) Ich ______ letzten Sommer in die Schweiz ______ . (*fahren*)
(d) Die Schüler ______ nach Köln ______ . (*fliegen*)
(e) Sein Opa ______ krank ______ . (*werden*)
(f) Johanna ______ meine beste Freundin ______ . (*bleiben*)

The imperfect tense

Digital resources

You can use the imperfect tense to describe and narrate events in the past. A number of common verbs are used in the imperfect tense in spoken language too.

Forming the imperfect tense

1. Take the infinitive, e.g. hören (to hear).
2. Take off the final -en ➡ hören = hör.
3. Add these endings:

ich hörte	I heard / was hearing
du hörtest	you heard / were hearing
er / sie / es / man hörte	he / she / it / one heard / was hearing
wir hörten	we heard / were hearing
ihr hörtet	you heard / were hearing
Sie / sie hörten	you / they heard / were hearing

At Foundation tier you only need to know the imperfect for **haben** and **sein** (all persons) and modal verbs for **ich**, **du** and **er/sie/es**.

Irregular verbs in the imperfect tense

Some verbs have irregular imperfect forms, as you will see in the tables on pages 108–109. The form shown in the tables is both the er / sie / es form and the ich form:

er fand / ich fand	he / I found
sie ging / ich ging	she / I went

- For the wir / Sie / sie forms, just add -en: sie ging**en** they went
  For the du and ihr forms, add -st and -t, respectively: du ging**st**, ihr ging**t** you went
- Note the impersonal verb es gab (there was / were), which does not change its ending even when referring to plurals: Es **gab** viele Leute. There **were** a lot of people.
- You should try to learn the imperfect tense forms of those verbs which will be most useful for expressing yourself in the past time frame for the Speaking and Writing exams. On the right are some handy examples.

Haben and sein in the imperfect tense

haben

ich hatte	I had
du hattest	you had
er / sie / es / man hatte	he / she / it / one had
wir hatten	we had
ihr hattet	you had
Sie / sie hatten	you / they had
Ich hatte Glück.	I was lucky.

sein

ich war	I was
du warst	you were
er / sie / es / man war	he / she / it / one was
wir waren	we were
ihr wart	you were
Sie / sie waren	you / they were
Es war teuer.	It was expensive.

Common irregular verbs in the imperfect tense

fahren ➡ fuhr	drove / travelled
gehen ➡ ging	went / walked
können ➡ konnte	could / was able to
müssen ➡ musste	had to
mögen ➡ mochte	liked
nehmen ➡ nahm	took
schreiben ➡ schrieb	wrote
sollen ➡ sollte	should / ought
sprechen ➡ sprach	spoke
wissen ➡ wusste	knew
wollen ➡ wollte	wanted to

Ich **wollte** mit meiner Freundin ausgehen, aber ich **musste** meine Hausaufgaben machen.

Als wir im Urlaub **waren**, **war** das Wetter sehr schön.

Die Musik **war** sehr laut!

Wir **hatten** zuerst eine Deutschstunde.

Now try this

Rewrite these sentences in the imperfect tense.

(a) Ich kaufe etwas zu essen.
(b) Wir wollen in die Stadt fahren.
(c) Er spielt in einer Band.
(d) Meine Freundin fährt nach Berlin.
(e) Mein Chef schreibt viele E-Mails.
(f) Ich spreche jeden Tag mit ihr.

Digital resources

The future tense

In both speaking and writing you will need to refer to the future time frame. You can do this by using the future tense or by using a future time marker and a present tense verb.

The future tense

Use the future tense to talk about plans for the future – whether later today or next year – and to say what you **will** do.

Use the present tense of werden plus an infinitive at the end of the clause.

Ich **werde** die Schule **verlassen**.

I will leave school.

ich	werde	*rest of sentence*	gehen
du	wirst		sein
er / sie / es	wird		helfen
wir	werden		fahren
ihr	werdet		spielen
Sie	werden		essen
sie	werden		zelten

Inversion in the future tense

A comment about the future often starts with a time marker, so the verb needs to invert, because it always needs to be in second place. Look at these examples.

1	2	3	4
In der Zukunft	werde	ich Geld	verdienen.
In the future I will earn money.			
Heute Abend	werde	ich	fernsehen.
This evening I'm going to watch television.			
Später	wird	er	ausgehen.
He's going to go out later.			

When you use a separable verb in the future tense the two parts join up again at the end of the sentence.

Present tense with future intent

You can use a present tense verb preceded by a time marker to say what you are going to do.

Morgen gehe ich einkaufen.

Tomorrow I'm going shopping.

Im Sommer macht er einen Fußballkurs.

In summer he's going to do a football course.

Heute Abend gehe ich mit Freunden aus.
Tonight I'm going out with friends.

Using the future tense with words like **wenn** or **weil** changes the word order:
Ich esse früh, weil ich heute Abend ausgehen werde.

Other ways of referencing the future

You can also use these structures to refer to future plans:

- wollen + infinitive
- hoffen + zu + infinitive
- ich möchte + infinitive.

In der Zukunft will ich nicht studieren.

I don't want to study in the future.

Ich hoffe, eine interessante Arbeit zu finden.

I hope to find an interesting job.

Ich möchte Schauspieler sein.

I would like to be an actor.

Now try this

Rewrite these sentences in the future tense using **werden**.

(a) Ich fahre ins Ausland.
(b) Er studiert Medizin.
(c) Was machst du?
(d) Wir finden eine neue Wohnung.
(e) Studiert ihr?
(f) Ich lebe mit meinem Freund zusammen.
(g) Sie arbeiten in Deutschland.
(h) Man schützt die Umwelt.

The conditional

H ONLY

Digital resources

The conditional is a verb form used to talk about things you would do or things that would happen in the future. At Foundation tier, the only conditional you need to know is ich möchte (I would like).

Forming the conditional

Once you can form the future tense (see page 116), the conditional is straightforward. There is still an infinitive at the end, but with a slightly different form of werden to express 'would' rather than 'will'.

ich	würde	+ infinitive
du	würdest	
er / sie / es	würde	
wir	würden	
ihr	würdet	
Sie	würden	
sie	würden	

Using gern

You can add gern(e) to say what you would **like** to do.

Ich würde gern nach Europa fahren.
I would like to travel to Europe.

Er würde gern Geschichte studieren.
He would like to study history.

Würden Sie gern reisen?
Would you like to travel?

Was würdest du lieber / am liebsten machen?
What would you prefer / most like to do?

The other way of expressing 'would' is to use these common subjunctive forms. They are based on the imperfect tense form, but also add an umlaut and an ending.

würde sein → wäre — would be
würde haben → hätte — would have
würde mögen → möchte — would like
würde können → könnte — would be able to

Wenn clauses

Using wenn (if) with the conditional will help you demonstrate more complex language.

Wenn ich mehr Zeit **hätte**, **würde** ich gerne ein Instrument lernen.
If I had more time, I would like to learn an instrument.

Wenn es möglich **wäre**, **würde** ich sofort eine Arbeit suchen.
If it were possible, I would look for a job right away.

Wenn ich **könnte**, **würde** ich Schauspieler werden.
If I could, I would become an actor.

Wenn er bessere Noten **hätte**, **würde** er lieber Arzt als Polizist sein.
If he had better grades, he would rather be a doctor than a policeman.

Wenn ich reich **wäre**, **würde** ich am liebsten in Amerika leben.
If I were rich, I would most like to live in America.

Note the verb – comma – verb structure in the middle of these sentences.

Ich **wäre** glücklich, **wenn** ich bessere Noten **hätte**.
I would be happy if I had better grades.

Mein Freund **würde gerne** in den Urlaub **fahren**, **wenn** er genug Geld **hätte**.
My friend would like to go on holiday if he had enough money.

Now try this

Rewrite these sentences using the conditional.
Example: Ich fahre nach Amerika. → Ich würde nach Amerika fahren.

(a) Ich gehe gern aus.
(b) Er studiert auf der Uni.
(c) Wir wohnen nicht in dieser Stadt.
(d) Ich bin Schriftsteller.
(e) Mein Freund und ich heiraten.
(f) Sie hat vier Kinder.
(g) Es gibt keine Umweltprobleme.
(h) Mein Opa hat einen Hund.

Vocabulary

This vocabulary section contains a comprehensive list of words that are in the Edexcel GCSE German vocabulary list. Verbs are included in their infinitive form only; please refer to the specification for more on the forms and tenses required.

To help you learn the words, they have been divided into subjects. However, words are flexible and you can use them for a variety of subjects. Remember, any vocabulary could appear in any of Edexcel's thematic contexts in the exam. Words that are shaded purple are Higher tier only.

Underlining indicates a separable prefix: aussehen = 'to look/appear'.

1 Basic vocabulary

Everyday phrases

Guten Tag	hello
hallo	hello
auf Wiedersehen	goodbye
ja	yes
nein	no
OK, okay	OK, alright
bitte (schön)	please; you're welcome
danke (schön)	thank you (very much)
Entschuldigung	excuse me
doch	yes, it is; however; but

Days, months and seasons

Montag (m)	Monday
Dienstag (m)	Tuesday
Mittwoch (m)	Wednesday
Donnerstag (m)	Thursday
Freitag (m)	Friday
Samstag (m)	Saturday
Sonntag (m)	Sunday
Januar (m)	January
Februar (m)	February
März (m)	March
April (m)	April
Mai (m)	May
Juni (m)	June
Juli (m)	July
August (m)	August
September (m)	September
Oktober (m)	October
November (m)	November
Dezember (m)	December
Frühling (m)	spring
Sommer (m)	summer
Herbst (m)	autumn
Winter (m)	winter

Numbers

null	zero
eins	one
zwei	two
drei	three
vier	four
fünf	five
sechs	six
sieben	seven
acht	eight
neun	nine
zehn	ten
elf	eleven
zwölf	twelve
dreizehn	thirteen
vierzehn	fourteen
fünfzehn	fifteen
sechzehn	sixteen
siebzehn	seventeen
achtzehn	eighteen
neunzehn	nineteen
zwanzig	twenty
einundzwanzig	twenty-one
dreißig	thirty
vierzig	forty
fünfzig	fifty
sechzig	sixty
siebzig	seventy
achtzig	eighty
neunzig	ninety
hundert	a hundred
tausend	a thousand
Million (f)	a million
erst	first
zweit	second
dritt	third
letzt- (er, e, es), letzte (pl)	last

Times of day

Uhr (f)	o'clock, clock, watch
Zeit (f)	time
Sekunde (f)	second
Minute (f)	minute
Stunde (f)	hour, lesson, class
Morgen (m)	morning
Mittag (m)	noon, midday
Nachmittag (m)	afternoon
Abend (m)	evening
Nacht (f)	night
Anfang (m); am Anfang	start; at the start
Ende (nt); am Ende	end / at the end
gestern	yesterday
heute	today
morgen	tomorrow
Tag (m)	day
Wochenende (nt)	weekend
Woche (f)	week
Monat (m)	month
Jahr (nt)	year
Jahrhundert (nt)	century
einmal	once
zweimal	twice

Colours

Farbe (f)	colour, paint
blau	blue
braun	brown
gelb	yellow
grau	grey
grün	green
orange	orange
rosarot	pink
rot	red
schwarz	black
weiß	white

Now try this

Look around you. Describe what you can see using as many colours and numbers as possible.

2 Basic vocabulary

Cultural and geographical words

Afrika	Africa
Amerika	America
Asien	Asia
Deutschland	Germany
EU (f)	EU
Europa	Europe
Großbritannien	Great Britain
Österreich	Austria
die Schweiz	Switzerland
die Türkei	Turkey
Berlin	Berlin
Köln	Cologne
München	Munich
Wien	Vienna
Donau (f)	Danube
Rhein (m)	Rhine
Kanton (m)	canton (Switzerland)
Karneval (m)	Carnival
Silvester (m or nt)	New Year's Eve
Viennale (f)	Vienna International FilmFestival

Short phrases

ab und zu	now and again
alles Gute	all the best
eigentlich nicht	not really
es gab	there was / there were / there used to be
Es geht mir …	I am …, I feel …
es gibt	there is / there are
Es ist mir egal	I don't mind, I'm not bothered
Es tut mir leid	I am sorry
Es tut weh	It hurts
gar nicht	not at all
Guten Appetit!	Enjoy your meal!
in der Nähe (von)	nearby, near
meiner Meinung nach	in my opinion
mit (meinen) Freunden	with (my) friends
morgen früh	tomorrow morning
nach Hause	home to one's home
sitzen bleiben	to repeat a year in school
so (alt) wie …	as (old) as …
sowohl … als auch …	both … and …
was für … ?	what kind of … ?
Wie geht's?	How are you?
zu Hause	at home at my / our house
alles (Andere)	everything (else)
auf diese Weise	in this way
bis bald	see you soon
etwas (Nettes)	something (nice)
im Großen und Ganzen	by and large, in general
statt … zu (+ infi nitive)	instead of (+ verb)
um … zu (+ infi nitive)	in order to (+ verb)
vor allem	above all

Names used in assessments

Girls

Alina	Johanna	Marie
Anna	Katharina	Mia
Charlotte	Lara	Mila
Elif	Layla	Paula
Emily	Lea	Samira
Hanna	Lena	Sofie
Jana	Leonie	Yasmin

Boys

Arda	Joel	Maximillian
Ben	Jonas	Milan
Can	Julian	Mohammed
Elias	Leon	Noah
Felix	Lukas	Paul
Finn	Malik	Tim
Jan	Matteo	Yusuf

Boys and girls

Bente	Sascha
Chris	Toni
Kim	Yannie
Mika	Yuki
Robin	

Female adults	Male adults
Frida	Helmut
Linda	Martin

Now try this

Choose five short phrases and write a sentence using each one.

3 Basic vocabulary

Useful words

alle	all
beide	both
danach	afterwards
dies- (er, e, es)	this, that
drinnen	inside
einige	some, a few
jed- (er, e, es)	every, each
jemand	someone
kein	not a, no
keine	not a, not any, no
niemand	no one
solch	such
viel	much
viele	many

Parts of the body

Arm (m)	arm
Auge (nt)	eye
Bauch (m)	stomach
Bein (nt)	leg
Finger (m)	finger
Fuß (m)	foot
Gesicht (nt)	face
Haar (nt)	hair
Hals (m)	neck
Hand (f)	hand
Kopf (m)	head
Mund (m)	mouth
Nase (f)	nose
Ohr (nt)	eat
Schulter (f)	shoulder
Stimme (f)	voice
Rücken (m)	back
Zahn (m)	tooth
Haut (f)	skin
Herz (nt)	heart
Körper (m)	body

Prepositions

an	on, at
auf	on, onto, at, to
aus	out, out of, from
bei	with
bis	until, till, up to
durch	through
für	for
in	in, into
mit	to, towards, after, according
nach	to
ohne	without
pro	by, per
um	at (+ time), at (the house of)
von	from, of
vor	in front of, before, ago
zu	to, too
zum (m, nt)	to the
zur (f)	to the
ab	from, as of
am	at the, in the process of, during, while
außer	except
außerhalb	outside of
bei	in the process of, during, while
beim (m, nt)	at the, in the process of, during, while
durch	by (way of)
entlang	along
hinter	behind
innerhalb	inside of, within
gegen	against
gegenüber	opposite
laut	according to
neben	next to, beside
ohne ... zu (+ infinitive)	without (+ verb)
seit	since, for
trotz	despite, in spite of
über	above, over, about
um	around, at (time)
unter	under
wegen	because of, due to
zwischen	between

Conjunctions

aber	but, however
als	than, when, as
dann	then
dass	that
denn	because
entweder	either
ob	whether, if
obwohl	although
oder	or
so	so, thus, in this way
und	and
weil	because
wenn	if, whenever
bevor	before
da	because, there
damit	so that
falls	in case, if
nachdem	after
sobald	as soon as
sondern	(but) rather
sowie	as well as
während	during, while
weder	neither

Some question words

wann?	when?
warum?	why?
was?	what?
wer?	who?
welch- (er, e, es), welche (pl)?	which?
wieviel(e)?	how much / how many?
wo?	where?

Now try this

To learn parts of the body, draw a picture of a person and label the different body parts.

4 General vocabulary

Abendessen (nt)	dinner	einfach	easy, simple, single (ticket)	hell	light
Aktivität (f)	activity	einzig	only, single	Herr (m)	Mr, gentleman
akzeptieren	(to) accept	empfehlen	(to) recommend	Hintergrund (m)	background
allgemein	general	enden	(to) end	hoch	high, tall
Alternative (f)	alternative	englisch	English	hoffen	(to) hope
ander- (er, e, es)	other	enorm	enormous	höher	higher, taller
ändern	(to) change	Erfahrung (f)	experience	hören	(to) hear
Anfang (m); am Anfang	start, beginning; in the beginning	eröffnen	(to) open, start	ideal	ideal
Angst (f)	fear	erzählen	(to) tell	Information (f)	information
Antwort (f)	answer, reply	europäisch	European	informieren	(to) inform
antworten (auf)	(to) reply (to)	Faktor (m)	factor	Interesse (nt)	interest
Artikel (m)	article	falsch	wrong, untrue	interessieren; sich interessieren für	(to) interest; (to) be interested in
Aspekt (m)	aspect	fantastisch	fantastic	international	international
aussehen	(to) look, appear	Farbe (f)	colour, paint	Jugendliche (pl)	young people
beantworten	(to) answer	fest	firm, solid	kalt	cold
bedeuten	(to) mean	finden	(to) find	kälter	colder
beginnen	(to) begin	Foto (nt)	photograph	kaputt	broken
bekommen	(to) receive, get	Frage (f)	question	kennen	(to) know
beschreiben	(to) describe	fragen	(to) ask	kennenlernen	(to) get to know
besonder- (er, e, es)	special	Franken (m)	(Swiss) franc	Kilometer (m)	kilometre
besser	better	fremd	strange, foreign	klar	clear
Bild (nt)	picture	Freude (f)	joy	klein	small
brauchen	(to) need	(sich) freuen (über); sich freuen auf	(to) be happy (about); (to) look forward to	komisch	funny, strange,
brechen	(to) break	führen	(to) lead, guide	kommen	(to) come
breit	broad	Garten (m)	garden	Kommunikation (f)	communication
Brief (m)	letter	geben	(to) give	kompliziert	complicated
bringen	(to) bring	gefallen (+ dative)	(to) please	können	(to) be able to
britisch	British	Gefühl (nt)	feeling	kurz	short, brief
bunt	colourful	gehen	(to) go, walk	lächeln	(to) smile
Chance (f)	chance	gemeinsam	common, together	lachen	(to) laugh
dauern	(to) last	genau	exact	Lage (f)	situation, location
Detail (nt)	detail	Geräusch (nt)	noise	lang, lange	long
deutsch	German	glauben	(to) think, believe	länger	longer
(der) Deutsche, (ein) Deutscher (m)	(the) German; (a) German	groß	big, tall, great	langsam	slow
dick	thick, fat	größer	bigger	langweilig	boring
Ding (nt)	thing	Grund (m)	reason	lassen	(to) let, allow,
direkt	direct	gut	good	laut	loud, loudly, noisy
Diskussion (f)	discussion	haben	(to) have	leer	empty
diskutieren (über)	(to) discuss	halb	half	legen	(to) lay, put
doppelt	double, twice	Haupt- (prefix)	main	leise	quiet, soft
dunkel	dark	Haus (nt)	house		
dünn	thin	heiß	hot		
echt	real, genuine	heißen	(to) be called, mean		
eigen	own	helfen	(to) help		

Now try this

Choose five words from this page that you find difficult to remember. Write a sentence using each one.

5 General vocabulary

Leute (pl)	people
Licht (nt)	light
Lieblings- (prefix)	favourite
Linie (f)	line
link- (er, e, es)	left
Liste (f)	list
Lust (f)	desire
machen	(to) do, make
Mal (nt)	time, occasion
Medien (pl)	media
meinen	(to) think, have an opinion
Meinung (f)	opinion
Mensch (m)	person, human
Meter (m)	metre
mitbringen	(to) bring along
mitnehmen	(to) take along
Mitte (f)	middle, centre
modern	modern
mögen	(to) like
möglich	possible
Möglichkeit (f)	possibility
Moment (m); im Moment	moment; at the moment
Nachricht (f)	news, message
nächst- (er, e, es) nächste (pl)	next
nah	near, nearby
näher	closer, nearer
national	national
negativ	negative
nehmen	(to) take
neu	new
normal	normal
nötig	necessary
notwendig	necessary, essential
Nummer (f)	number
offen	open
Öffentlichkeit (f)	public
öffnen	(to) open
organisieren	(to) organise
passieren	(to) happen
perfekt	perfect
Person (f)	person
persönlich	personal
Plan (m)	plan
planen	(to) plan

Platz (m)	square, seat, space, place
positiv	positive
praktisch	practical
präsentieren	(to) present
probieren; anprobieren; ausprobieren	(to) try; (to) try on; (to) try out
Problem (nt)	problem
Projekt (nt)	plan, project
Prozent (nt)	percent
Qualität (f)	quality
Raum (m)	room, space
recht- (er, e, es)	right
Recht (nt)	right
reden	(to) talk
reich	rich
Rest (m); Reste (pl)	rest, remainder, leftovers
richtig	right, correct
rufen	(to) call, shout
rund	round, around
Sache (f)	thing, issue
scharf	sharp, spicy
schlecht	bad
schließen	(to) close, shut
schnell	quick
schön	beautiful
schreiben	(to) write
schwach	weak
Schweizer	Swiss, Swiss man
Schwierigkeit (f)	difficulty
See (m)	lake
Seen (pl)	lakes
sehen	(to) see, watch
Seite (f)	side, page
seltsam	strange, weird
setzen	(to) place, put
sich (hin)setzen	(to) sit down
sicher	safe, sure
Situation (f)	situation
sitzen	(to) sit, be seated
Spaß (m)	fun
spielen	(to) play
sprechen	(to) speak
Sprecher (m)	speaker
stammen (aus)	(to) come from
stark	strong

Stärke (f)	strength
Start (m)	start
stecken	(to) put (in)
stehen	(to) stand
stellen	(to) put, place
stimmen	(to) be correct
stolz (auf)	proud (of)
Suche (f)	search
suchen	(to) look for
super	super
Süden (m)	south
System (nt)	system
Tasche (f)	bag, pocket
Teil (m, nt)	part
teilen	(to) share
Telefon (nt); am Telefon	(tele)phone; on the phone
tief	deep
toll	great, terrific
total	total
traurig	sad
Treppe (f)	stairs, staircase
treten (auf)	(to) step (on)
Tür (f)	door
türkisch	Turkish
typisch	typical
üblich	usual
unglaublich	incredible
Union (f)	union
unmöglich	impossible
verändern	(to) change
Veränderung (f)	change
(sich) verbessern	(to) improve
Vergangenheit (f)	past
vergessen	(to) forget
vergleichen	(to) compare
verlassen	(to) leave
Verständnis (nt)	understanding
versuchen	(to) try
Viertel (nt)	quarter
voll	full

Now try this

Test yourself by covering the German words and saying the German word. Then cover the English words and say the English word.

6 General vocabulary

Vordergrund (m)	foreground
Vorstellung (f)	performance, idea, introduction
wählen	(to) choose, vote
Wahrheit (f)	truth
weinen	(to) cry
weit	far, wide
wenig	little
wenige	few
werfen	(to) throw
Westen (m)	west
wichtig	important
wissen	(to) know (something)
wollen	(to) want (to)
Wort (nt)	word
wunderbar	wonderful
Zahl (f)	figure, number
zahlen	(to) pay
zeigen	(to) show
Zeit (f)	time
Zeitung (f)	newspaper
ziehen	(to) pull, move
zufrieden	content, pleased
zuhören	(to) listen
zweit	second

ähnlich	similar
aktuell	current
(an)bieten	(to) offer
anfangen	(to) start
anschauen, sich anschauen	(to) look at, watch
Art (f)	type, species
aufhören	(to) stop
Aufmerksamkeit (f)	attention
aufregen	(to) excite, upset, annoy
Augenblick (m)	moment
Ausrüstung (f)	equipment
auswählen	(to) choose
beenden	(to) end
Beginn (m); zu Beginn	beginning; in the beginning
behandeln	(to) treat
Behandlung (f)	treatment
behaupten	(to) maintain, claim
bemerken	(to) notice
beobachten	(to) observe, watch
beschließen	(to) decide
besitzen	(to) own
betrachten	(to) look at, consider
bitten (um)	(to) request
Blick (m)	view, glance
Boden (m)	floor, ground
danken	(to) thank
das Gute (nt)	the good (thing)
Decke (f)	ceiling, blanket
deutlich	clear
ehemalig	former
Einrichtung (f)	furnishings
enthalten	(to) contain
entscheiden	(to) decide
Entscheidung (f)	decision
(sich) entschuldigen	(to) apologise, excuse
Ereignis (nt)	event

Now try this

Choose some verbs from this page and learn the past forms.

7 General vocabulary

erfahren	(to) experience
erfolgreich	successful
erhalten	(to) receive
erinnern; sich erinnern an	(to) remind, (to) remember
Erinnerung (f)	memory
erklären	(to) explain
Erklärung (f)	explanation
erwähnen	(to) mention
erwarten	(to) expect
Fall (m)	case
fehlen	(to) lack, be absent, miss
Fehler (m)	mistake, error
fertig	ready, finished
Folge (f)	consequence
folgen	(to) follow
Gedanke (m)	thought
Gegenstand (m)	object
Gegenteil (nt); im Gegenteil	opposite; on the other hand
Gegenwart (f)	present
gehören (+ dative)	(to) belong (to)
Gelegenheit (f)	opportunity
generell	general
genießen	(to) enjoy
genügen	(to) be enough
gering	low, small
gesamt	whole, entire
geschehen	(to) happen
gesellschaftlich	social, socially
gewiss	certain
gleich	same, equal, immediately
Glück (nt)	luck
gründen	(to) start, found
Hälfte (f)	half
häufig	frequent
Hoffnung (f)	hope
Inhalt (m)	content, plot
jährlich	yearly, annual
Kilo(gramm) (nt)	kilo(gram)
klingen	(to) sound, ring
kriegen	(to) get, receive
kritisieren	(to) criticise
liefern	(to) deliver

lösen	(to) solve
Mehrheit (f)	majority
Menge (f)	quantity, amount, crowd
Nachteil (m)	disadvantage
niedrig	low
nutzen	(to) use
nützlich	useful
Phase (f)	phase
Publikum (nt)	public, audience
Rand (m)	edge
Rede (f)	speech
regelmäßig	regular
schauen	(to) watch, look
schlimm	bad, serious
schmal	narrow
schweigen	(to) be silent
sich beschweren	(to) complain
sich sorgen (um)	(to) worry, care (about)
Sieg (m)	victory
Sinn (m)	sense, meaning
sinnvoll	meaningful
sogenannt	so-called
stattfinden	(to) take place
Stoff (m)	material, fabric
Szene (f)	scene
Titel (m)	title
Ton (m)	sound, tone
träumen	(to) dream
tun	(to) do, put
unbekannt	unknown
Unterschied (m)	difference
unterschiedlich	different
Veranstaltung (f)	event
vermeiden	(to) avoid
verrückt	mad, crazy
verschieden	different / diverse
(sich) verstecken	(to) hide
vorbereiten	(to) prepare
Vorschlag (m)	suggestion
vorschlagen	(to) suggest
Vorteil (m)	advantage
wagen	(to) dare, risk
wahr	true

Weile (f)	while, moment
weitergehen	(to) continue
wert	worth
Wert (m)	value, worth
wiederholen	(to) repeat
Wirklichkeit (f)	reality
Wirkung (f)	effect
wöchentlich	every week
Wunsch (m)	wish
wünschen, sich wünschen	to want, wish
zählen	(to) count
zahlreich	numerous
Zeichen (nt)	sign
Zweifel (m)	doubt

Now try this

Choose ten words from this page and make learning cards for them with English (or a picture) on one side and German on the other.

8 Adverbs

allein	alone
also	so, therefore
auch	also, too, as well
besonders	particularly
damals	then, at that time
deshalb	therefore
deswegen	therefore
dort	there
draußen	outside
einander	each other
einmal	once
endlich	finally, at last
ungefähr	about, approximately
fast	almost, nearly
früh	early
früher	previously, in the past
ganz	whole, quite
genauso	just as
genug	enough
geradeaus	straight ahead
gern, gerne	gladly, (with a verb) like to
her	from something, in this direction, here
heute	today, nowadays
hier	here
hin	to something, in that direction
immer	always
immer noch	still
insgesamt	altogether
jetzt	now
leider	unfortunately
lieber	rather
links	to the left
manchmal	sometimes
mehr	more
meistens	mostly
natürlich	of course
nicht	not
nie	never
noch	still, yet
normalerweise	normally
nur	only
oft	often
online	online
rechts	on / to the right
schon	already
sehr	very
selbst, selber	self
sicherlich	certainly
sonst	otherwise, else
spät	late
täglich	every day, daily
überall	everywhere
unbedingt	absolutely
unterwegs	on the way
vielleicht	perhaps
vorne	at / to the front
weg	away, vanished
weiter	further
wieder / nochmal	again
ziemlich	quite, fairly
zuerst	first of all, firstly
zurück	back
zusammen	together
zweimal	twice
ab	off, away
allerdings	though, indeed
andererseits	on the other hand
anders	differently
außerdem	moreover, besides, in addition
äußerst	extremely
bald	soon
beinahe	almost, nearly
bereit	ready
bereits	already
bestimmt	special, certainly
bisher	until now
dahin	there, to that place
eben	just, now
eigentlich	actually
einerseits	on the one hand
entfernt	away, distant
erst	only, not until
gerade	straight, just
gleichzeitig	at the same time
hinten	at the back
inklusive	including
inzwischen	in the meantime
irgendwann	sometime
irgendwo	somewhere
jedoch	however
mindestens	at least
neulich	recently
nun	now
oben	above, upstairs
riesig	huge, great
schließlich	finally, after all
seitdem	since then, since
selten	rare, rarely
sofort	immediately
sogar	even
teilweise	partly
trotzdem	nevertheless
überhaupt	at all, generally
übrigens	by the way
unten	below, downstairs
völlig	completely
vorbei	past, over
vorher	beforehand, earlier
wahrscheinlich	probably
wenigstens	at least
wohl	well, happy, probably

Now try this

Describe a typical day in your life, using as many adverbs of time as possible.

9 Family, friends, identity and equality

alt	old
älter	older
Alter (nt)	age
Behinderung (f)	disability
beliebt	popular
bisexuell	bisexual
böse	angry, bad
Bruder (m)	brother
Charakter (m)	character
Eltern (pl)	parents
Familie (f)	family
feiern	(to) celebrate
fleißig	hard-working
Frau (f)	Mrs, wife, woman
Freund (m)	friend, boyfriend
Freundin (f)	friend, girlfriend
freundlich	friendly, nice
geboren	born
Geburtstag (m)	birthday
Generation (f)	generation
Geschwister (pl)	siblings
glücklich	happy, fortunate
Großeltern (pl)	grandparents
Großmutter (f)	grandmother
Großvater (m)	grandfather
Gruppe (f)	group, gang
Halb- (prefix)	half (e.g. brother)
heiraten	(to) get married
hetero(sexuell)	straight
Hund (m)	dog
... jährig	... years (old)
jung	young
Junge (m)	boy
jünger	younger
Katze (f)	cat
Kind (nt)	child
Kontakt (m)	contact
lesbisch	lesbian
lieb	kind, dear
Liebe (f)	love
lieben	(to) love
lustig	funny, enjoyable
Mädchen (nt)	girl
Mama (f)	mum
Mann (m)	man, husband
müde	tired
Mutter (f)	mother
Nachbar (m)	neighbour
Name (m)	name
nett	nice, kind
nicht binär	non-binary
Onkel (m)	uncle
Paar (nt)	pair, couple
Papa (m)	dad
Partner (m)	partner
Party (f)	party
privat	(in) private
Rollstuhl (m)	wheelchair
Schwester (f)	sister
schwul	gay
Sohn (m)	son
sportlich	sporty, athletic
Stief- (prefix)	step-
Tante (f)	aunt
Tochter (f)	daughter
Töchter (pl)	daughters
Transgender-	transgender
(sich) treffen (mit)	(to) meet (with)
Treffen (nt)	meeting
Typ (m)	type, guy
Vater (m)	father
warten (auf)	(to) wait (for)
wohnen	(to) live, stay
begeistern	(to) inspire, be enthusiastic
behindert	disabled
Beziehung (f)	relationship
Brille (f)	glasses
ehrlich	honest
Eigenschaft (f)	characteristic
Eindruck (m)	impression
Einfluss (m)	influence
einladen	(to) invite
Einstellung (f)	attitude
erkennen	(to) recognise
ernst	serious, earnest
Erwachsene (pl)	adults
froh	happy, glad
(sich) fühlen	(to) feel
Jugend (f)	youth, young people
Oma (f)	grandma, granny
Opa (m)	grandad
pflegen	to care (for)
plaudern	(to) chat
schenken	(to) give (as a present)
Streit (m)	argument, fight
streng	strict
überraschen	(to) surprise
überzeugen	(to) convince
unabhängig	independent
(sich) unterhalten	(to) chat / amuse oneself
unterstützen	(to) support
Unterstützung (f)	support
verantwortlich	responsible
Verhältnis (nt)	relationship
versprechen	(to) promise
vertrauen	(to) trust
Verwandte (m/f)	relative, relation
Vorbild (nt)	role model
vorsichtig	careful
(sich) vorstellen	(to) introduce (oneself)
zuständig	responsible
Zwilling (m)	twin

Now try this

Write a description of your family, using as many words on this page as possible.

10 Interests, wellbeing and technology

Interests

Ball (m)	ball
Band (f)	band, group
Bühne (f)	stage
Fan (m)	fan, supporter
Freizeit (f)	free time
Fußball (m)	football
gewinnen	(to) win
Handball (m)	handball
Instrument (nt)	instrument
Konzert (nt)	concert
Leichtathletik (f)	athletics, track and field
lesen	(to) read
Lied (nt)	song
malen	(to) paint
Mannschaft (f)	team
Musical (nt)	musical
Musik (f)	music
Popmusik (f)	pop music
Preis (m)	price, prize
Rockmusik (f)	rock (music)
Roman (m)	novel
Sänger (m)	singer
singen	(to) sing
Sport (m)	sport
Stadion (nt)	stadium
Tanz (m)	dance
tanzen	(to) dance
Team (nt)	team
Tennis (pl)	tennis
Theater (nt)	theatre, drama
Trainer (m)	coach
aufführen	(to) perform
auftreten	(to) appear (on stage)
Konkurrenz	competition
Mitglied (nt)	member
teilnehmen an	(to) take part in, participate in
treiben	(to) do (sport)
Verein (m)	association, club
Wettbewerb (m)	competition
zeichnen	(to) draw

Wellbeing

aktiv	active
arm	poor
Arzt (m)	doctor
(sich) bewegen	(to) move, exercise
Doktor (m)	doctor
fallen	(to) fall
Fieber (nt)	fever
Fitnesszentrum (nt)	gym
Form (f); in Form	form, shape; in shape, fit
gesund	healthy
gesünder	healthier
Gesundheit (f)	health
Hilfe (f)	help
Knochen (m)	bone
krank	ill, sick
Krankenhaus (nt)	hospital
laufen	(to) run
Medizin (f)	medicine
Muskel (m)	muscle
Muskeln (pl)	muscles
Pause (f)	break
rauchen	(to) smoke
schlafen	(to) sleep
Schmerz (m)	pain
schwimmen	(to) swim
Schwimmen (nt)	swimming
spazieren (gehen)	(to) (go for a) walk
(Arznei)mittel (nt)	medicine
aufgeben	(to) give up
Bewegung (f)	exercise, movement
Blut (nt)	blood
fürchten; sich fürchten vor	(to) fear
geistig	mental
körperlich	physical
leiden	(to) suffer
(sich) verletzen	(to) injure (oneself)

Technology

anrufen	(to) call, phone
App (f)	app
chatten	(to) chat online
Computer (m)	computer
elektrisch	electric
funktionieren	(to) function, work
Gaming (nt)	gaming
Handy (nt)	mobile phone
herunterladen	(to) download
Internet (nt)	internet
Ladung (f)	charge, load
Laptop (m, nt)	laptop
Netz (nt)	network
Passwort (nt)	password
schicken	(to) send
Smartphone (nt)	smartphone
Spiel (nt)	game, match
Spieler (m)	player
Spielkonsole (f)	games console
Tablet (nt)	tablet
Text (m)	text
virtuell	virtual
Virus (m, nt)	virus (computer)
Webseite (f)	website
WLAN (nt)	Wi-Fi
Bildschirm (m)	screen, monitor
Cyberkriminalität (f)	cybercrime
digital	digital
elektronisch	electronic
Fortschritt (m)	progress
Gerät (nt)	appliance, piece of equipment
Kritik (f)	review, criticism
Ohrhörer (pl)	earbuds
Sicherheit (f)	security, safety

Now try this

Make a list of your top five interests. Use adjectives to give your opinion of them.

11 Food and drink and shopping

Food and drink

Abendessen (nt)	dinner
allergisch	allergic
bedienen	(to) serve
bestellen	(to) order
Brot (nt)	bread, loaf
Café (nt)	café
Durst (m)	thirst
Ei (nt)	egg
Eis (nt)	ice, ice cream
essen	(to) eat
Essen (nt)	food, meal, eating
Fastfood (nt)	fast food
Fisch (m)	fish
Flasche (f)	bottle
Fleisch (nt)	meat
frisch	fresh
Frühstück (nt)	breakfast
Gemüse (nt)	vegetable(s)
günstig	cheap, good
Hunger (m)	hunger
Kaffee (m)	coffee
Käse (m)	cheese
Kellner (m)	waiter
kochen	(to) cook
Küche (f)	kitchen, cuisine
Kuchen (m)	cake
lecker	delicious
Mittagessen (nt)	lunch
Obst (nt)	fruit
Pommes (frites) (pl)	chips
probieren	(to) try
Rechnung (f)	bill
Restaurant (nt)	restaurant
Schokolade (f)	chocolate
Stück (nt)	piece, play
Tee (m)	tea
trinken	(to) drink
Veganer (m)	vegan
Vegetarier (m)	vegetarian
Wasser (nt)	water
Wurst (f)	sausage
Würste (pl)	sausages
Butterbrot (nt)	sandwich
Dose (f)	tin, can
Gabel (f)	fork
Gericht (nt)	dish, course
Getränk (nt)	drink
Löffel (m)	spoon
Mahlzeit (f)	meal
Messer (nt)	knife
Milch (f)	milk
Nachtisch (m)	dessert
riechen	(to) smell
sauer	sour
schmecken	(to) taste
Schnitzel (nt)	schnitzel, escalope
süß	sweet
Teller (m)	plate
Vorspeise (f)	starter

Shopping

Angebot (nt)	offer
anprobieren	(to) try on
bezahlen	(to) pay
billig	cheap
einkaufen	(to) shop
Euro (m)	euro
Geld (nt)	money
Geschäft (nt)	shop, business
Geschenk (nt)	present, gift
Größe (f)	height, size
Hut (m)	hat
Kasse (f)	checkout, till
kaufen	(to) buy
Kleid (nt)	dress
Kleidung (f)	clothing
Kosten (pl)	costs
kosten	(to) cost
kostenlos	free (of charge)
Kurs (m)	exchange rate
Laden (m)	shop
Mode (f)	fashion
modisch	fashionable
passen	to fit, suit
Preis (m)	price, prize
Pullover / Pulli (m)	pullover, jumper
Schuh (m)	shoe
Socke (f)	sock
sparen	(to) save (money)
Supermarkt (m)	supermarket
teuer	expensive
T-Shirt (nt)	T-shirt
verkaufen	(to) sell
Ware (f)	goods
wechseln	(to) change, exchange
ausgeben	(to) spend (money)
Bargeld (nt)	cash
eng	narrow, tight (clothes)
Kleingeld (nt)	change
Kreditkarte (f)	credit card
Kunde (m) / Kundin (f)	customer
locker	loose (clothing), relaxed
Marke (f)	brand
Produkt (nt)	product
Stil (m)	style
Tüte (f)	bag

Now try this

Make a list of your favourite and least favourite food and drink. Try to memorise it all!

12 In the town and transport

In the town

Apotheke (f)	chemist's
Besuch (m)	visit
besuchen	(to) visit, attend (school)
Besucher (m)	visitor
Bibliothek (f)	library
Brücke (f)	bridge
Dorf (nt)	village
Ecke (f)	corner
Einkaufszentrum (nt)	shopping centre
Fenster (nt)	window
Gegend (f)	region, area
historisch	historical
Höhe (f)	height, hill
Industrie (f)	industry
Kino (nt)	cinema
Kultur (f)	culture
kulturell	cultural
Kunst (f)	art
lokal	local
Markt (m)	market
Mauer (f)	wall
multikulturell	multicultural
Museen (pl)	museums
öffentlich	public, municipal
Ort (m)	place, location
Park (m)	park
Post (f)	post office
Region (f)	region
Richtung (f)	direction
Rolle (f)	role
Schloss (nt)	castle
Schwimmbad (nt)	swimming pool
sich befinden	(to) be (situated)
Stadt (f)	town, city
Städte (pl)	towns, cities
Straße (f)	street, road
Straßenplan (m)	map (street)
Weg (m)	way, route, road
zentral	central
Zentrum (nt)	centre
Ausstellung (f)	exhibition
Bäckerei (f)	bakery
bauen	(to) build
Bereich (m)	area
Bevölkerung (f)	population
Bürger (m)	citizen
Dach (nt)	roof
Einwohner (m)	inhabitant
Fest (nt)	festival, holiday, fair
Gebäude (nt)	building
Hauptstadt (f)	capital city
Kreis (m)	circle, district
Umgebung (f)	surroundings
Wand (f)	wall

Transport

ankommen	(to) arrive
Auto (nt)	car
automatisch	automatic
Bahn (f)	railway, rail
Bahnhof (m)	station
Boot (nt)	boat
Bus (m)	bus
Einzelkarte (f)	single ticket
fahren	(to) go (by transport)
Fahrkarte (f)	ticket
Fahrrad / Rad (nt)	bicycle, bike
Fahrt (f)	journey, trip
Flug (m)	flight
Flughafen (m)	airport
Flugzeug (nt)	plane
Fuß (m); zu Fuß	foot; on foot
Karte (f)	ticket, card, menu
landen	(to) land
Radfahren (nt)	cycling
reservieren	(to) reserve
Reservierung (f)	reservation
Rückfahrkarte (f)	return ticket
Schiff (nt)	ship, boat
Strecke (f)	distance, route
U-Bahn (f)	underground
Unfall (m)	accident
Verkehrsmittel (nt)	means of transport
verpassen	(to) miss (the bus)
Wagen (m)	car, carriage
Zug (m)	train
Abfahrt (f)	departure
Ankunft (f)	arrival
erreichen	(to) reach, catch (the bus)
Fahrzeug (nt)	vehicle
fliegen	(to) fly
Straßenbahn (f)	tram
Verkehr (m)	traffic

Now try this

Make a map of your local area. Label it with places of interest.

13 School and work

Alltag (m)	everyday life
anhaben	(to) have on
(sich) anziehen	(to) get dressed
Arbeit (f)	work
arbeiten	(to) work
aufstehen	(to) get up, stand up
Ausbildung (f)	training
Austausch (m)	exchange
Beruf (m)	occupation, job
beruflich	professional
bestehen	(to) pass (an exam)
Bildung (f)	education
Buch (nt)	book
Büro (nt)	office
Chef (m)	boss, leader
Club / Klub (m)	club
Einkommen (nt)	income, pay
erlauben	(to) allow
Fach (nt)	subject
Firma (f)	firm, business
Gang (m)	corridor, course
Geschichte (f)	history, story
gestresst	stressed
hart	hard
Hausaufgabe (f)	homework
Heft (nt)	exercise book
Hemd (nt)	shirt
Hochschule (f)	college, university
Hose (f)	trousers
Interview (nt)	interview
Jacke (f)	jacket
Job (m)	job
Karriere (f)	career
Klasse (f)	class, year (in school)
Kollege (m)	colleague
Konzentration (f)	concentration
(sich) konzentrieren (auf)	(to) concentrate (on)
Krawatte (f)	tie
Kuli (m)	pen
Künstler (m)	artist
Kurs (m)	course
Lehrer (m)	teacher
leicht	easy, light
Leistung (f)	achievement
lernen	(to) learn
Manager (m)	manager
Mathe(matik) (f)	maths
Papier (nt)	paper
Polizei (f)	police
Position (f)	job, position
Regel (f)	rule
Schule (f)	school
Schüler (m) / Schülerin (f)	pupil, student (school)
schwer	heavy, difficult
schwierig	hard, difficult
Sprache (f)	language
Stelle (f)	position, job
Student (m)	student (university)
Studie (f)	study
studieren	(to) study (at university)
Studium (nt)	studies
Stuhl (m)	chair
Stunde (f)	lesson, hour
Test (m)	test
Thema (nt)	theme, subject
Tisch (m)	table
tragen	(to) wear, carry
Traum (m)	dream
üben	(to) practise
Übung (f)	practice
Uniform (f)	uniform
Universität (f) / Uni	university
Unterricht (m)	lesson, teaching
verbieten	(to) forbid
verdienen	(to) earn, deserve
Wissenschaft (f)	science
Zukunft (f)	future

Abschluss (m)	leaving qualification
Aufgabe (f)	task, assignment, exercise
ausbilden	(to) train
Ausflug (m)	excursion, trip
(aus)füllen	(to) fill (in)
Blatt (nt)	sheet, leaf
Direktor (m)	headteacher, director
Druck (m)	pressure
Erfolg (m)	success
Ergebnis (nt)	result
erleben	(to) experience
ermüdend	tiring
Fähigkeit (f)	skill, ability, capability
gelingen	(to) succeed
Gesellschaft (f)	society, company
Hochschulbildung (f)	higher education
Kenntnis (f)	knowledge
leisten	(to) achieve
Mitarbeiter (m)	employee
Mobbing (nt)	bullying
Note (f)	grade, note
Oberstufe (f)	sixth form, college
prüfen	(to) test, examine, check
schaffen	(to) manage
Schriftsteller (m)	writer
Stundenplan (m)	timetable
übersetzen	(to) translate
Unternehmen (nt)	company, business
unterrichten	(to) teach
vorhaben	(to) intend, plan
Wahl (f)	choice
Ziel (nt)	destination, goal

Now try this

Describe your school. Use as many words on this page as possible.

14 Holidays, TV and film

Holidays

Bad (nt)	bathroom, bath
bequem	comfortable
Bett (nt)	bed
bleiben	(to) stay, remain
Campingplatz (m)	campsite
Doppelzimmer (nt)	double / twin room
Einzelzimmer (nt)	single room
Ferien (pl)	holidays, vacation
frei	free, available
Hotel (nt)	hotel
Koffer (m)	suitcase
Meer (nt)	sea, ocean
mieten	(to) hire, rent
Pass (m)	passport
Reise (f)	journey, trip
reisen	(to) travel
Sand (m)	sand
Schlafzimmer (nt)	bedroom
Service (m)	service
Stock (m)	floor (e.g. of a hotel), storey
Strand (m)	beach
Tourist (m)	tourist
Touristeninformation (f)	tourist information office
Tradition (f)	tradition
traditionell	traditional
Urlaub (m)	holiday, vacation
verbringen	(to) spend (time)
Wohnung (f)	flat, apartment
Zelt (nt)	tent
zelten	(to) go camping
Zimmer (nt)	room
zurückkommen	(to) return
ausländisch	foreign
besichtigen	(to) view, visit
fern	far, distant
Gepäck (nt)	luggage
übernachten	(to) spend the night, stay

TV and film

ansehen, sich ansehen	(to) watch, look at
bekannt	well-known
berühmt	famous
Dokumentarfilm (m)	documentary
fernsehen	(to) watch television
Fernsehen (nt); am Fernsehen	television; on television
Horror (m)	horror
Komödie (f)	comedy
Krimi (m)	detective story, thriller
Sendung (f)	programme
Serie (f)	series
spannend	exciting
Star (m)	celebrity, star
streamen	(to) stream
Streaming (nt)	streaming
Video (nt)	video
Programm (nt)	channel
Schauspieler (m)	actor
Spannung (f)	suspense, tension
Stimmung (f)	mood, atmosphere
Zuschauer (m)	viewer

Now try this

Think about a memorable holiday. Write a description using some of the words on this page.

15 Issues in the world, the natural world and the countryside

Aktion (f)	campaign
Alternative (f)	alternative
Änderung (f)	change
ärmer	poorer
Baum (m)	tree
Berg (m)	mountain
dicht	thick, dense
Diskriminierung (f)	discrimination
Energie (f)	energy, power
Erde (f)	earth
Feld (nt)	field
Feuer (nt)	fire
Fluss (m)	river
Freiheit (f)	freedom
Gefahr (f)	danger, risk
gefährlich	dangerous
Glas (nt)	jar, glass
global	global
Grad (m)	degree (temperature)
Grenze (f)	border
Himmel (m)	sky
Insel (f)	island
Kaninchen (nt)	rabbit
Konflikt (m)	conflict
Kraft (f)	strength, power, energy
Küste (f)	coast
Land (nt)	country, land, countryside
leben	(to) live
Luft (f)	air
nass	wet
Natur (f)	nature, countryside
neblig	foggy
Norden (m)	north
Osten (m)	east
Pferd (nt)	horse
Pflanze (f)	plant
Plastik (nt)	plastic
Rassismus (m)	racism
recyceln	(to) recycle
Recycling (nt)	recycling
reduzieren	(to) reduce
regnen	(to) rain
rein	pure, clean
Religion (f)	religion
religiös	religious
respektieren	(to) respect
retten	(to) save (e.g. the world)
Risiko (nt)	risk
Ruhe (f)	silence, peace
ruhig	quiet, calm,
sauber	clean
scheinen	(to) shine, to seem
schmutzig	dirty
Schnee (m)	snow
schneien	(to) snow
Schutz (m)	protection
schützen	(to) protect
See (m)	lake
Sexismus (m)	sexism
Sonne (f)	sun
steigen	(to) climb, increase
Strom (m)	electricity
Temperatur (f)	temperature
Tier (nt)	animal
trocken	dry
Umwelt (f)	environment
umweltfreundlich	eco-friendly
Wald (m)	wood, forest
wandern	(to) hike
warm	warm
wärmer	warmer
Welt (f)	world
Wetter (nt)	weather
Wind (m)	wind
abnehmen	(to) reduce
(sich) äußern	(to) express (oneself)
Beitrag (m)	contribution
beitragen zu	(to) contribute to
bewusst	conscious, aware
Blume (f)	flower
drohen	(to) threaten
durchschnittlich	(on) average
entdecken	(to) discover
entwickeln	(to) develop
erneuerbar	renewable
existieren	(to) exist
Experte (m) / Expertin (f)	expert
Flüchtling (m)	refugee
Frieden (m)	peace
Gesetz (nt)	law
Gewalt (f)	violence, force
Heimat (f)	home country
Initiative (f)	initiative
Integration (f)	integration
Kampf (m)	fight, struggle
kämpfen	(to) fight
Klima (nt)	climate
Klimawandel (m)	climate change
knapp	scarce
kontrollieren	(to) check
Krise (f)	crisis
Landschaft (f)	countryside
Lösung (f)	solution
Minderheit (f)	minority
Müll (m)	waste, rubbish
nachhaltig	sustainable
Opfer (nt)	victim
produzieren	(to) produce
Risiken (pl)	risks
Schaden (m)	damage
Sorge (f)	worry
Stern (m)	star
Tatsache (f)	fact
tot	dead
trennen	(to) separate / sort
überleben	(to) survive
Ursache (f)	cause
Verantwortung (f)	responsibility
verhindern	(to) prevent
Verlust (m)	loss
Verschmutzung (f)	pollution
verschwinden	(to) disappear
verursachen	(to) cause
warnen	(to) warn
weltweit	worldwide
zerstören	(to) destroy
zunehmen	(to) increase
zurückkehren	(to) return
Zustand (m)	state, condition

Now try this

Choose ten words to describe issues in the world that you are concerned about. Learn them and then practise them by saying sentences describing the problem.

Answers

The answers to the Speaking and Writing activities below are sample answers – there are many ways you could answer these questions.

1 Physical descriptions

Mein Großvater heißt Georg und ist fast siebzig Jahre alt, aber er sieht viel jünger aus. Er ist groß und dünn und sehr aktiv. Er hat graue Haare, braune Augen und er trägt ziemlich altmodische Kleidung. Er hat auch einen Hund. Er heißt Bertie.

2 Character and personality

Meiner Meinung nach bin ich eine freundliche und nette Person. Ich spreche gern mit anderen Leuten und ich denke, ich bin sehr aktiv and ich habe viel Energie.
Manchmal bin ich böse, aber nur, wenn ich müde bin.
Meine Freunde finden, dass ich immer lustig und fleißig bin.

3 My family

Meine Familie ist keine typische Familie mit zwei Eltern und zwei Kindern. Ich wohne / lebe mit meinem Papa und seinem Partner Helmut und mit meinem Stiefbruder, der Noah heißt. Wir verstehen uns gut und treiben oft Sport zusammen. Ich sehe meine Mama jedes Wochenende, und das macht immer Spaß.

4 Friends

1 Ich habe **viele** Freunde und **Bekannte**, die mir **wichtig** sind.
2 Ich bin **seit** elf Jahren mit Lea **befreundet** – wir waren zusammen in der **Grundschule**.
3 Wir sind sehr enge Freunde und können über alles sprechen.

5 Relationships

Ich verstehe mich gut mit meinem Zwillingsbruder, weil wir dieselben Interessen haben. Er ist ein sehr netter Typ.
Mit meiner Schwester habe ich ein schwieriges Verhältnis. Sie ist älter als ich und interessiert sich gar nicht für ihre Brüder.
In der Zukunft werde ich neue Freunde auf der Uni finden.

6 Dealing with problems

SPEAKING TRACK 93

Listen to the recording

a Ich versuche, mit ihm darüber zu sprechen.
Ich versuche, mit ihm zu reden.
Ich versuche, seine Stimmung zu verbessern.
Ich helfe ihm, keine Angst zu haben.
b Wir gehen ins Kino.
Wir sprechen über Probleme.
Wir trinken gern Kaffee.
Wir spielen gern zusammen.

7 Daily routine

a very difficult / hard
b he's always tired
c leaves the house at 6:25 am

8 Clothing and fashion

SPEAKING TRACK 94

Listen to the recording

Auf dem Foto gibt es vier Leute, die in der Stadt sind. Vielleicht gehen sie einkaufen. Sie sehen glücklich aus und tragen modische Kleidung. Links ist eine junge Frau. Sie hat braune Haare und trägt eine schöne Jacke. Der Mann neben ihr trägt eine schwarze Jacke und ein blaues T-Shirt. Er hat kurze schwarze Haare. Die andere junge Frau hat ein grünes Kleid.
a Ich finde Mode total uninteressant, weil ich meinen eigenen Stil habe.
b Am liebsten trage ich praktische Kleidung, die mir gut passt, weil sie bequem ist.

9 Identity

Ich habe viele Freunde / Freundinnen, die alle unterschiedlich sind. Sie sind mir alle sehr wichtig. Mein bester Freund, Mika ist sportlich und auch sehr fleißig. Gestern sind wir mit Mikas Schwester einkaufen gegangen. Layla ist immer glücklich und benutzt einen Rollstuhl. Wir haben alle neue Kleidung gekauft und haben dann in einem Café zu Mittag gegessen.

10 Celebrations

A, B, D

11 When I was younger

a When I was a child, I had a rabbit.
b I often used to play in the garden.
c I liked watching children's programmes.
d I often painted pictures.
e I also had a small black dog, which I loved.

12 My life in the future

A, D, F

13 Food and drink

1 Am **liebsten** esse ich **Fisch** und **Kartoffeln**.
2 Zum **Frühstück** mag ich **Brötchen** mit **Honig**.
3 Wir essen kein Fleisch zu Hause, weil wir alle Vegetarier sind.
4 In der Mittagspause habe ich ein Butterbrot mit Käse gegessen.
5 Grüner Tee ist mein Lieblingsgetränk.
6 Gestern hat mein Bruder ein tolles Abendessen gekocht.

14 Meals at home

Zum Frühstück esse ich immer Brot mit einem Ei oder mit Käse und ich trinke normalerweise Kaffee.
Ich muss immer sehr schnell essen, denn ich stehe jeden Tag zu spät auf.
Mein Lieblingsessen ist das Abendessen mit meiner Familie, weil wir dann alle zusammen sind und miteinander sprechen können. Ich mag es sehr, wenn es Fisch mit Pommes gibt.
Gestern Abend haben wir Würste gegessen, die mir sehr gut geschmeckt haben. Dann haben wir ein Schokoladeneis gegessen. Ich weiß nicht, was wir heute Abend essen werden – vielleicht ein Gemüsegericht oder Fleisch.

15 Shopping for food

SPEAKING TRACK 95

Listen to the recording

16 Eating out

1 Ich gehe ganz selten mit meiner Familie essen.
2 Aber wenn jemand Geburtstag hat, gehen wir in unser Lieblingsrestaurant in der Nähe.
3 Wir genießen den Abend, weil die Kellnerinnen freundlich und die Gerichte lecker sind.

17 A healthy diet

Ich versuche, meistens gesund zu essen, und ich esse selten Kuchen oder Fastfood. Ich mag Fleisch und Gemüse, aber ich hasse Bananen und vermeide sie immer! Ich trinke normalerweise Tee oder Wasser und manchmal Kaffee oder heiße Schokolade. Ich denke, es ist sehr wichtig, richtig zu essen, um gesund zu bleiben und nicht krank zu werden. Ich treibe oft Sport und ich muss genug Energie haben, um jeden Tag Fußball zu spielen. Wenn man nicht gut isst, kann man dick werden, und das will ich vermeiden.
Gestern Abend haben wir in einem Restaurant gegessen, denn mein Vater hatte Geburtstag. Das Essen war lecker und hat mir geschmeckt. Nach dem Abendessen gab es einen leckeren Kuchen, der mir sehr geschmeckt hat.
In der Zukunft werde ich versuchen, mehr Obst zu essen, weil es gut für die Gesundheit ist und Energie gibt. Ich werde auch kein Fastfood essen.

18 Sport

Ich finde Sport wichtig und auch nötig, wenn man gesund bleiben will. Meiner Meinung nach braucht man regelmäßig Bewegung, um nicht gestresst zu sein und nicht dick zu werden. Wenn man Sport macht, ist man oft mit Freunden in einer Mannschaft, und es ist gut, zusammen zu arbeiten. Ich bin aber böse, wenn eine Person in der Mannschaft fehlt!
Letztes Wochenende sind wir am Strand spazieren gegangen und ich bin im Meer geschwommen. Das war toll, obwohl das Wasser sehr kalt war.
Nächsten Sonntag werde ich mit meinem Vater Fahrrad fahren.

19 Advantages of sport

Ich treibe regelmäßig Sport und bewege mich fast jeden Tag. Ich mag Fußball und bin in der Schulmannschaft. Das heißt, dass ich sehr oft trainiere.
Ich finde Sport sehr wichtig und ich weiß, dass es viele Vorteile gibt. Ich fühle mich glücklich, ich verbringe Zeit mit Freunden, und das macht Spaß. Wenn man keinen Sport macht, kann man negative Gefühle haben oder vielleicht dick werden.
Letzte Woche bin ich auf dem Land spazieren gegangen.
In der Zukunft werde ich gesünder sein, werde weniger krank und werde länger leben.

20 Physical wellbeing

SPEAKING TRACK 96

Listen to the recording

21 Mental wellbeing

Ich versuche, positiv zu sein, aber ich akzeptiere, dass es normal ist, manchmal Probleme zu haben. Ich finde, dass Musikhören, Spazierengehen oder Lesen mir helfen, glücklicher zu sein.
Dieses Jahr gibt es viel Leistungsdruck in der Schule, und ich bin oft sehr gestresst und habe Angst, dass ich nicht alles schaffen kann.
Neulich habe ich Streit mit einer Freundin gehabt. Es war schwer, weil es über einen Jungen war.
In Zukunft werde ich versuchen, Streit zu vermeiden. Wenn es ein Problem gibt, werden wir sofort darüber reden.

22 Feeling unwell

a Ich bin nicht oft krank.
b Heute habe ich Kopfschmerzen.
c Meine Schwester kann nicht schlafen und ist immer müde.
d Am Wochenende hat mein Vater Rückenschmerzen gehabt. / Am Wochenende hatte mein Vater Rückenschmerzen.
e Er will die Ärztin / den Arzt sehen.

23 Avoiding health risks

a Drink more water! Your body needs eight glasses a day.
b I should try to go to bed earlier.
c I know young people who take drugs, but I think it's dangerous and would never try it.
d I have never smoked and I won't smoke in the future.
e We try to eat less chocolate.

24 Sports stars

a I like a lot of sports stars.
b Sometimes I go to the football match with friends.
c In summer I go running three times a week.
d Yesterday I saw wheelchair tennis on television.
e It was really fast and very exciting.

25 Hobbies and interests

1 In meiner **Freizeit** gehe ich mit **Bekannten** wandern.
2 Ich **stricke** gern und mache **jetzt** einen **Schal**.
3 Ich interessiere mich sehr für Mode.
4 Musik gefällt mir auch, und ich singe in einer Band.
5 Sport ist mir immer wichtig gewesen.
6 Ich bin Mitglied in einem Leichtathletikverein.

26 Music and dance

1 Ich **höre** sehr **oft** Musik.
2 Mein **Lieblingssänger** spielt **Gitarre**.
3 Ich **möchte** in der Zukunft **Klavier** spielen.

27 Arranging to go out

a Friday evening.
b See a detective film (at the cinema).
c At 7:30 at the corner of the street.

28 Reading

1 Lesen gefällt mir sehr und ich versuche, jeden Tag etwas zu lesen.
2 Am liebsten lese ich Krimis, weil es viel Abenteuer und Spannung gibt.
3 Ich genieße vor allem eine spannende Geschichte mit einer überzeugenden Hauptperson.

29 Television

Ich sehe heute nicht so oft fern, weil ich es besser finde, Filme und Dokumentarsendungen auf meinem Tablet anzuschauen. Das ist praktischer, weil ich die Sendungen sehen kann, wenn ich will. Jeden Samstag sehe ich mit meinem Vater fern, denn wir schauen beide gerne Fußballspiele an.
Viele andere Fernsehsendungen interessieren mich nicht, aber ich sehe manchmal gern Krimis an, denn sie sind spannend.
Gestern Abend habe ich mit meinen Eltern einen alten Liebesfilm gesehen – er war in Schwarz-weiß!
Nächstes Wochenende werde ich wie immer das Fußballspiel im Fernsehen anschauen.

30 Film and cinema

a The big screen / seeing better.
Hearing the film music clearly.
b That tickets are quite expensive.
Other people eat / talk during the film.

31 Mobile technology

Ich liebe mein Handy und kann mir ein Leben ohne Handy nicht vorstellen. Ich finde die vielen Apps sehr nützlich, besonders die Apps wie Spotify, wo man überall Musik hören kann.
Meiner Meinung nach ist es ein großer Vorteil, dass man mit der Familie in Kontakt bleiben kann. Wenn ich spät nach Hause ankomme, rufe ich meine Eltern an, damit sie sich nicht sorgen.
In der Schule darf man kein Handy benutzen, aber in der Mittagspause habe ich Infos im Internet gesucht.
Ich möchte nächstes Jahr ein neues Handy bekommen, um Filme zu streamen.

32 Social media

Die sozialen Medien können eine positive Erfahrung für Jugendliche / junge Leute sein, aber es gibt auch Risiken, und man soll online vorsichtig sein. Es ist keine gute Idee, persönliche Daten mit Leuten / Menschen / Personen zu teilen, die man nicht kennt. Es macht aber Spaß zu sehen, was deine / seine Freunde / Freundinnen machen / tun. Gestern habe ich Ferienfotos / Urlaubsfotos hochgeladen.

33 Internet

SPEAKING TRACK 97

Listen to the recording

Sample responses to follow-on questions:

a Ich benutze das Internet täglich, oft um E-Mails zu schicken und um meine Hausaufgaben zu machen.
b Manchmal verbringen Jugendliche zu viel Zeit vor dem Computer. Ich denke, das ist nicht gesund.

34 Computer games

1. Es gibt einen Jungen, vielleicht einen Teenager.
2. Er ist Gamer und spielt ein Computerspiel.
3. Ich denke, er ist in seinem Zimmer.
4. Es ist spät, und das Zimmer ist dunkel.

35 Pros and cons of technology

1. Die Technologie hat viele positive Aspekte.
2. Ich finde es praktisch, dass man schnell kommunizieren kann.
3. Es gibt aber auch Gefahren.

36 Films on the internet

SPEAKING TRACK 98

Listen to the recording

Ich sehe einen jungen Mann und seine Freundin.
Die Frau hat lange braune Haare und ist schön.
Der Mann hat braune Haare und trägt ein graues T-Shirt.
Sie sind zu Hause.
Sie sehen etwas online an.
Es ist vielleicht ein Fußballspiel.
Sie sind sehr glücklich.

37 My home

Ich wohne in einer ziemlich großen Wohnung mit meiner Mutter. Wir haben einen kleinen Garten und zwei Schlafzimmer.
Ich mag die moderne Küche, denn ich koche sehr gern, aber das Wohnzimmer ist zu klein. Mein Schlafzimmer ist schön und bequem. Ich mache meine Hausaufgaben in meinem Zimmer.
Gestern habe ich das Abendessen gekocht, denn meine Mutter hatte Geburtstag. Wir haben Fleisch mit Gemüse gegessen, und es war sehr gut.
In der Zukunft will ich ein großes modernes Haus haben. Ich möchte eine Garage für mein Auto.

38 My town

SPEAKING TRACK 99

Listen to the recording

Auf dem Foto sieht man eine Straße in einer Großstadt. Das sieht wie London aus. Ich denke, es ist früh am Morgen. Ich sehe viele Leute, die zu Fuß gehen. Vielleicht gehen sie ins Büro oder zur Arbeit. Es gibt auch große Geschäfte. Es ist ein schöner Tag und die Sonne scheint.

39 Facilities in town

a Ich mag meine Stadt.
b Es gibt viel zu sehen.
c Wir haben einen schönen Park mit einem See.
d Man kann das Schloss und das Museum besuchen.
e Letzte Woche bin ich mit Freunden ins Kino gegangen.

40 Finding the way

1. Es gibt drei Mädchen.
2. Sie sind in der Stadt.
3. Zwei suchen etwas.
4. Das andere Mädchen zeigt den Weg.

41 Shops and shopping

B, D, E

42 At the market

1. Der **Markt** ist am **Sonntag**.
2. Ich gehe **gern einkaufen**.
3. Man **kann** Obst und **Gemüse** kaufen.
4. Manchmal kaufe ich Kleidung.
5. Ich mag die T-Shirts.
6. Die Preise sind billig.

43 Transport

1. Ich **fahre** jeden Tag mit dem **Rad**.
2. Das ist **gesund** und gut für die **Umwelt**.
3. Mein **Vater** findet sein Auto schnell und **bequem**.

44 Buying tickets for travel

a Berlin, 30
b 9
c 8

45 Places of interest near me

a B
b C

46 The environment

Meine Stadt hat viele positive Aspekte, und die Verschmutzung ist meistens nicht so schlimm. Wir haben einen kleinen Wald, wo man an der frischen Luft spazieren gehen kann.
Aber in dem Stadtzentrum sieht es nicht so gut aus. Es gibt so viele Autos, und die Luft ist nicht gesund, denn die Verschmutzung ist ein Problem.
Letzte Woche habe ich mit Freunden Papier und Plastik in der Stadt gesammelt.
In der Zukunft werde ich kein Auto fahren und werde zu Fuß gehen oder mit dem Rad fahren. Das ist umweltfreundlicher.

47 Environmental problems

SPEAKING TRACK 100

Listen to the recording

48 The dangers of pollution

a They use wind power / energy.
b By bus.

49 The natural world

a Lena likes the beach(es), because she goes swimming / she swims (every day).
b She dislikes the small streets, because there are no good shops.

50 Individual actions for the environment

1 Auf dem Foto gibt es eine Familie zu Hause.
2 Sie recyceln Flaschen und Papier.
3 Es gibt zwei Frauen und zwei Kinder.
4 Eine Frau trägt ein weißes Hemd.

51 How to recycle

1 Zu Hause **recyceln** wir fast **alles**.
2 Der **gelbe** Müllcontainer ist für **Dosen**.
3 **Pappe** kommt in den **blauen** Müllcontainer.
4 Wir werfen nicht viel weg.
5 Ich denke, wir sind umweltfreundlich.
6 Man muss versuchen, die Umwelt zu schützen.

52 My school

Meine Schule ist etwa eine halbe Stunde von meinem Haus entfernt. Ich fahre normalerweise mit dem Bus zur Schule, aber wenn ich Zeit habe und das Wetter schön ist, kann ich zu Fuß gehen.
Die Schule ist groß und ganz neu. Die Gebäude sind sehr modern und hell. Es gibt auch Tennisplätze und eine Sporthalle, was ich toll finde.
Meine letzte Schule war viel kleiner, und das Schulgebäude war alt. Wir hatten einen schönen Garten mit einem Spielplatz.
Meine Traumschule wäre klein mit fantastischen Lehrern und Lehrerinnen. Wir hätten ein Schwimmbad!

53 School subjects

A, C, E

54 My teachers

Meine beste Lehrerin ist meine Englischlehrerin. Sie ist jung und cool, und ihre Stunden sind immer interessant.
Mein Kunstlehrer ist nicht sehr freundlich. Er interessiert sich nicht für seine Klassen und hilft uns nicht, wenn wir ein Problem haben.
Ich will nicht Lehrerin werden. Das ist eine sehr schwierige Arbeit!

55 The school day

a B
b B

56 School uniform

a Everyone looks the same despite all being different.
b It makes a good impression when students are in town. / No one is allowed to wear branded clothing, which is too expensive for most young people.

57 School rules

Ich denke, dass einige Schulregeln nötig sind, weil sie das Schulleben sicher machen. Zum Beispiel ist es verboten, im Gang zu laufen, um Unfälle zu vermeiden, und natürlich darf niemand rauchen. Gestern hat ein Mädchen in meiner Klasse ihr Handy im Unterricht benutzt und hat ein Video aufgenommen.

58 School clubs

1 In meiner Schule gibt es nach dem Unterricht viele Aktivitäten, die man machen kann.
2 Ich bin Mitglied des Klubs für Umweltschutz. Diese Woche sammeln wir im Park Müll.

59 School trips

Ich mag Schulreisen. Die beste Reise ist, wenn wir zu einer anderen Schule fahren, um ein Fußballspiel zu spielen.
Ich finde Schulreisen toll, denn man ist mit vielen Freunden zusammen, und es macht Spaß.
Meine nächste Reise geht in ein Museum in Manchester. Wir fahren mit dem Zug. Das ist mit meinem Geschichtslehrer.

60 Homework

B, C, F

61 Stress at school

A, B, E

62 Preparing for exams

B, D, F

63 My ideal school

a Meine Schule ist sehr alt.
b Die Klassenzimmer sind kalt und dunkel.
c Ich mag die Uniform nicht.
d Unsere Lehrer sind gut, aber manchmal streng.
e Ich hätte gerne mehr Sportstunden.

64 Plans for next year

A, C, F

65 Future studies

Ich denke, es ist toll, auf die Uni zu gehen und etwas Interessantes zu lernen. Man hat viel Freiheit, wenn man in einer anderen Stadt wohnt.
Aber es kostet viel, wenn man studieren will, und für viele Leute ist es einfach zu teuer.
In der Schule mag ich Geschichte, und wir haben gestern über Berlin gelernt. Das war sehr interessant.
Ich werde nicht auf die Uni gehen, weil ich kein Geld habe.
Ich möchte eine Arbeit in einem Büro finden und sofort Geld verdienen.

66 Future career

In der Zukunft möchte ich / würde ich gern(e) Zahnarzt / Zahnärztin werden, obwohl die Ausbildung lang ist. Es ist mir wichtig / Es ist wichtig für mich, viel Geld zu verdienen, und Zahnärzte / Zahnärztinnen sind / werden gut bezahlt. Ich hoffe, in einer schönen Umgebung zu arbeiten und freundliche Kollegen / Kolleginnen zu haben. Meine Mutter / Mutti / Mama ist Zahnärztin und liebt ihre Arbeit / ihren Job / ihren Beruf.

67 Pros and cons of some jobs

a it is useful / it is well paid
b (two of) at least 7 years' study / difficult exams / long working hours / little free time

68 My dream job

Speaking Track 101 — Listen to the recording

a Mein Traumberuf ist Polizist.
b Ich finde es langweilig.

69 Gap year

1 Ich werde in zwei Jahren die Schule verlassen.
2 Ich will nicht direkt auf die Uni gehen.
3 Ich möchte anderen Menschen helfen.

70 Equality and helping others

a Checkpoint Charlie Museum (in Berlin).
b It was the most famous border crossing.
c 1990.
d That many families were separated.

71 Holiday activities

Speaking Track 102 — Listen to the recording

a Ich fahre gern nach Österreich, aber das ist nicht immer möglich. Manchmal bleiben wir zu Hause und machen Ausflüge in der Gegend.
b Es ist wichtig, Zeit mit Familie und Freunden zu verbringen und auch keinen Stress zu haben.
c Diesen Sommer fahre ich nach London, wo meine Tante wohnt. Wir werden ins Theater und einkaufen gehen.
d Letztes Jahr war ich mit meinem Freund am Meer. Seine Eltern haben einen kleinen Wohnwagen.

72 Camping

Speaking Track 103 — Listen to the recording

73 Holiday accommodation

When I was younger, we always stayed at home in the summer holidays, but in recent years we have often spent our holidays in Switzerland. Last year we were in a holiday house right on the beach, which was great because I could easily get / travel to the lake in my wheelchair.

74 Other holiday accommodation

1 Es gibt eine Familie.
2 Es gibt Eltern und zwei Kinder.
3 Sie sind im Urlaub.
4 Es gibt ein Berg.

75 Making a complaint

1 Ich habe keine **Geduld** mehr. Ich **warte** jetzt **seit** vierzig Minuten.
2 Wir haben die **Forelle** mit **Gemüse** und **Kartoffeln** bestellt.

76 Pros and cons of travelling

A, C, F

77 Plans for next summer

a C
b B
c B

78 Past holidays

1 Wir **waren** in den **Ferien** in **Deutschland**.
2 Ich **habe** ein paar **Andenken** in der alten **Kirche** gekauft.
3 Wir haben zehn Tage in der Nähe von Berlin verbracht.
4 Es hat häufig geschneit.
5 Auf dem Markt gab es viele schöne Sachen.
6 Das Museum und die alte Brücke waren interessant.

79 Holiday problems

a C b B

80 Lost property

1 Ich kann **seit** gestern **Abend** meinen Pass und meinen **Regenschirm** nicht finden.
2 Ich brauche **dringend** meinen Pass, weil ich morgen **geschäftlich** nach **Österreich** fliege.

81 Places to visit

Ich wohne in einer Gegend, die bei Touristen beliebt ist. Jedes Jahr kommen viele Leute, um die historischen Gebäude und die schöne Altstadt / alte Stadt zu sehen. Die Straßen sind eng, und es gibt überall tolle Geschäfte und Restaurants. Letztes Wochenende war das Wetter gut, und wir sind den Fluss entlang gewandert / spazieren gegangen.

82 Holiday jobs

This year I decided to spend the summer holidays differently / in a different way. I wanted to earn a bit of money, as I'm saving up to buy my own car. Jobs are not easy to find; however, in the end I was lucky and found a job in a sports shop, where one of the sales assistants was on holiday.

83 Buying gifts and souvenirs

Wenn ich im Urlaub bin, bringe ich immer Geschenke für meine Freunde und Familie zurück. Es sind keine teuren Sachen und sie müssen klein sein, denn mein Koffer ist nicht groß / da (weil) mein Koffer nicht groß ist. Letztes Jahr war ich in der Schweiz. Ich habe für meine Großeltern eine Uhr und für meine beste Freundin / meinen besten Freund Schokolade gekauft.

84 Weather

Tomorrow morning it will stay cold in the north with a light wind from the east. During the day it will become even colder with evening temperatures around 7 degrees. In the next two days the situation will improve and at the weekend it will be warmer with sunshine in all areas.

85 Tourism and the environment

a A week in (sunny) southern Europe.
b They shouldn't fly.
c Bad effect on the environment; She doesn't want to make situation worse.
d Travelling by rail.

94 Gender and plurals

a das Tier / die Tiere
b die Pause(n)
c der Bus / die Busse
d die Wohnung(en)

e das Buch / die Bücher
f das Glas / die Gläser
g die Reise(n)
h der See / die Seen
i der Supermarkt / die Supermärkte

95 Indefinite articles and possessives

1 a ein Mann
b eine Schule
c ein Haus
d ein Mädchen
2 a kein Hotel
b keine Hausaufgaben
c kein Kind
d keine Schwester
3 a meine Freunde / Freundinnen
b ihr Bruder
c ihre Lehrerinnen / Lehrer
d deine Eltern

96 Nominative and accusative cases

a einen
b Das / einen
c Mein / das
d meine
e der
f Das / ein
g seinen

97 Other cases and prepositions

a den
b dem
c des
d eine
e einer
f eines

98 Prepositions with the accusative or dative

a dem / der
b den
c dem
d das
e der
f dem
g den
h der
i dem

99 *Dieser*, *jener* and *jeder*

1 a This week I have a lot to do.
b Which dress did you buy?
c Which bus is he travelling on?
d We have a party in December every year.
e Do you know that teacher?
2 a accusative
b accusative
c dative
d accusative
e accusative

100 Adjective endings

a alte / kleinen
b bester / älteren
c unglückliche
d schwarzen
e netten

101 Comparative and superlative adjectives

a jünger
b besser
c interessanter
d länger

102 Personal pronouns

a mir
b ihn
c ihr
d mich
e ihm
f uns
g ihnen
h euch

103 Word order 1

a Jeden Sommer fährt mein Freund mit seiner Familie in den Urlaub.
b Gestern haben wir ein spannendes Fußballspiel gesehen.
c Ich werde in der Zukunft auf die Uni gehen.
d Letztes Jahr bin ich auf dem Land zelten gegangen.
e Wir müssen immer viele Hausaufgaben machen.
f Kannst du später ins Kino kommen?
g Er will mit dem Zug nach Berlin fahren.

104 Conjunctions

a Wir haben auf dem Land gewohnt, als ich jünger war.
b Er wird in der Schweiz leben, weil er eine neue Arbeit gefunden hat.
c Ich habe Essen gekauft, da meine Mutter krank ist.
d Ich verstehe nicht, warum er das gesagt hat.
e Es freut mich, dass meine Noten jetzt viel besser sind.

105 Word order 2

a Ich mache / treibe Sport, um gesund zu sein.
b Wir gehen ins Kino, um einen neuen Film zu sehen.
c Ich hoffe, eine Arbeit / einen Job zu finden.
d Sie versucht, fleißig zu arbeiten.
e Das Mädchen, das blonde Haare hat, heißt Anna.
f Die Leute / Menschen, die hier wohnen, sind freundlich.

106 The present tense

a fahre
b Spielst
c gibt
d gehen
e sieht
f macht
g wohnen
h hört

107 Reflexive and separable verbs

1 a dich
b mich
c uns
d sich
2 a Wann kommt dein Zug an?
b Ich stehe immer früh auf.
c Meine Eltern kommen morgen zurück.
d Sie sieht einen lustigen Film an.

110 Using irregular verbs in different tenses

a gefahren
b geholfen
c gesprochen
d vergessen
e gegeben

111 *Sein* and *haben*

1 a hat
b hatte
c haben / gehabt

2 a ist
b war / war
c sind / gewesen

112 Modal verbs in the present tense

a Ich will eine Geburtstagsparty haben.
b Er darf nicht in die Bar in der Stadt gehen.
c Man soll / sollte die Umwelt schützen.
d Das können wir nächste Woche machen.
e Alle Schüler müssen täglich Hausaufgaben machen.
f Ich mag / möchte im Meer schwimmen.

113 The perfect tense with *haben*

a hat / gemacht
b hast / gegessen
c haben / getroffen
d Habt / gesehen
e hat / gekauft

114 The perfect tense with *sein*

a ist / angekommen
b ist / passiert
c bin / gefahren
d sind / geflogen
e ist / geworden
f ist / geblieben

115 The imperfect tense

a Ich **kaufte** etwas zu essen.
b Wir **wollten** in die Stadt fahren.
c Er **spielte** in einer Band.
d Meine Freundin **fuhr** nach Berlin.
e Mein Chef **schrieb** viele E-Mails.
f Ich **sprach** jeden Tag mit ihr.

116 The future tense

a Ich werde ins Ausland fahren.
b Er wird Medizin studieren.
c Was wirst du machen?
d Wir werden eine neue Wohnung finden.
e Werdet ihr studieren?
f Ich werde mit meinem Freund zusammenleben.
g Sie werden in Deutschland arbeiten.
h Man wird die Umwelt schützen.

117 The conditional

a Ich würde gern ausgehen.
b Er würde auf der Uni studieren.
c Wir würden nicht in dieser Stadt wohnen.
d Ich würde Schriftsteller sein. / Ich wäre Schriftsteller.
e Mein Freund und ich würden heiraten.
f Sie würde vier Kinder haben. / Sie hätte vier Kinder.
g Es würde keine Umweltprobleme geben. / Es gäbe keine Umweltprobleme.
h Mein Opa würde einen Hund haben. / Mein Opa hätte einen Hund.

Credits

Published by Pearson Education Limited, 80 Strand, London, WC2R 0RL.

www.pearsonschoolsandfecolleges.co.uk

Copies of official specifications for all Pearson qualifications may be found on the website: qualifications.pearson.com

Edited by Pearson and Just Content
Designed and typeset by Integra

Cover illustration by Subrayan. R (Creative Artist)
Audio recorded at Tom, Dick and Debbie Productions
Written by Heather Murphy

First published 2024

28 27 26 25 24
10 9 8 7 6 5 4 3 2 1

British Library Cataloguing in Publication Data
A catalogue record for this book is available from the British Library

ISBN 978 1 292 471679

Printed in the UK by Bell & Bain Ltd, Glasgow

Acknowledgements
The author and publisher would like to thank the following individuals and organizations for permission to reproduce photographs.

Non-Prominent Photo Credit(s) for this book:
123RF: Iakov Filimonov iii, Michaeljung 11, Ljupco 14, Scott Griessel 16, Dolgachov 21, 116, Adam121 33, Vadymvdrobot 34, Michael Charles 38, Mirko Vitali 42, vectorplus 43, Guruxox 44, Maleeescape 45, Niserin 47, Iuliia Kvasha 50, Lucadp 51, Antonio Guillem 54, Stockbroker 56, Fizkes 60, Michaeljung 61, Dean Drobot 62, Dimaberkut 64, Maridav 71, Tonobalaguer 73, Goodluz 74, Arkadijschell 76, Sborisov 78, Fei Wong 81, Belchonock 95; **Alamy Images:** Wavebreakmedia Ltd IP-230411/Wavebreak Media Premium 4, Igor Mojzes 27; **Getty Images:** Triloks/iStock/Getty Images Plus 17, Maskot 19, Moto Yoshimura/Getty Images Sport 24, SolStock/E+ 25, 32, 59, COROIMAGE/Moment 35, The Good Brigade/DigitalVision 37, KALA STUDIO/Moment 40, SeventyFour/iStock/Getty Images Plus 64, Anand purohit/Moment 91; **Pearson Education Ltd:** Ann Cromack, Ikat Design 41, Studio 8 57; **Shutterstock:** PeopleImages.com - Yuri A ii, 18, DoublePHOTO studio 1, Absolute-india 2, SeventyFour 5, Stockfour 8, Brian Mueller 9, Oneinchpunch 12, Shutterstock 13, 30, 82, Artemisphoto 14, MinDof 15, Galina Barskaya 20, Pressmaster 22, Cookie Studio 23, Anna Omelchenko 26, Susan Stevenson 28, Fizkes 32, Sabphoto 35, Helen Fields Hotelfoxtrot 36, Antonio Guillem 36, PHOTOCREO Michal Bednarek 37, Maroke 37, AnnaStills 37, P.Alex19 37, Smileus 38, BABAROGA 38, Nick_Nick 39, Dragon Images 42, RonGreer.Com 44, Elizaveta Galitckaia 46, Martin D. Vonka 48, Kevin Eaves 49, CRStocker 50, TAGSTOCK1 50, ShutterPNPhotography 51, Alexandre Zveiger 52, SeventyFour 55, shisu_ka60, John Roman Images 66, Rawpixel.com 67, 87, VGstockstudio 68, PR Image Factory 68, Bernd.neeser 70, Studio 1One 72, Elxeneize 73, Jo Ann Snover 73, CREATISTA 77, Prostock-studio 79, 92, PhotographyByMK 79, 80, DSerov 83, Vitaly Goncharov 85, SpeedKingz 87, Wavebreakmedia 90, Nataly Reinch 95, Cat Box 111.

Non-Prominent Photo Credit(s) for the Quick Quizzes:
Shutterstock: Avesun (Quiz 48 Question 4).

Notes from the publisher
Pearson has robust editorial processes, including answer and fact checks, to ensure the accuracy of the content in this publication, and every effort is made to ensure this publication is free of errors. We are, however, only human, and occasionally errors do occur. Pearson is not liable for any misunderstandings that arise as a result of errors in this publication, but it is our priority to ensure that the content is accurate. If you spot an error, please do contact us at resourcescorrections@pearson.com so we can make sure it is corrected.